MUSICOLOGY

ಆ§ ಕಿಖ

FRANK LL. HARRISON
MANTLE HOOD
CLAUDE V. PALISCA

PRENTICE-HALL, INC.   ENGLEWOOD CLIFFS   NEW JERSEY

C

PRENTICE-HALL INTERNATIONAL, INC, LONDON
PRENTICE-HALL OF AUSTRALIA, PTY, LTD, SYDNEY
PRENTICE-HALL OF CANADA, LTD, TORONTO
PRENTICE-HALL FRANCE, S A R L., PARIS
PRENTICE-HALL OF JAPAN, INC, TOKYO
PRENTICE-HALL DE MEXICO, S.A, MEXICO CITY

FOREWORD

What is the purpose of humanistic scholarship? What, in fact, does the humanist scholar do?

The job of the humanist scholar is to organize our huge inheritance of culture, to make the past available to the present, to make the whole of civilization available to men who necessarily live in one small corner for one little stretch of time, and finally to judge, as a critic, the actions of the present by the experience of the past.

The humanist's task is to clear away the obstacles to our understanding of the past, to make our whole cultural heritage—primitive, pre-Columbian, African, Asian, aboriginal, Near Eastern, classical, medieval, European, American, contemporary, and all the rest—accessible to us. He must sift the whole of man's culture again and again, reassessing, reinterpreting, rediscovering, translating into a modern idiom, making available the materials and the blueprints with which his contemporaries can build their own culture, bringing to the center of the stage that which a past generation has judged irrelevant but which is now again usable, sending into storage that which has become, for the moment, too familiar and too habitual to stir our imagination, preserving it for a posterity to which it will once more seem fresh.

The humanist does all this by the exercise of exact scholarship. He must have the erudition of the historian, the critical abilities of the philosopher, the objectivity of the scientist, and the imagination of all three. The scholar who studies the history of science, for example, must combine a knowledge of languages, history, and philosophy with the knowledge of a scientist. And so on with the scholars who study music, art, religion, literature, and all the rest.

The job is, obviously, impossible for any man; and the humanist scholar, knowing he can never attain his true goal, is always tempted to run after wooden idols whose cults are less exacting and which proffer an easy bliss.

Sometimes the humanist is tempted to bypass the rigorous training of the scholar and to wrap himself in the cloak of the sophist. Then he lapses into a painful wooliness and becomes the "literary" sort of humanist whose only accomplishment is a style which achieves the appearance of sublimity at the cost of an actual inanity. His opposite number is the hardheaded humanist who reacts against empty loftiness by becoming a pedant: he devotes himself to antiquarian detail no less trivial than the banalities of some social science or the mere collecting spirit which is sometimes found in the natural sciences. "Physical science can be at least as trivial as any other form of inquiry· but this is less obvious to the outsider because the triviality is concealed in the decent obscurity of a learned language."

Given the magnitude of his task and the impossibility of total perfection, the humanist scholar must, of course, specialize and his works will often be esoteric. But the belief persists that somehow specialization must be converted to generalization if the humanist scholar is to complete his job. Humanist scholars have not solved the problems of excessive specialization and must share the blame for that catastrophe of communication which besets modern learning.

Humanist scholars have been accused of being overly genteel, contemptuous of popular culture, snobbish and antidemocratic after the fashion of their aristocratic Renaissance progenitors, backward looking, hostile to the present, fearful of the future, ignorantly petulant about science, technology, and the Industrial Revolution—"natural Luddites." "It is a sad thought indeed that our civilization has not produced a *New Vision*," a modern technologist complains, "which could guide us into the new 'Golden Age' which has now become physically possible, but only physically. . . . Who is responsible for this tragi-comedy of Man frustrated by success? . . . Who has left Mankind without a vision? The predictable part of the future may be a job for electronic predictors but the part of it which is not predictable, which is largely a matter of free human choice, is not the business of the machines, nor of scientists . . . but it ought to be, as it was in the great epochs of the past, the prerogative of the inspired humanists." (Dennis Gabor, "Inventing the Future," *Encounter,* May 1960, p. 15.)

Scholars in the humanities may modestly reject the suggestion that they can ever be the inspired prophets of a new age. But their scholarship is essential to enable us to distinguish the inspired prophets from the fanatical Pied Pipers.

The Ford Humanities Project under the direction of the Council of the Humanities of Princeton University is looking at American humanistic scholarship of recent decades, describing it, and attempting to sift the imaginative, the original, and the admirable from the pedantic, the conventional, and the superficial.

We have commissioned about a dozen volumes by recognized scholars in each field. These volumes will give us an account of American humanistic scholarship enabling us to see just what that scholarship has contributed to the culture of America and the world.

Musicology is one of the newest of the scholarly disciplines in the American university. Imported from Germany in the twentieth century, quickened by the work of excellent scholars who fled from the Nazis, musicology, like art history, has had to be domesticated in the United States. The three essays in this volume tell the story of that domestication and draw some morals for the future.

Professor Palisca writes about the study of the Western musical tradition in the United States; Professor Hood tells us about the struggle to found a disciplined study of non-Western music in this country; and Mr. Frank Harrison of Oxford University allows us to see ourselves as others see us. The three together tell us the story of musicology's growth from infancy to adolescence, give us a glimpse of the problems of that difficult age, and tell us about the promise of the future.

RICHARD SCHLATTER
General Editor

CONTENTS

CONTENTS

ILLUSTRATIONS

AMERICAN MUSICOLOGY AND
THE EUROPEAN TRADITION

⊸ξ℘⊱

FRANK LL. HARRISON

READER IN THE HISTORY
OF MUSIC
UNIVERSITY OF OXFORD

INTRODUCTION

"Musicians in the United States receive a one-sided education . . . in general . . . their whole attention is directed towards the technical side of musical art." This was the "European view" taken by Frederic Louis Ritter, author of the first *History of Music* (Boston, 1870-74) written on American soil. Ritter was in some position to make comparisons. Born in Strasbourg and educated in France and Germany, a professor of music in Lorraine before coming to Cincinnati in 1856, he spent eleven years as a choral and orchestral conductor there and (from 1861) in New York before becoming Director of Music at Vassar in 1867. As far as the training of professional performers is concerned, Ritter's strictures are still largely valid. As a rule American conservatories give little place to the historical and theoretical sides of music, and American performers are stronger in technique than in interpretation. The college study of the history of music, on the other hand, which Ritter pioneered, has had a remarkable growth. Undergraduate courses in the subject are now a normal provision in the college curriculum and the past three decades have seen the development of higher studies in the subject in an increasing number of graduate schools, as well as the founding and growth of the American Musicological Society. Official recognition at home came with the acceptance of the American Musicological Society as a constituent member of the American Council of Learned Societies in 1951. Ten years later the international standing of American musicology was confirmed by the holding of the Eighth Congress of the International Musicological Society in New York, and its election of an American-born president, Professor D. J. Grout.

It would be gratifying if one could say that the recognition and growing cultivation of musicology are proof of the maturity of musical life in the United States. It would be agreeably flattering to American musicologists to suggest that they symbolize the ripe fruit of the tree of musical culture in their society. An observer from across the Atlantic might sometimes believe that music in America has achieved an almost ideal state, were it not for the occasional voices of doubt from within that culture itself. The musicologist who both visits and observes might expect that the ardent cultivation of the leaven of his subject would soon leaven the whole lump, until he becomes aware of a mutual isolation of the parts of American musical life.

Most of the fifteen contributors to the most recent survey of the American musical scene (*One Hundred Years of Music in America*, New York, 1961—issued for the centennial of the music publishers G. Schirmer, Inc., edited and with an introduction by Paul Henry Lang and an epilogue by Hans W. Heinsheimer), while celebrating the achievements of a time of extraordinary progress, also express some degree of doubt and concern about the present state of their subject. Although, or perhaps because, musicology as such is not one of the topics of the book, the panorama presented by these essays is pertinent to our subject. We shall not see musicology in America in its true perspective unless we make some attempt to see it as a part of the whole musical culture of the nation. Still less may we assess its trends and judge its potentialities without considering the special characteristics of the society in which it exists.

The first formal review of the state of musicology in America was made in 1929-31 by Oliver Strunk for the Committee on Musicology of the American Council of Learned Societies, and was printed by the council in 1932. It was an inquiry into the *State and Resources of Musicology in the United States* as revealed in the teaching of the subject at universities and the attention paid to it by librarians. Its effect was to draw the attention of the ACLS to inconsistencies in practice and limitations in range in musicological studies as then carried on, and to arouse the interest of and support for librarians in providing adequate collections. It was the appeal of a new discipline to the parent body for understanding and support. Meanwhile, in the field of college music, there was developing a schism between those who supported the cause of performance and re-creation and those who advocated liberal study of the history and theory of the art. The resulting confusion of aims and purposes was clarified in Randall Thompson's survey *College Music: An Investigation for the Association of American Colleges* (New York, 1935), which championed the humanistic conception, but the conflict was still not entirely resolved some twenty years later, when Manfred Bukofzer proposed, in *The Place of Musicology in American Institutions of Higher Learning* (Publications in the Field of Musicology Sponsored by the American Council of Learned Societies, New York, 1957), a "traditional curriculum" for college music.

In this study, Bukofzer divides his curriculum into the areas of theory, history, performance, and music education, but expresses grave doubts about the liberal qualities of the two latter divisions as they are most frequently treated. Recognizing the function of school and college music in American society as that of mass education in music, and thinking mainly of the first two of his divisions, he observes that "this type of musical education was not intended for the training of professional musicians, although this may not have been entirely clear to its early proponents. Its logical aim could only be to foster more intelligent listening habits in the same

5

way as a general education seeks to produce a more intelligent human being. It is therefore the idea of music as a liberal art, of music as part of the humanities, that underlies the idea of mass education in music." This is the aim of what Bukofzer distinguishes as "Education *for* Music," as distinct from "Education *in* Music." "In its purest and highest forms education in music means the training of the three most specialized representatives in the field: the composer, the virtuoso performer, and the musicologist. Both the cultural and the professional aims are necessary and justified; though they differ in nature, they are in fact interdependent."

It is an unfortunate consequence of this kind of division between two parts of what should be a continuous and coherent educational process that it tends to impose itself and perpetuate itself in practice. While Bukofzer's analysis is incontrovertible, the pursuit in practice of these divisions in isolation accentuates the gap between the mass-oriented "cultural" approach and the "professional" aim essential to graduate study. The gap is acceptable only if it be agreed that the aim of college music is to present the subject drained of its true nature as a discipline and that the aim of musicology is to create and protect a reserve for specialized and uncommunicative scholarship.

Should there be, then, a wider aim for musicology? Should there be a social aim broad enough to bridge the gap between the cultural and the professional approach? To some, a "social aim" implies utilitarianism—and one is quick to agree with Bukofzer that "the utilitarian justification of musicology must not be overstressed"—but a social aim, in the broader sense, is not contained within a purely utilitarian approach. Bukofzer endorses, while explaining, such an aim in this assertion:

> It goes without saying that such studies [as are contained in his six divisions of musicology] will gradually shape and

6

determine the public and professional attitude toward music and lead to a clearer and more profound insight into music altogether. The purely emotional and sentimental approach of those who teach and preach music as an entertainment will then slowly give way to a more enlightened and serious conception, such as has long been adopted without question in literature and the fine arts.

This is an aim for musicology within the society of the musical culture of its time. The doubt that arises today is whether the results Bukofzer predicted will in fact come about if musicology, in America and elsewhere, is pursued in the way he describes. And this involves a larger question, implicit in the eloquent conclusion of Bukofzer's essay: "The goal of the humanities, the understanding of man, although approached in each age in a different way, is timeless. The future of this ideal is also the future of musicology." The question today is that of the social aim of musicology in this larger context. It is the question of the role of the humanities, as keys to communication and understanding between man and man and between the present and the past, in the American society of the future and therefore in the world of the future, of the quality of the contribution musicology may make to that role, and how musicology may best be helped and guided to its fullest and most effective contribution.

A musical culture may be thought of as the totality of musical "events" within a society or social unit, using the word *events* in the widest sense. In Western musical culture the most important kinds of events have been the production of music by composers and its communication by performers. All other musical activities were ancillary to these two and existed for their sakes. Traditionally the function of musicology has been in the first place to contribute to the fostering of composition and performance by adding to the sum of knowledge about music. As a branch of history it has also the function of enlarging man's knowledge of himself by widening the bounds of historical writing and so throwing light on Western man's cultural and intellectual development.

The relevance of musicology to composition derives from the nature of the Western art of "composition," which is largely the manipulation of musical ideas that have themselves a recorded history. The function of musicology for the composer is to make this record available, and so provide him with a means of enriching his musical vocabulary with whatever ideas his aesthetic sense leads him to choose. The sources of these ideas may lie in earlier music made "obsolete" through social change, in the "folk music" of social strata in which oral tradition still exists, or in the "popular" music of composers whose currency was confined to a particular social group. By adding such kinds of music to the store of recorded sound, whether the record be on paper or also realized in sound, musicology supplements the composer's experience of his own musical culture. Analogies with the influences of literary record on writers and of visual record on architects, painters, and sculptors are clear and valid. In its relatively short history, musical scholarship has contributed demonstrably to the stylistic development of many significant composers.

For performers in our musical culture the importance of musicology lies even more in the nature of their activity, which makes of almost every performance a historical enterprise, so little are they concerned with contemporary music. In all music but that of the recent past, performance aims, at least ideally, at the re-creation in every detail and nuance of an actual musical event of the past, that is, of the composer's original concept in terms of sound. In practice the attempt to realize this original concept is an extremely complex matter, calling for a judicious balance of compromises between a number of interlocking factors. All music before

8

the gramophone record comes to us in an approximate form, not in actual sound. As Béla Bartók put it in connection with his transcriptions of Hungarian folk song: "The only true notations are the soundtracks on the record itself." Many of the shades of musical meaning that give life and authenticity to performance cannot be shown in the written symbols of notation. They must be distilled from the historical evidence in the case of an "obsolete" style, or from both history and oral tradition in the case of style that is still current. Again, ideas about the quality and technique of the human voice and of instruments are just as subject to change as other factors in musical style and taste. Many things we can learn about these ideas from surviving instruments of the past and from writers about them are of immediate concern to performers today. Finally, the acoustical conditions for which music was designed are an essential part of its original concept, and must be taken into account in a performance given under different conditions.

THE EUROPEAN TRADITION

THE ORIGINS OF MUSICAL HISTORY

In a society that draws so much of its artistic sustenance from the past it would be natural to expect that the historical approach to the arts would have an important place. Two centuries ago the normal repertory of public and court music was almost entirely by contemporary composers, and was unlikely to include music by any composer earlier than Corelli, who died in 1713. In the sixteenth century Palestrina reworked material by composers who had published music some forty to fifty years earlier. In the previous century Johannes Tinctoris wrote that no music was considered worth listening to that was more than forty years old. The anthology of Italian music made by Tinctoris's older contemporary Antonio Squarcialupi is quite exceptional among medieval collections in preserving music written around a century before his time. By contrast, the ever increasing historical coverage of musical performances during the past century reflects a profound social and cultural change in which the rise of musicology has been one of the symptoms.

In spite of what may seem to be a lack of interest in the history of the arts, it is nevertheless true that it was largely through the symbols of art that medieval society expressed and fostered its consciousness of the past. The ritual of Christian worship and the architecture that housed it provided both a framework for the arts and an aural and visual representation of Christian history and belief. In music the stable and recurring part of the yearly cycle of the liturgy was the monophonic plainsong, reaching back in its origins to the beginnings of the church itself. Ornamenting and supplementing it at prescribed points, the newly "composed" music of polyphony was sanctioned and justified by the psalmist's injunction to sing a new song to the Lord (Cantate Domino canticum novum). Against the unchanging background of ritual and plainsong, styles of polyphony played their parts and succeeded one another, rose and were eclipsed, as emphasis shifted from one aspect of devotional fervor to another. Likewise the secular monophonic song of the chivalric tradition, deriving its musical notation from plainsong, was the tree on which flowered the secular polyphony of the French courts and the Italian city-states. The almost wholly unwritten songs and dances of minstrels and ordinary people certainly interpenetrated both kinds of recorded music, sacred and secular, thus exercising their bonding force between the generations and between the social strata.

In a culture of this kind, artistic history was interwoven with and inseparable from artistic activity. Musical history in the modern sense of the recovery and interpretation of past styles was unnecessary and irrelevant. The history of music so far as it existed was a marginal concern of theorists and writers on music who traced the authority and liberality of their art to the ancient philosophers and after them to Boethius, the church fathers, and earlier theorists of almost mythological renown like Guido of Arezzo. Italian and French humanists in the sixteenth century were preoccupied with the nature of the music of the Greeks and with the possibilities of reviving it. Not all of this was speculation, for Girolamo Mei wrote in his *De modis musicis antiquorum* (finished by 1574) what is probably the first history of a period of music based entirely on documentary evidence, and also discovered the four Greek hymns printed in 1581 by Vincenzo Galilei. The significant outcomes of humanist interest in the antique art of music and words were Italian opera and French *vers mésurées*.

It was in the Lutheran church, where music suffered no interruption but was even more vigorously cultivated than before the breach with Rome, that the stirrings of a historical view of music made themselves felt. In 1600 Seth Calvisius, one of J. S. Bach's distinguished predecessors at St. Thomas's in Leipzig, printed a pedagogical work, *Exercitationes musicae* (one of a long line of musical theory treatises for Lutheran schools), and appended to it an outline of the history of music entitled *De origine et progressu musices*. Luther had given a high place to music in worship and in education, and had expressed admiration for the craft of polyphony and explicitly for the work of Josquin des Prés (d. 1521). While Lutheran musical culture thus retained a continuity with the past and a community with the contemporary musical culture of the Roman Catholic Church, it was at the same time concerned to avow its own character in relation to the pre-Lutheran past. Calvisius echoes Luther in admiring the craft of polyphonic composition, and he praises Josquin, Clemens non Papa, and Orlandus Lassus. He also follows Luther in justifying, by the biblical precedent of Jubal, the use of instruments in church, a development of the greatest importance in Lutheran Germany. The history of music in this same sense was a significant though relatively small part of the encyclopedic activity of Michael Praetorius (d. 1621), whose father was a pupil of Luther in theology and an associate of Johann Walther, Luther's musical ally. Praetorius planned all his work, in composition, theory, history, and organology (the second volume of the *Syntagma musicum* is the first comprehensive handbook of musical instruments, brilliantly carried out; see Fig. 1), as the products of a life dedicated to the enrichment and distinction of the musical culture of his church.

XXI

1. 2. Kleine Poschen / Geigen ein Octav höher. 3. Discant-Geig ein Quart höher.
4. Rechte Discant-Geig. 5. Tenor-Geig. 6 Bas-Geig de bracio. 7. Trumscheidt.
8. Scheidtholtt.

FIG 1 A page from *De organographia* (1619), Volume II
of Michael Praetorius's *Syntagma musicum*, showing art, popular, and folk instruments two sizes of violin (3, 4), a viola
(5), a five-string cello (6), a pocket fiddle (2), a rebec (1), a
four-string tromba marina (7), and a partly fretted zither (8).

The next phase of the recording of musical history belongs to a period when national and even local musical styles had acquired distinctive characteristics that were fully recognized in their own time. The three most important styles had their respective centers in the continuing creative tradition of Lutheran church music, in the *conservatori* (originally institutions of charity), which trained the singers and players for Italian opera houses and churches, and in the monarchic cultural unity of France, controlled by the court and the Académie Royale de Musique et de Danse. Alone of these three, Italian practice used both a *stile antico,* perpetuating the polyphonic vocal style of the sixteenth century, and a *stile moderno,* each with its appropriate contexts.

The *Historische Beschreibung der edelen Sing- und Klingkunst* (Dresden, 1690) of Wolfgang Caspar Printz set out for the first time in chronological order the achievements of great musicians up to his own generation, and added an interesting analysis of the functions of music in society. Printz gave much weight to Luther's views on music, and even quoted Luther's encomium on Josquin, whose music was still known in Germany, though not elsewhere. In 1695 Giovanni Andrea Bontempi, like Printz an experienced practical musician, printed in Perugia his *Historia musica.* Bontempi, a versatile writer and scholar, was also the author of a *Storia della ribellione d'Ungheria* and a *Historia dell'origine dei Sassoni.* In the tradition of the Italian humanist academies his history was concerned with the differing qualities of ancient and modern music, and with proving that the Greeks did not have part-music. But while sixteenth century academicians like Vincenzo Galilei had been strongly antipathetic to vocal polyphony on the ground that it confused the meaning of the words, Bontempi could record the survival of polyphony in the *stile antico,* and speak of "la practica moderna che contiene la scientia del contrapunto." The *Histoire de la*

14

musique of Pierre Bourdelot (d. 1685), completed by his nephews Pierre and Jacques Bonnet and printed in Paris in 1715, was partly a compilation of ancient and biblical music and partly a partisan comparison of French and Italian styles, a controversy that was pursued with increased polemic in the *querelle des Bouffons* in the circle of Jean-Jacques Rousseau and the *encyclopédistes*.

THE FOUNDING OF MUSICAL HISTORIOGRAPHY

The second half of the eighteenth century saw the creation of musical historiography in the modern sense. The first volume of Dr. Charles Burney's *General History of Music* and all four volumes of Sir John Hawkins' *History of the Science and Practice of Music* appeared in 1776, and Burney completed the publication of his four volumes in 1789. The Abbot Martin Gerbert's two-volume work *De cantu et musica sacra* had been published by his Abbey of St. Blaise in Switzerland in 1774. The three volumes of the *Storia della musica* by the Franciscan "Padre" Giambattista Martini of Bologna came out between 1757 and 1781. Johann Nicolaus Forkel's *Allgemeine Geschichte der Musik* was published in two volumes in Leipzig in 1788 and 1801.

In the work of these five pioneers, who gave to music a written history and to historiography a new branch, the basic principles and requirements of the modern humanistic approach to music were laid down. The primary "art objects" of a musical historian until the present age of recording were the manuscripts and prints in which music was preserved in the symbols of notation. The gathering and copying of these materials were the overriding tasks of the musical historians of many generations to come. The work of the pioneers provided the earliest extensive anthologies of music compiled

15

for a historical rather than a practical purpose, and the first
clear outlines of a chronology of composers and styles. All
five had some degree of presupposition in their views of the
development of music in its historical framework, but all
were humanists in their object of treating that development
as a progress in human reason, expression, and communication.

It was only after a varied professional life—as protégé
of the opera composer Thomas Arne, as adapter of an English version of Rousseau's *Le Devin du village,* as composer,
church organist, and fashionable teacher—that Burney at
the age of forty-four decided to travel to Italy in search of
material for a history of music. The state of his project at that
time was, he wrote, "a chaos to which God knows whether
I shall have life, leisure, or abilities to give order. . . . I
shall consult the public Libraries at Milan, Florence, Venice,
Rome, Naples &c for the first rise & progress of Music since
Guido's time; & I shall endeavour, by hearing & conversing
with the most ancient Professors, to inform myself of its
present state." To every likely musician he met in his travels,
Burney put the inquiry "Where and when did counterpoint
or modern harmony begin?" In the eighteenth century as in
the Middle Ages, Guido of Arezzo was the reputed "inven-
tor" of part-music, but Burney's interest in its beginnings
arose mainly from his conviction, highly fashionable in England then, that the art of melody supported by harmony had
attained perfection in the Italianate style of the day. Another
historical problem that engaged him, rather from the intellectual fashion of the Augustan age than from any inner conviction, was the long-standing one of the music of the ancient
Greeks. Above all, Burney was a professional observer of the
contemporary world of music. "Learned men and books may
be more useful as to ancient music, but it is only *living musicians* that can explain what *living music* is," he wrote, with

16

an authentic note of real enthusiasm. On his journeys he occupied himself both as a reporter and as a researcher to such
good effect that the *reportage* in his *Journals* has become
source material in its own right.

Hawkins' view of the history of music, on the contrary,
was anticontemporary. Among Burney's manuscript writings,
not intended for publication, there is a satire on Hawkins'
History called the *Trial of Midas, the 2nd, or Congress of
Musicians*. Burney used the term *Gothic* to lampoon Hawkins' taste:

> Hence every rule he draws from Gothic works,
> From barb'rous Jargon & unmeaning Quirks,
> Produc'd in impious and ill-fated Days
> When all thy Sacred altars ceas'd to blaze.

It is strange that no writer on the Burney-Hawkins rivalry,
a subject of keen public interest in their day and of frequent
comment since, has pointed to the first period of the Gothic
revival in England, with all it held for the future of the arts
there, as the stage on which the protagonists took their stand.
For Burney was clearly right that this is where Hawkins belongs, as a figure in the movement for the study and use of
the Gothic that also produced Bentham's *History of Ely*
(1771), Grose's *Antiquities* (from 1773), Buck's *Antiquities and Venerable Remains* (1774), and Horace Walpole's
house at Strawberry Hill. This too goes some way to explain
why Hawkins, condemned by the majority in his own time,
was twice reprinted in the nineteenth century (1853, 1875),
while Burney, whose arrogant championship of his contemporaries could not but be antipathetic to the romantic sensi-
bility, remained unedited until 1935.

Reflecting as they do the aesthetic philosophies of their
day, the English pioneer histories raise the question whether
a work of interpretive scholarship in the arts suffers from

aesthetic prejudices in the writer. If this be charged on the one side, it can be argued on the other side that the impulse to make a contribution to knowledge is the more effective for being based on individual preference. Burney for one was quite frank in stating his:

> Grace, Fancy, Feeling and clearness, are to me superior to all other merits. There are times for shewing learning and contrivance; but I think that the best of all contrivances in Music, is to please people of discernment and taste, without trouble. A long and laboured Fugue, *recte et retro* in 40 parts, may be good entertainment for the *Eyes* of a Critic, but can never delight the *Ears* of a Man of Taste. I was no less surprised than pleased to find Mr. C. P. E. Bach get out of the trammels of Fugue and crowded parts in which his father so excelled.

This was the positive aesthetic view behind the seeming shallowness, which some have taken as an almost sinful frivolity, of Burney's definition of music as "an innocent luxury, unnecessary, indeed, to our existence, but a great improvement and gratification to the sense of hearing." In the accepted view of his time this definition is in keeping with Burney's object of restoring music to a place in the cultural and intellectual circles of society.

Having given such frank statements of his tastes, Burney did not scruple to express them forcefully in particular cases: on the English madrigalists ("there is doubtless more verve, more science, and fire in the worst of Handel's choruses, than in the greatest efforts of these old madrigalists"), on the English virginalists ("in Virginal Books, we find no attempts at invention, in point of Air or melody: the business of our best Composers for keyed-instruments, such as Bird, Morley, Bull, Giles Farnaby, and Gibbons, being to make variations upon old and well-known tunes"), and on John Blow (Burney made a collection of "Specimens of Dr. Blow's Beastialities"). A positive aesthetic tenet of the intellectual and artistic circles of his day could be his justification for likening the "crudities" of Purcell's harmony to "some words and phrases which Shakespeare tried unsuccessfully to render current" but which "have been rejected by posterity." Burney's successes in critical estimation also owed something to his prejudices, since few composers among those who showed "learning and contrivance" elicited his admiration. They included Josquin and Robert White, then unknown but since recognized as great, and Jean Mouton and Antoine de Fevin, still known only to specialists.

Hawkins' lack of involvement with the musical life of his time—he was knighted as a magistrate of the county of Middlesex and divided his life between writing and dispensing justice—caused his writing to be less informative about eighteenth century music and more motivated by a disinterested antiquarian spirit. He called his work a history of the "Science and Practice" of music, and saw his task as "the investigation of the principles, and a deduction of the progress of a science . . . intimately connected with civil life" and one "deservedly ranked among those, which . . . have long been dignified with the characteristic of liberal." But, he observes, music "has scarce ever been so well understood by the generality, as to be thought a fit object, not to say of criticism but of sober discussion."

The absence of understanding and calm discussion of music he puts down to the prevalence of Burney's favorite criterion of Taste, in the place of reason based on discovered principles. "Instead of exercising the powers of reason, [music] has in general engaged only that faculty of the mind, which, for want of a better word to express it by, we call Taste; and which alone and without some principle to direct and controul it, must ever be deem'd a capricious arbiter." His object in the *History* was "above all, to demonstrate that [the] principles [of music] are founded on certain general and universal laws, into which all that we discover in this material world, of harmony, symmetry, proportion and order, seems to be resolvable." His purpose in writing the *History* was to provide "an explanation of fundamental doctrines, and a narration of important events and historical facts, in a chronological series, with such occasional remarks and evidences, as might serve to illustrate the one and authenticate the other. With these are intermixed a variety of musical compositions, tending as well to exemplify that diversity of styles which is common both to music and speech or written language, as to manifest the gradual improvements in the art of combining musical sounds " Hawkins' "variety of musical compositions" comprised some one hundred and fifty pieces, almost all previously unknown They form the first true anthology of the history of music in examples, which has been drawn upon by many later historians, as have Hawkins' extensive quotations from theorists. As a new enterprise in the history of the arts they stand worthily beside Padre Martini's more specialized musical *Esemplare* (1774-75), Grose's *Antiquities* (1773), and Percy's *Reliques of Ancient English Poetry* (1765).

None of the other pioneers of musical historiography achieved a complete general history of the subject. Martin Gerbert, one of the great churchmen of his time and Prince-Abbot of the Benedictine Abbey of St. Blaise from 1764, devoted his life and energies to the revival of the great traditions of monastic scholarship. He believed that the monasteries of his time should be "workshops of learned industry; and their inmates should disprove the contemptuous reproach of an idle, useless life by scientific works"; they should "shake off the old scholastic dust and discontinue the pseudo-erudite disputes from which no good can ever result either for Church or State." Under Gerbert, St. Blaise became the intellectual center of monasticism, and his own researches in liturgies and liturgical music represent one of the greatest single achievements in a long and still vital monastic tradition. In musical scholarship he laid the foundations of the history of theory in the *Scriptores ecclesiastici de musica sacra potissimum* (1784). By giving the full texts of treatises by more than forty writers, this accomplished what Hawkins had attempted in a cursory fashion. With Edmund de Coussemaker's *Scriptorum de musica medii aevi, nova series* (1864-76), Gerbert's work provides the basic material for the history of musical theory and remains an essential item in the musicology of the Middle Ages and the Renaissance.

Gerbert's history of church music (*De cantu et musica sacra a prima ecclesiae aetate usque ad praesens tempus*) was formed on the strictest canons of exact scholarship and objective recording. Burney turned to it for answers to many medieval questions, though he could not accept the aesthetic basis of its music. Some two-part motets of the thirteenth century printed by Gerbert were in Burney's opinion "of so coarse a texture, that if a specimen were given here it would be of no other use than to raise the reader's wonder how such music could ever be composed or performed, and still more, how it should ever have been listened to with pleasure." Gerbert's inclinations, like those of Hawkins, were anti-contemporary; but Gerbert was in a position to exercise them by reforming the music used in his monastery. He deplored the effect on church music of the worldly taste of the Italians and he anticipated modern reforms by persuading his community to banish all instruments but the organ and to sing the plainsong as it was sung in the papal choir. (It had been customary to have a flourish of trumpets at the elevation and the singing of an aria after it.)

Gerbert was on friendly terms with Padre Martini, like

so many in the musical world of his time. The two exchanged information to their mutual advantage, and at one time thought of collaborating on a complete history of music. Martini was certainly the most erudite musician of his day; he owned a library that Burney put at seventeen thousand volumes and that has since his death been the basis of the famous library of the Liceo Musicale in Bologna. A true exponent of modern musicology in his systematic research, critical method, and command of technical musicianship, Martini was a combination of historian, composer, teacher, and practicing *maestro di capella,* to a degree that made him a legend in his lifetime. As a historian and teacher his taste was for the *stile antico,* which he taught and studied both as a consciously "sacred" church style and as a technical craft. On the other hand, as a composer he was a man of his age, writing chamber music, oratorios, and intermezzi in the current styles. His *Storia della musica* was planned on a lavish scale and left unfinished, so that only a portion of his researches was printed. In addition he published an anthology of examples illustrative of the *stile antico* in choral music from Palestrina to his own time in the *Esemplare ossia saggio fondamentale pratico di contrappunto* and a *Dissertatio de usu progressionis geometricae in musica.*

As a teacher of counterpoint with a comprehensive knowledge of the history of the *stile antico* Martini was an important formative influence on composition in his day. He instructed and inspired the admiration of J. C. Bach (the "London" Bach, youngest son of J. S. Bach), of the fourteen-year-old Mozart, and of many less renowned composers. In a valuable *Study of Fugue* (Rutgers University Press, 1958) the American musicologist Alfred Mann sums up the historical position of Martini in these terms:

Thus Martini's role is that of the mentor who established a standard for the student through example rather than assignment and correction. In this spirit he quotes the writing of his own teachers and of the masters of the past. The manner in which he introduces the student to the great heritage of his art heralds a new age, a thoroughly modern and enlightened approach to musical instruction.

In this sense Martini realized a new social aim for musical scholarship in the changing society of his age. He represented a new creative relationship between musical history and composition by which they were united in a humanistic whole.

Johann Nicolaus Forkel was the only one of our group of five who wrote as a member of a university. The decline of music as a university subject had begun, strangely enough, with the rise of Renaissance humanism. Clearly, the reason was not that the humanism of the Renaissance was disinterested in music, but rather that in the necessary revision of the university curriculum no approach to music was found to replace that of the Middle Ages. Even before the founding of universities the *musica speculativa* of Boethius's *De musica,* treating of numerical proportions as revealed in the nature of sound, was recognized as one of the *artes liberales.* In the curriculum of the medieval university Boethius was read as one of the subjects of the *quadrivium* with arithmetic, geometry, and astronomy. Music was not confined to such purely routine and speculative treatment, however, but was treated at greater length by such men as John of Garland at Paris, Robert Grosseteste, Roger Bacon, and Walter Odington at Oxford, and Prosdocimus de Beldemandis at Padua. The last exposition of university music in the medieval sense was the *Dodecachordon* (1547) of Henricus Glareanus, a figure of importance equally in the history of humanism and of musical theory, who brought the medieval theory of music into conformity with the practice of Renaissance composers.

By the end of the sixteenth century the reading of Boethius

had been discontinued and in the seventeenth century the lecturer in music was replaced, in Germany by an *akadem-ischer Musikdirektor* who concerned himself almost entirely with performance and in England by a Professor of Music (the Heather Professorship at Oxford dates from 1626, the Cambridge chair from 1684) who lectured and examined compositions submitted for the degrees of Bachelor and Doctor of Music. Meanwhile the traditional *musica speculativa,* though no longer a part of the university curriculum, was continued and reinterpreted, notably in the work of Descartes (*Compendium musicae,* written 1618, printed 1650), Mersenne (*Harmonie universelle,* 1636-37), Kircher (*Musurgia universalis,* 1650), and Rameau, whose *Traité de l'harmonie réduite à ses principes naturels* of 1722 is the basis of the modern theory of harmony.

Forkel's thinking about the history and theory of music owed much to the intellectual vigor of Gottingen University, which was then quite outstanding. He lectured in music in addition to his functions as *Musikdirektor,* and in 1787 was given the degree of *Magister.* This gave official recognition to his lectures more than a century before the first professorship in music was founded at a German university. In the late eighteenth century the famous Historical School of Gottingen applied scholarly methods of historical research to the humanities. Its methods brought about a union of the ideas of reason and progress in the philosophy of history. Through historical research, the dogma of steady progress toward the Enlightenment was modified by taking into account the events of national histories and the appearances of individual genius. Forkel's history is much concerned with the music of peoples, both Eastern and Western, and with high points in the musical culture of nations.

His comprehensive view of university music as having a historical and a "scientific" side has led recent biographers to call Forkel the founder of musicology, though the word *musicology* did not exist during his time. On the theoretical side he laid down the first methodology (in *Über die Theorie der Musik,* 1777), dividing the subject into five sections: physical sound (acoustics), mathematical sound (construction of instruments), musical grammar (notation and theory), musical rhetoric (form and style), and musical criticism (aesthetics and performance practices). He also provided the first comprehensive bibliography of the whole subject of music in the *Allgemeine Literatur der Musik* (1792), a work of basic importance to later historians and bibliographers.

Forkel considered that music in his own time had entered a period of decadence and was moving toward a low point. The high point had come in the first half of the eighteenth century, when "music was indisputably from every point of view in its most beautiful and virile maturity." He believed that the expression of religious devotion in music was "the most important and useful application of our art," and that J. S. Bach was the culminating genius of the great traditions of German music. He extended his *Allgemeine Geschichte der Musik* to the end of the seventeenth century—his biography of Bach (the first great work of its kind) acted as the final volume—and completed the first volume of a pioneer history of music in examples, which was engraved and in the hands of the Vienna publishers in 1805 when unfortunately the plates were made into cannonballs by the French soldiers. A complete edition of the works of Bach was also among his plans, some half century before this enterprise was actually begun.

It is a further tribute to the thoroughness of Forkel's conception of musical history that he compiled material about the social milieu of the "production" and "consumption" of music. This was in the form of lists not only of composers,

performers, and writers on music but also of orchestras, publishers, musical academies and societies, and instrument
makers. He seems to have foreseen the idea of a social history
of music and the need for as systematic an approach to it as
to other aspects of the art. In all, Forkel charted with a remarkable approach to completeness the configurations and
depths of the great sea of musical facts upon which Burney
had set out with such misgivings not so long before.

ROMANTIC RE-CREATION

It was more than two decades after Forkel's second volume
that the call to a romantic involvement in the musical past
was sounded, not yet by a musical historian but by a passionate
and unscholarly amateur. In 1825 Anton Thibaut, Professor
of Jurisprudence at Heidelberg, published a small book called
Über Reinheit der Tonkunst (English translation as *Purity
in Musical Art*, 1877). The word *pure* in Thibaut's aesthetics,
which were much influenced by Kant, his Konigsberg teacher,
and Schiller, his Jena colleague, conveyed among other meanings the purity of the vocal medium, the purity of religious
music, and the purity of the music of the folk. About 1814
he formed in Heidelberg a *Singverein* to perform choral
music from Palestrina, Lasso, and Victoria to Handel, Bach,
and Cherubini. Schumann and Mendelssohn were moved by
Thibaut's ideas and enthusiasm, while recognizing his ama-
teurishness. Though he had but a myopic view of Bach, for
example, knowing the motets but not the passions and can-
tatas, there is no doubt that his meetings had some influence
on the Bach revival and his book on contemporary ideas
about musical history. His library, which was acquired by
the state of Bavaria for its library in Munich, included a
series of folk songs of many countries.

To the philosophical musical historian of the eighteenth

26

century, history had been a means of marking himself off from the past, of distinguishing himself from men who had not attained the state of reason. "Outgrown" stages of music, like plainsong, trouvère melody, and folk song, were "fruits of nature not of art" and so were provided, most unhistorically, with a bass and other parts in the style of the eighteenth century. The bizarre efforts of early polyphony were unquotable and were replaced by elegant paraphrases of the course of musical events. Similarly, the aesthetic values of the past could perfectly well be expressed in modern terms and judged by modern criteria. For the musical historian of what we may call the romantic phase of musical history—say from Thibaut (1825) to Adler (1885)—the subject had a different aim. To them it was a means of plunging back, mentally and spiritually, into the past. They strove to immerse themselves in the music of the past and to identify themselves with its social setting and aesthetic ideals. Archaic musical language and the idioms of oral tradition acquired value for their own sakes. The lives of composers and the musical cultures of particular places and periods took on a new relevance because of the need for absorption in past ages. Consequently the characteristic productions of the time were complete editions of composers' works, studies of their lives, and local and period histories. Almost all these were contained within the period from the sixteenth century to Mozart. The attitude to musical history in this phase was especially congenial to the gifted amateur, with his devoted enthusiasm and keen desire for insight. Kiesewetter and Ambros were civil servants, von Winterfeld was a magistrate, Otto Jahn a professor of archaeology and philology, while Chrysander was musically self-taught.

In 1828 Raphael Kiesewetter and François Fétis were both given awards by the Royal Belgian Institute of Sciences, Literature, and the Fine Arts in a competition for a Prize

Essay that should answer the question "What contribution did Netherlands composers make to music, especially in the fourteenth, fifteenth, and sixteenth centuries?" These essays were the first important contributions to special research in regional musical cultures. Kiesewetter's paper put an end to the prevalent notion that the Italians had been the musical preceptors of all Europe. He showed that the Roman and Venetian schools of the sixteenth century took over the style of their Netherlands predecessors, and thus put the achievement of Palestrina in a new perspective. In his subsequent *History of the Modern Music of Western Europe* (1834; English translation, London, 1848) Kiesewetter proposed a division of the history of music into periods named according to their dominating creative figure, such as the "Epoch of Dufay" (1380-1450), the "Epoch of Ockeghem" (1450-80), the "Epoch of Josquin" (1480-1520), the "Epoch of Willaert" (1520-60), followed by the "Epoch of Palestrina" (1560-1600) and later epochs. The delineation of periods in terms of the style of one or two composers has ever since been one of the dominant ideas in the writing of musical history. Kiesewetter also wrote a history of secular song (*Schicksale und Beschaffenheit des weltlichen Gesanges vom fruhen Mittelalter bis zur Erfindung des dramatischen Styles und den Anfangen der Oper,* 1841) that is the earliest significant essay in the history of forms.

Like Forkel, Kiesewetter conceived the plan of publishing an anthology of the history of music in examples of part-music from its origins to his own time. As well as accumulating a large collection of transcriptions of choral music of the fifteenth and sixteenth centuries, he formed a choir to perform them in his home. Performance of old music was an essential part of the romantic re-creation of the musical past. The lead of Kiesewetter and Thibaut in this enterprise was later followed by Baini in Rome, von Winterfeld in Berlin, and Karl Proske (editor of the important collection *Musica divina*) in Ratisbon. The first notable figure in the history of musicology in Vienna, Kiesewetter was prominent in the musical life of the city. As vice president of the Gesellschaft der Musikfreunde (founded in 1812-13) he sent to Schubert the society's grant of one hundred florins in recognition of the dedication of a symphony. His performances enabled Beethoven to gain a knowledge of and admiration for Palestrina, an experience that undoubtedly had an effect on the writing of the choral movement of the *Ninth Symphony*. In 1847 some of his transcriptions of polyphonic choral music were printed in his *Gallerie der alten Contrapunctisten*. He bequeathed his collection to the Royal Library, where it became the basis of the researches of his nephew Ambros. Kiesewetter's researches in the sources of Arabian music (*Die Musik der Araber*, 1842) and in musical paleography should also be mentioned. Both stood alone for many years after his death in 1850.

The researches of men like Kiesewetter and Carl von Winterfeld (1784-1852) revealed great gaps in the knowledge of earlier historians and a vast amount of music still to be transcribed and studied. Von Winterfeld thought that "the production of the history of a single art is a problem which hardly any individual can solve in the full sense." He himself made detailed studies of the Roman and Venetian schools of the sixteenth century as represented by their outstanding figures (*Palestrina*, 1832; *Giovanni Gabrieli and his Time*, 1834) and he achieved the first comprehensive history of Lutheran music (*Der evangelische Kirchengesang*, 1843-47). His work on Gabrieli and Baini's more famous *Palestrina* (1828) were models for a new genre, the musical biography. Its object was to place a musical personality in the context of his time and culture, and also in the context of musical history in relation to his forerunners and contemporaries. The idealization of Palestrina brought about by Baini—priest, composer, and director of the papal choir—was greatly to the taste of the romantic period. At the same time his account of life and society in Rome in Palestrina's time makes his book a milestone in musical biography in a social context. Baini projected a complete edition of the composer he called "Il principe della musica," but published only two volumes before his death.

The versatile professional musicianship of François Joseph Fétis (1784-1871) was matched by an encyclopedic approach to all the aspects of music. Historian and musical lexicographer, theorist, composer, and director of the Brussels Conservatory, Fétis thought of all his writing as part of one great purpose. This he expressed as the accomplishment of "un art nouveau, étendu, varié, immense, qui embrassera toutes les nuances de l'art et qui sera conforme à l'objet illimité de la musique." These words are both grand and vague, but they do reflect his purpose: to affect the future of the art of music. The unfinished *Histoire générale de la musique* (1869-76) was the first attempt at a history of the music of all peoples, regarding the music of the West as the expression of one culture among many; in this work, by relating music to linguistics and ethnography, Fétis became one of the prophets of ethnomusicology. He also achieved distinction as the author of the first everyman's history of music, *La Musique mise à la portée de tout le monde* (1830), which was published in several later editions and was translated into six languages. It is a further measure of his success that he was the subject of a contemporary caricature, under which was written:

> O! Fétis! si jamais par ton rare génie,
> Tu m'enleves du sol,
> Je m'y cramponnerai comme un maure à la vie,
> Ut, Ré, Mi, Fa, Sol! . . . .

30

In the preliminary essay to his *Biographie universelle des musiciens* (1835-44) Fétis printed a draft of a contemplated work on the philosophy of music. Entitled *Résumé philosophique de l'histoire de la musique,* it set the goal of the musical historian as a logically organized history of the language of music, based on studies of composers and institutions. He saw the need for such projects as scholarly editions of plainsong, a collection of treatises on musical theory, and comprehensive publication of the music of the Netherlands schools. Fétis also founded the first entirely musical periodical in France (*Revue musicale,* 1827-35), wrote biographies of Paganini (1854) and Stradivarius (1856), and made an important collection of historical material, which passed at his death to the Royal Library in Brussels.

Like Fétis, August Wilhelm Ambros (1816-76) cherished the idea of a universal and organic history of music. Though constrained to follow a career in law and public service, he succeeded in combining state duties with an ardent devotion to the arts as a critic, essayist, researcher, and historian. He carried out extensive musical researches in Austria, Germany, and Italy and in 1869 was appointed Professor of the Theory and History of Music at Prague University. This appointment was short-lived, for in 1871 he was called to the Ministry of Justice in Vienna where he became one of the teachers of the Crown Prince Rudolph. His life and writings show a dual professional allegiance and a voracious intellectual curiosity.

As a critic and essayist Ambros concerned himself keenly with contemporary music by such composers as Mendelssohn, Schumann, Berlioz, Liszt, and Wagner. Though welcoming the spread of musical education through the press, festivals, concert halls, and music in the home, he dreaded the "semiculture" (*Halbcultur*) which seemed to him to result from the popularizing of artistic and intellectual things:

The great public in our hurrying, railway-travelling, tele-graphing times certainly does not object; it wants to polish off everything in a hurry and without effort, otherwise no matter how, and this also applies to its education. [*Ge-schichte der Musik,* preface to the second volume, dated Prague, 1864.]

In Ambros's circles, the difficulty of arriving at a phi-losophy of history was complicated by the new idea of the "equality" of all cultures, which ruled out the postulation of a "progress" or "goal." The arts were now viewed as ex-pressions of their times. Each was thought to come to the front of the stage of history in a different period, the historical sequence of leadership being architecture, sculpture, painting, music, and poetry. Music developed late and was considered a special achievement of the Western world as its expression of the higher experiences of self-knowledge. But the historian of an art is almost inevitably attracted to the work of some par-ticular period, and for Ambros this was the Renaissance. Given the ideal of equal treatment of all periods, Ambros could still consider himself justified in redressing the balance of ideas on musical history in his time by stressing the great-ness of the Renaissance. Outraged by Berlioz's relegation of Josquin to a person of merely "historical interest," he counters:

Anyone who still thought of Cologne Cathedral or of the Ghent Altar as merely "historically" interesting, because the former does not look like a crystal palace for industrial ex-hibitions and the latter like a salon picture of Winterhalter, would disgrace himself for all time [*Geschichte der Musik,* p. 15.]

Ambros's ideal historian of the arts was one who should in-fluence contemporary artistic thought and trends. Therefore, "understanding, love, correct evaluation of everything noble, even though it lie outside the taste of our time, is one of the tasks of the historian of art. But he must be the right person to do so, and not imagine, as Oulibicheff did for example, that God created the world in order that the overture to the *Magic Flute* might be composed in it."

Since Ambros regarded music and the visual arts as "externalisation of one and the same spiritual stream," it was part of his method to call on the visual arts as aids to the understanding of musical style, wherever he found common criteria. This he did for example between the motets of Josquin and Italian altarpieces, and between the Venetian polychoral-instrumental style of Gabrieli and the element of the "colossal" in the art of the early baroque. His work was directly influenced by contemporary historians of the visual arts, especially Franz Kugler and Moritz Carrière (author of *Art in Correlation with Cultural Development*), by archaeologists of non-European cultures (Rosellini, Layard), and by the "Historical School" of law (Eichorn, Thibaut, Savigny) with which he had professional acquaintance. He was conscious of being the first to bring the new nineteenth century classical culture (von Humboldt, Muller) to bear on the musical history of ancient Greece, by attempting to show what Greek music must have been, in view of the character of the civilization as a whole. He explained the arrangement of the first volume of the *Geschichte der Musik* as an adaptation of Franz Kugler's arrangement in the *Handbuch der Kunstgeschichte.*

EDITIONS AND BIOGRAPHIES

Ambros did not succeed in finishing his brave attempt to bring the whole of musical history under examination in terms of the intellectual outlook of his time. His history, completed and revised by other hands, remained until after the turn of the century the outstanding achievement in the historical re-creation of music on such a scale. His period of musical historiography also saw the completion or initiation of some of the greatest projects in the editing and publishing of music that have been carried out in modern times. The most formidable of these in size as well as the most influential in its effects was the complete edition of the works of J. S. Bach. The first cantata by Bach to be printed after his death was issued in 1821, and even Zelter, the greatest Bach enthusiast in Germany at the time, regarded this as a lost cause; he could not believe that Bach's religious music had anything to communicate to the musical public of the 1820's. In 1823 Zelter had a copy of the *St. Matthew Passion* made for Mendelssohn and in 1829 Mendelssohn conducted the Berlin Singakademie in the first performance since Bach's death, a hundred years after its composition. This momentous event was far from being an accurate re-creation. The work was shortened and simplified, and performed with the kind of dynamic effects appropriate to early romantic music. (See Figs. 2 and 3.) Nevertheless its impact greatly accelerated the revival of Bach, who was then known only through some of the instrumental music. Researches, performances, and some publications awoke increasing interest until in 1850 the Bach Gesellschaft was founded for the purpose of publishing a complete critical edition. This task took fifty years and forty-six volumes to accomplish. A century after it was begun, the effects that this unfolding revelation of the whole creative personality of Bach had on the musical culture of the West were summarized by Professor Friedrich Blume:

> The complete edition of Bach's works was an achievement of incalculable significance. It not only became the gateway to a new understanding, to an historical correction and deepening of the accepted ideas of Bach, to a new and glorious chapter in musical research in general, but it also inspired a surprising advance in practical music making. It inspired

34

also a new interest in the other masters of the age of the Baroque and the rediscovery of the whole of the older music; in fact it stimulated all modern research into musical sources to a much greater extent than Chrysander's complete edition of Handel, which, appearing at the same time as the Bach edition, failed to direct the attention of musicians and scholars to anything but Handel himself. All the innumerable complete editions of the old masters, the great serial publications, the editions of the *Denkmaler Deutscher Tonkunst* are indebted to the Bach edition in one way or another. It also gave a powerful stimulus to the study of the practical problems involved in the performance of the older music. All the efforts of the last fifty years devoted to the revival of the old instruments and the authentic performance of the music were all ultimately inspired by the Bach edition. But this epoch-making achievement has also had immense influence in the sphere of composition. Which of the great composers from Schumann to Reger, from Mendelssohn to Strauss and Pfitzner, from Brahms to Wagner, and from Bruckner to Verdi had not somewhere been deeply influenced by the complete edition of the works of Bach? It opened the sluice through which his art and technique, as well as his mind and faith, poured into the creative work of the neo-Romantics and neo-Classicists. The *Rosenkavalier* is as inconceivable without this influence as Mendelssohn's *St. Paul*, the *Mastersingers*, the *German Requiem*, Reger's *Hiller Variations,* or Bruckner's masses and symphonies. For the first time in history creative minds in music experienced the overwhelming influence of past greatness so profoundly that it set the whole direction and standard for their own work. An epoch-making change took place in the half-century covered by the Bach editions, since for the first time European music was part of a definite historical process Musical historians began to interpret Bach as the centre of gravity of the whole history of music. Wagner saw in Bach "the history of the innermost life of the German spirit during the cruel century in which the German people

FIG. 2. Part of a page of the manuscript score of Bach's *St. Matthew Passion* used by Mendelssohn for his performance in 1829. The copy was made for Zelter. The phrasing and dynamics pencilled in by Mendelssohn impose a romantic conception on the music. Reproduced by kind permission of Miss Margaret Deneke.

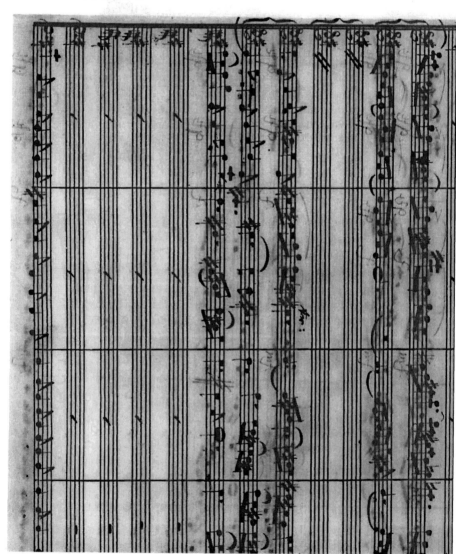

FIG. 3. Another page from Mendelssohn's performance score. In this aria he used A clarinets instead of the oboi da caccia, which had become obsolete by his time. He also penciled out the grace notes, thus depriving the tune of one of its most essential rhythmic and harmonic features. Reproduced by kind permission of Miss Margaret Deneke.

were completely blotted out." Brahms declared that it would grieve him if the whole of music, the works of Schubert, Schumann and Beethoven were to disappear, but that he would be utterly inconsolable if he were to be deprived of Bach. Reger called him "the beginning and end of all music," and Beethoven had already declared "He ought not to be called Bach (brook) but ocean." It is still impossible to estimate the full significance of this irruption of Bach into the musical world of the nineteenth century as an historical event. It is, indeed, an event without parallel in the whole of history, and it has transformed the musical world from its very depths. [*Two Centuries of Bach*, trans. Stanley Godman (Oxford, 1950).]

The transformation worked by the Bach revival on the writing of musical history is clearly seen in Philipp Spitta's biography (1873-80). This work placed Bach's achievement in the context of Lutheran history, and viewed it in the light of the work of his Lutheran predecessors. The most important of these were Heinrich Schütz and Dietrich Buxtehude, whose works Spitta also edited. The revelation of the genius of Handel as the other dominating figure of the late baroque period was carried out with single-handed heroism by Friedrich Chrysander, who edited the works (1859-94) and wrote an unfinished biography (1858-67). Kiesewetter's "Age of Leo and Durante" was henceforth to be the "Age of Bach and Handel."

THE REVIVAL OF CHURCH MUSIC

The effects of the Bach revival, profound as they were, may yet be equaled by the creative influence of the musical culture of still earlier ages. This revival had its first beginnings in the same circles of early romantic enthusiasm as did that of Bach. The Berlin Singakademie performed the works of Palestrina and other sixteenth century composers, and

Anton Thibaut spoke of the decline of true church music from the sublimities of Palestrina and Lasso to the rococo masses with orchestra of the eighteenth century. The first center of the church music revival was Munich, where Allegri's *Miserere* was sung in St. Michael's Church in 1816. As organist there from 1816 to 1847, Caspar Ett introduced a newly discovered mass (the *Missa cuiusvis toni*) by Ockeghem, performed regularly music of the sixteenth century, and produced a practical edition of Gregorian chant, albeit in a much truncated form. Ratisbon was the next focus of the movement; King Ludwig I of Bavaria took a direct interest in the cathedral and in 1839 ordered that the chant should be specially cultivated there. The reform movement was greatly furthered by the writings of Kiesewetter, Baini, Fétis, and von Winterfeld, and by the publication of some massive anthologies—the *Musica sacra* (28 vols., 1839-87) of Franz Commer; the *Musica divina* (4 vols., 1853-64) of Karl Proske, canon and Kapellmeister of Ratisbon, and F. X. Haberl; and the *Trésor musical* (29 vols., 1865-93) of R. J. van Maldeghem. Societies for the restoration of early church music were founded in most European countries and in the United States, where the periodical *Caecilia* was begun at Milwaukee in 1873.

For most of the revivalists the ideal qualities of church music were to be found in Gregorian chant, in Palestrina, and in Lasso. F. X. Haberl, one of Proske's successors as Kapellmeister at Ratisbon and founder of its School of Church Music, was engaged in all three of these subjects of research. He took over at the tenth volume the edition of Palestrina's works and brought it to completion with the thirty-third volume in 1894. In that year he initiated with Adolph Sandberger an edition of the works of Lasso, and he had earlier begun a series of new editions of Gregorian chant. In this last field, however, his work was overtaken and re-

placed by the more fundamental researches of the Benedictine monks of Solesmes. Beginning in the abbacy of the
founder Dom Guéranger (d. 1875), the monks carried out
a full-scale work of restoration based on the most important
early manuscripts, which they have continued to publish in
a series of facsimiles. In 1904 the community of Solesmes
saw their work crowned by papal recognition of their editions.
In the following year the *Motu proprio* of Pope Pius X on
sacred music also set the seal of approval on the century-
old movement of reform. It recognized Gregorian chant as
"the supreme model for sacred music" and noted the same
qualities in "Classic Polyphony, especially of the Roman
School, which reached its greatest perfection in the sixteenth
century, owing to the works of Pierluigi da Palestrina, and
continued subsequently to produce compositions of excellent
quality from a liturgical and musical standpoint."

The re-creation of Gregorian chant and of "classic" polyphony had its indirect effects on composition through the
teaching of the new conservatories, among which were those
of Vienna, Leipzig, Berlin, Dessau, and Munich, and the
Royal Academy and Royal College of Music in London. The
direct effects were most noticeable in the sacred works of
composers like Liszt, Peter Cornelius, Joseph Rheinberger,
and Anton Bruckner, the *Sanctus* of whose *Mass in E Minor*
is based on a theme from Palestrina's *Missa brevis*. Like the
Bach revival, its effects on the musical culture of the present
century have been pervasive and continuous.

MUSICAL SCHOLARSHIP

Universities played but a minor part in this first period of
collecting, editing, and performing the musical monuments
of the past. Though Forkel had mapped out the history,
theory, and bibliography of music as a university discipline,

the subject could not be developed in this direction until the music of at least the chief composers and periods was made available. If the motivation of many of the revivalists was romantic nostalgia for an idealized lost state of art rather than strict historical interpretation, the products of their enthusiasm in editions and anthologies were nevertheless prerequisite to the development of musical scholarship. By midcentury the editions completed or in course of publication provided materials for the study of some of the high points and great figures of musical history. The high points and great figures represented mature phases of musical history that were clearly marked off from each other, so that differences of style and technique could be described in broad and general terms. The new period of musical historiography would have to concern itself also with composers of so-called transition phases, those whose style appeared to combine some of the characteristics of each of the high points on either side. Consequently the musical historian would be more closely occupied than before with techniques and methods of composition, and with the analysis, description, and comparison of large numbers of single compositions. His attention would be focused on the music as a product of certain processes of composition that were exhibited in a style with distinctive technical and expressive characteristics. When the consequent need for more systematic and penetrating methods of analyzing musical styles was felt, the idea and the name of "musicology" were born, almost exactly a century ago.

The term was first used in the nineteenth century by Chrysander in founding his *Jahrbuch fur musikalische Wissenschaft* in 1863. His chief concern was to establish the principle that the music of past ages should be edited and performed in a scholarly spirit, without introducing additions or modifications to cater to the tastes of the present. Chrysander brought out only one further *Jahrbuch* (1867), and the next step in furthering the new scientific and professional attitude to musical scholarship was the founding in 1885 of the *Vierteljahrsschrift für Musikwissenschaft* by Chrysander, Spitta, and Guido Adler. The key article in the first issue was contributed by Adler, the youngest of the trio. In this paper ("Umfang, Methode und Ziel der Musikwissenschaft"), Adler defined the idea of a scientific approach to the study of music along lines that have governed musical scholarship until the present time.

The chief object of the co-founders of the new *Vierteljahrsschrift* was to see scholarship in the arts (*Kunstwissenschaft*) accepted into the family of the humanities. Adler countered the idea that the growth of learning in an art is a sign of the creative decadence of the art by maintaining that on the contrary creative art is not possible, and never has been possible, without such a body of knowledge based on reflection and research. He quoted from Chrysander (in the introduction to the first *Jahrbuch für musikalische Wissenschaft*) to combat the delusion that the "indefinite" nature of music made it impossible to apply to it the requirements of a rigorous scholarship, and from Spitta (in a formal address on "Kunst und Kunstwissenschaft" given in the Royal Academy of Arts in Berlin in 1883) to state the claims of these young disciplines to exercise their independence. In the preamble to his article and its superbly ordered marshaling of the particular aims and methods of musical scholarship, Adler placed the subject of music in its new guise in the direct tradition of Greek mathematical learning about music and the musical studies of the medieval *artes liberales*. The focus of the new musical learning, he emphasized, was the musical work of art itself, and the central aim of all research in music was to elucidate the theoretical and aesthetic principles of the art in the various periods of its history. The systematic side of musical scholarship (comprising musical theory, musical aesthetics, and musical pedagogy) is dependent on the historical side, and has as its object the systematizing of the artistic principles that for the time being acquire stability within the process of historical change. Throughout the essay Adler's main concern is with the investigation of the changing laws of musical style and design in the light of an organic historical process. It is part of the thinking of his time that he saw in this process something analogous to natural growth and decay:

Wie von den Anfangen der einfachen Melodie ausgehend der Bau der Kunstwerke allmahlich wachst, wie von den einfachsten Thesen ausgehend die in den Tonproducten latenten Kunstnormen kompliziert und komplizierter werden, wie mit entschwindenden Kulturen die Tonsysteme vergehen, wie an das Glied sich nach und nach eine Kette von Zellen anschliesst und so organisch wachst, wie die ausserhalb der fortschrittlichen Bewegung stehenden Elemente, weil nicht lebensfahig, untergehen—dies darzulegen und nachzuweisen ist die dankbarste Aufgabe des Kunstgelehrten.

[How starting from the beginnings of simple melody the structure of works of art grows by degrees, how proceeding from the simplest postulates the artistic norms latent in the production of sound become more and more complicated, how sound systems vanish with disappearing cultures, how a series of cells gradually attaches itself to the limb and so grows organically, how elements which stand outside the movement of progress become extinct because not viable— to demonstrate and trace these principles is the most profitable exercise of the scholar in the arts.]

Adler's ideas had a profound influence, primarily through his teaching (for which he founded the Vienna Musikhistorisches Institut), through his organizing of editions in the

series of *Denkmaler der Tonkunst in Oesterreich* (83 volumes
from 1894 to 1938), and through the effects of his training
on young composers, among them Arnold Schönberg, Anton
Webern, Egon Wellesz, and Paul Pisk. His methods were
practiced and taught in turn by a long list of eminent dis-
ciples: Lach, Orel, Haas, Botstiber, von Ficker, Besseler, and
Rietsch in Austria and Germany; Smijers in Holland; Jeppesen in Denmark; Wellesz in Britain; Nettl and Geiringer
in the United States. If one adds that the pupils of Spitta
included Johannes Wolf, Peter Wagner, Fleischer, Seiffert,
and Sandberger, and if one were further to add the names of
Riemann, Ludwig, and Einstein in Germany, Pirro and
Aubry in France, van den' Borren in Belgium, Torchi in
Italy, Pedrell in Spain, and Wooldridge and Dent in England, one would have mentioned the authors of most of the
basic works on which modern musical scholarship depends.

MUSICAL PALEOGRAPHY AND REPERTORY

Adler's concept of musicology took for granted that musical
historians would continue to edit and publish the music of
the past, in order to make available the "art works" that are
the subject of their studies. He himself provided for this,
as far as his own country was concerned, by establishing the
Austrian *Denkmaler,* many of which were edited by his
pupils. (Composers were not exempt from this enterprise—
Webern edited part of Heinrich Isaac's *Choralis Constantinus.*) In fact, editing inevitably became an integral part of
musical scholarship, since most projects involved, and many
still involve, the study of unpublished music. In the case of
medieval and earlier music, and of music written in a special
notation such as lute tablature, the scholar's work belongs
to a division of musical research that Adler placed first on
the historical side of his scheme, the subject of musical

44

paleography. The period between 1885 and about 1930 saw the solution of the main problems, the establishment of the general principles of transcription, and the writing of a history of musical notation, largely through the work of Johannes Wolf (*Geschichte der Mensuralnotation 1250-1460,* 1905; *Handbuch der Notationskunde,* 1913-19). The researches of the monks of Solesmes in the paleography of Western chant were complemented by pioneer studies in Byzantine chant by Fleischer (Professor at Berlin) and others. The solution of the problems of transcribing Byzantine notation was achieved by Wellesz (Professor at Vienna until 1938, and since then at Oxford) as the result of studies which he began in 1916.

Allied to these researches in notation, Ludwig (Professor and *Rector magnificus* at Gottingen) and Besseler (formerly Professor at Heidelberg and now at Leipzig) carried out fundamental studies in what may be called repertory-research, the investigation of groups of manuscripts or prints of a particular time, place, or composer. Through their studies in the sources of the thirteenth and fourteenth centuries entirely new avenues to the musical past were opened. For a period nearer the present this kind of research is represented notably by the great index by numbers of Mozart's works (*Chronologisch-thematisches Verzeichnis samtlicher Tonwerke W. A. Mozarts,* 1862) made by the professional botanist and mineralogist Ludwig Kochel. The most comprehensive of all bibliographical achievements in music was the dictionary of musical sources of all periods compiled by Robert Eitner, a teacher of music in Berlin who was self-taught in musical history. It is interesting to remark that this fundamental work (*Biographisch-bibliographisches Quellen-lexikon der Musiker und Musikgelehrten der christlichen Zeitrechnung bis zur Mitte des 19. Jahrhunderts,* 10 vols., 1900-1904) had in its first volume a list of subscribers for one hundred and forty-six copies. Its replacement by a new *Répertoire international des sources musicales* is now in progress under an international commission with its secretariat in Paris.

Besides his bibliographical work, Eitner organized a Society for Musical Research that published under his direction the first important series of editions of music and musical treatises of the fifteenth and sixteenth centuries (*Publikationen alterer praktischer und theoretischer Musikwerke vorzugsweise des XV. und XVI. Jahrhunderts,* 29 vols., 1873-1905). Alongside Adler's Austrian *Denkmaler* there were series of *Denkmaler deutscher Tonkunst* (1892-1931) and *Denkmaler der Tonkunst in Bayern* (1900-31), both with music of various periods. In 1926 Theodore Kroyer, a pupil of Sandberger and Professor at Heidelberg, began a new series of *Publikationen alterer Musik* in which appeared works of Guillaume de Machaut edited by Ludwig (the literary works of Machaut had been edited by Hoepffner, 1908-21), of Ockeghem edited by Plamenac, and of Luis Milan edited by Schrade. France had its *Les Maîtres musiciens de la renaissance française* in twenty-three volumes edited by Expert from 1894 to 1908, and a further series of *Monuments de la musique française au temps de la renaissance* by the same editor from 1924 to 1929. Much Italian music of the sixteenth and seventeenth centuries was first made known by Torchi's *L'Arte musicale in Italia* (7 vols., 1897-1907), while Pedrell edited sacred Spanish music of the fifteenth and sixteenth centuries in *Hispaniae scholae musica sacra* (8 vols., 1894-98). For his time Pedrell had remarkably comprehensive views of musical culture. His work also included studies in the musical folklore of Spain, which have had a deep effect on Spanish composers, researches in the music of the Spanish theater, and the complete edition of the works of Victoria.

After the turn of the century the music of the Middle Ages,

46

previously little known and much misunderstood, became more and more the subject of scholarly editions, monographs, and articles. Fifty compositions by *Dufay and his Contemporaries* from an Italian manuscript in the Bodleian Library were printed in 1898 by Sir John Stainer, Professor of Music at Oxford, and his son and daughter. Pierre Aubry, lecturer at the École des Hautes Études Sociales in Paris, published a facsimile edition of the *Roman de Fauvel* (1316) and a volume of *Estampies et danses royales* in 1907, and the thirteenth century Bamberg motet manuscript in facsimile with transcriptions and analytical commentary in 1908. Facsimiles of chansonniers containing troubadour and trouvère music were published by Aubry, Jeanroy, and Beck, and two volumes of transcriptions and texts by Gennrich in his *Rondeaux, Virelais und Balladen* (1921, 1927). In 1935-39 the motet manuscript in Montpellier was published by Éditions de l'Oiseau-lyre in a splendid three-volume edition, with complete facsimile, by Yvonne Rokseth, pupil of Pirro and Professor at Strasbourg.

A complete edition of the large repertory of English music for the virginals contained in the *Fitzwilliam Virginal Book* was brought out (1894-99) by Barclay Squire of the British Museum and Fuller-Maitland of the *Times*. From 1913 to 1924 E. H. Fellowes, an Oxford graduate in music and Minor Canon of Windsor, reprinted all the English madrigal prints of 1593 to 1624 in the thirty-six volumes of *The English Madrigal School,* as well as all the lute song prints of the same period in *The English School of Lutenist Songwriters* (1920). Ten volumes of *Tudor Church Music* were published by a committee of editors with the support of the Carnegie United Kingdom Trust in 1923-29, and the celebrated *Old Hall Manuscript* of the Royal Chapel in the early fifteenth century by three editors for the Plainsong and Mediaeval Music Society in 1933-38. The sacred music in the

Bodleian manuscript that the Stainers had drawn on earlier for chansons by Dufay and others was edited for the same society by van den Borren in 1932 under the title *Polyphonia sacra*. The editions of courtly chansonniers of the fifteenth century that appeared included the Copenhagen Chansonnier by Jeppesen and the Dijon Chansonnier by Eugenie Droz, Geneviève Thibault, and Yvonne Rokseth.

When one considers that, besides these and other editions of music of earlier periods and in earlier forms, many complete editions of single composers were also made available between the 1880's and the 1930's, one begins to realize how much the musical culture of the mid-twentieth century owes to the musical scholarship of those decades. A summary list by countries would have to include among composers of Austria and Germany the works of Mozart (1876-1907), Schumann (1879-93), Schubert (1883-97), Schein (1901-23, unfinished), Liszt (1907-36, unfinished), Buxtehude (1925-37, unfinished), Brahms (1926-28), and Praetorius (1928-40); among those of France and the Netherlands the works of Sweelinck (1894-1901), Rameau (1896-1924), Berlioz (1900-07), Obrecht (1908-21), de Monte (1927-35, unfinished), and Couperin (1932-33); of Italy Corelli (1888-91) and Monteverdi (1926-42); of England Purcell (1878-1928, unfinished but now resumed); of Spain Victoria (1902-13); and of Poland Chopin (1878-80).

STYLE IN STRUCTURE AND SOUND

Beyond any doubt the most signal achievement of post-Adler musicology has been to provide musical "works-of-art" on this grand scale. Because the primary purpose of these editions was to nourish the scholar with food for stylistic analysis and critical-historical comment, they were normally designed for the library shelf rather than for the performer's stand. Like scholarly editions in the other humanities they included information on the character and content of all the sources, on variants, and on necessary editorial changes. Their usefulness did not end there, however, for many have been used as the basis of "practical" editions in more convenient format, which thus place the findings of musical research in the hands of conductors and performers. Unfortunately, many such performing editions are disfigured by speed and expression marks that are historically invalid and research in the appropriate media and manners of performance is not always available to the user of a performing edition. The historical study of musical instruments and of methods of performance (*Auffuhrungspraxis*) are comparatively recent branches of musical scholarship, and many questions remain only partially answered.

The concept of style criticism implicit in Adler's article in the *Vierteljahrsschrift* pervaded the historical writing of the following period. He himself returned to and elaborated the subject in *Der Stil in der Musik* (I, 1911; the second volume, which was to deal with historical style periods, did not appear) and in *Methode der Musikgeschichte* (1919). The study of musical forms and genres, which Adler placed second in the historical division of his scheme, viewed musical works as the "compositional products" of a historical process at a certain stage, rather than as manifestations of the human will-to-beauty. This notion of a "morphology" of forms betrays a pattern of thinking derived from current theories of biological evolution. Nevertheless, the viewing of musical forms in the context of the processes of growth and decay did lead to researches in the history of specific genres. By working across the usual divisions of composer, time, and place, these studies formed threads in the pattern of historical knowledge. Keyboard music, for example, was the subject of a history written by Max Seiffert in 1899. The first volume of Peter

Wagner's comprehensive and still immensely valuable work on Gregorian chant (*Einfuhrung in die Gregorianischen Melodien*) appeared in 1895, and the second and third volumes in 1905 and 1921 respectively. Wagner's history of the mass (*Geschichte der Messe*, 1914; only the first volume appeared) was one of a notable series of handbooks on the histories of the various genres ("Kleine Handbucher der Musikgeschichte nach Gattungen") that also included historical studies of the motet (by Leichtentritt), the overture (by Botstiber), the concerto and the oratorio (by Schering), the secular cantata (by Schmitz), the symphony and suite (by Nef), and the opera (by Kretzschmar, who was the general editor).

The third part of Adler's plan was the study of the "Principles of Composition in their Historical Succession." Much of the historical research and writing of this period consisted of detailed studies in style within a limited framework, some of which have already been mentioned in connection with editions. Other studies of fundamental value were Riemann's on the *History of Theory* (1898), Dent's on Alessandro Scarlatti (1905) and on early English opera (1928), Charles van den Borren's on English virginal music (1912) and on Dufay (1925), and Jeppesen's on the style of Palestrina (1927). Few scholars attempted to write a general history of music unassisted. The only significant exception was the prolific Riemann, whose *Handbuch der Musikgeschichte* (2 vols., 1901-13) was criticized by followers of Adler on the ground that its approach to the psychology of the composer through a study of the art of musical creation could "never completely explain the complex ingredients which make up a musical composition," but rather opened the door "to fruitless aesthetic speculation." (Wellesz in *Grove's Dictionary of Music and Musicians*, 4th ed., supplementary volume 1948, p. 461.) With increasing specialization and the accumulation of editions and detailed studies, it became clear that larger histories that would take new knowledge into account depended on collaboration.

England produced a pioneer work in *The Oxford History of Music* (6 vols., 1901-05). In the first two volumes a notable contribution to the understanding of medieval music was made by H. E. Wooldridge, painter and musical historian, who was Slade Professor of Fine Art at Oxford. The other periods were dealt with by Sir Hubert Parry, Fuller-Maitland, Edward Dannreuther, and Sir Henry Hadow, the general editor. Hadow was an influential figure in education (he was Vice-Chancellor of Sheffield University from 1919 to 1930) who had convictions about the importance of musical history in general education. He held that "we should admit musical history to the same place in our annals that we now accord to the history of literature." (*The Education of the Adolescent*, 1927.) In France Alexander Lavignac enlisted more than a dozen co-workers for the historical part (in five volumes) of the *Encyclopédie de la musique* (1913-31). Adler's own *Handbuch der Musikgeschichte* (1924; 2nd ed. in 2 vols., 1930) had contributions from thirty-five historians of various countries. The modern musical anthology was represented by Schering's *History of Music in Examples* (1931), while George Kinsky's *History of Music in Pictures* (1929) was a new departure in the presentation of visual material. The work that most fully presented the scholarly findings of the period was the *Handbuch der Musikwissenschaft* edited by Ernest Bücken (a pupil of Sandberger and Professor at Cologne) and printed in Potsdam between 1928 and 1931. In the first of the thirteen volumes, Robert Lachmann wrote on non-Western music and, in the second, Curt Sachs dealt with the music of antiquity. The other volumes included a history of Western music by Besseler, Haas, Bücken, and Mersmann as well as studies on practices of performance by Haas, on the music of the Roman Catholic Church by Ursprung, on the music of the Lutheran Church by Blume, and on the history of musical instruments by Heinitz.

The scholarly study of the musical instruments of the West was the fourth and last part of the historical side of Adler's scheme of musical research (the study of non-Western music appears as *Musikologie* on the systematic side). This was the one subject in which comparative and overlapping studies of Eastern and Western cultures were unavoidable, and the only one in which the rift between musicology and ethnomusicology was closed. A classification of instruments, applicable to all cultures, was worked out by Victor Mahillon (*Catalogue descriptif et analytique du musée instrumental du conservatoire royale de musique de Bruxelles*, 1888) and this was adapted and developed by E. M. von Hornbostel and Curt Sachs ("Systematik der Musikinstrumenten," in *Zeitschrift für Ethnologie*, 1914). On this basis Sachs went on to lay the foundations of modern research in musical instruments in a dictionary of the instruments of all periods and cultures (*Reallexikon der Musikinstrumente*, 1913) and in a historical account of European instruments (*Handbuch der Musikinstrumentenkunde*, 1920). Some of the earliest research of permanent value in this subject was done in England by Canon F. W. Galpin, who published *Old English Instruments of Music* in 1912, a *Textbook of European Musical Instruments* in 1937, and monographs on such diverse topics as *The Musical Instruments of the American Indians of the N. W. Coast* (1903) and *The Music of Electricity* (1938).

WESTERN MUSICOLOGY TAKES STOCK

On the initiative of Oskar Fleischer and Max Seiffert the first International Musical Society was formed in 1899. There were already in existence a Society for Musical History in

Holland and a Musical Association (now the Royal Musical Association) in Great Britain, and these became affiliated societies. A number of national groups were organized, and four international congresses were held before the war of 1914-18 caused the disruption of the organization. A congress was held at Basel in 1924, a year which gave a special timeliness to one of the three public addresses, in which Adler made a plea for a balance between nationalism and internationalism in music:

> Internationalism, in art as in life, is opposed to nationalism. Every nation undeniably has its peculiar disposition, out of which arise, on the one hand, the simple natural products—folk-music—and, on the other, those highest forms of art which are likewise influenced by it. Some few investigators have recently extended their researches, more especially in the field of poetry, to a scientific exploration of regions and localities. So long as these researches are not influenced by political motives or their value exaggerated by local patriotism, they appear unobjectionable. Indeed, all artistic phenomena can be gathered together into time-groups and place-groups
>
> Thus, while nationalism directs its chief attention to the ascertainment of and insistence upon national qualities, with a tendency to racial narrowness, it is incumbent on internationalism to ascertain and set forth those artistic phenomena which are common property. Objective research should endeavour successfully to bring the two species into accord. And this can be effected by closely following up the organic processes of art—how nature and culture unite, blend, balance each other, and so combined reach full fruition from time to time.

In 1927 the Beethoven Centenary celebrations in Vienna gave an opportunity for forming an international organization, and the International Society for Musical Research was founded, with Adler as honorary president, Peter Wagner as president, and Dent, Pirro, and Wolf as vice presidents. The bulletin that commenced publication in 1928 became the quarterly journal *Acta musicologica* in 1930.

In the early volumes some representative musicologists contributed their reflections on the state of musicology in their country and their views on the place of musicology in musical culture. For Italy, F. Torrefranca pointed out that the teaching of history of music there dated only from the war, and that the political convulsions of the time were unpropitious for its development. He thought that Italy's special activity in research would be in the history of musical forms, since almost all musical forms were Italian creations. André Pirro saw musical writing in France afflicted by a "style de causerie" that tainted many potentially useful studies. But he looked forward to the part musicology would have in writing anew the history of the Middle Ages and the Renaissance in France, and gave specific examples to show that musical historians had worked in too narrow a range of sources, neglecting material to be found in literature, in general history, in paintings, in catalogs and inventories of documents, and in archives of institutions. E. J. Dent of Cambridge deplored the lack of official organization of English research, which had been largely carried on by amateurs for fifty years. His thoughts on the needs and functions of musicology were succinct and unpretentious: the practical study of old music was indispensable to the inner understanding of all music; music research was useless unless it was directed toward the practical benefit of the art of music in general; and there was great need of a general history of music for ordinary readers. To Arnold Schering, such thoughts made Dent a fanatical utilitarian. Musicological research could deal with matters not directly related to practice. In Germany its object was to inculcate in the aspiring student respect for facts and awareness of problems, and to lead him to positive and public achievements as a scholar. Schering noted that reform of school music in Germany had greatly increased knowledge of older music, and that a fruitful interchange existed between university musicians and performers in the musical world at large. He was not ready, however, to foretell whether there would be any perceptible effect of this on the general public.

ơ§ 3 ƍ

MUSICOLOGY IN AMERICA

THE IMPACT OF EUROPEAN TRADITION

Beginning in the 1930's a number of European musical scholars emigrated to the United States and found positions in American institutions. This addition to the relatively small band of American-born musicologists greatly hastened not only the adaptation of European traditions of research in Western music to the American scene but also the reception of musicology into the community of the humanities. Among these bearers of the European outlook—some already renowned for their scholarship—were Apel, Bukofzer, David, Alfred Einstein, Geiringer, Gombosi, Hertzmann, Lang, Lowinsky, Nathan, Paul Nettl, Plamenac, Sachs, Schrade, and Winternitz. Besides giving a powerful impulse to teaching and research, they added notably to production in musical scholarship. They came with established concepts of the nature and scope of musicology and of the place of the musical scholar in the world of learning. Many if not most came from societies in which the very foundations of the humanistic view of their subject were being attacked and undermined. By the fact of their coming, therefore, they declared convictions about the place of the scholar in the society of his time and the necessity of keeping scholarship free of social dogma.

Because of their presence, as well as the fact that virtually all American-born musicologists active in the 1930's had had to seek their training in Europe, American musicology accepted *en bloc* the current traditions and aims of European musicology. In common with the immigrant scholars they organized their research and teaching according to the established lines of division between general history, period history and the history of forms, biography and bibliography, and scholarly editions of music. The only important change was a greatly increased use of photography, made necessary by the almost total absence of original sources.

Though the work of immigrant scholars was founded on earlier training and research, the completion and publication of an imposing number of important studies must be counted among the achievements of musicology in America, and due credit must be given to the institutions and foundations that gave their support. Musicology everywhere has been greatly enriched and musical history in the English language has for the first time been provided with some of the key items of a musical library through these publications. In a period richer in important musical publications than any other in American history, some of the outstanding works were Lang's *Music in Western Civilization* (1941), Sachs's *The Rise of Music in the Ancient World* (1943) and his *History of Musical Instruments* (1940), Bukofzer's *Music in the Baroque Era* (1947), Apel's *The Notation of Polyphonic Music* (1942) and his *Harvard Dictionary of Music* (1944), Einstein's *The Italian Madrigal* (1949), Lowinsky's *Secret Chromatic Art in the Netherlands Motet* (1946), Geiringer's *The Bach Family* (1954), Schrade's *Monteverdi* (1950), and editions of music by Apel and Plamenac.

ACTIVITY AND COMMUNICATION

While the work of European scholars who settled in the United States must be counted a part of the American achievement, it is on the native scholar and researcher that the pattern of musicological development ultimately depends.

The strong influence of European methods and criteria, combined in some cases with an approach matured in other fields of study, is apparent in the achievements of American-born musicologists between about 1930 and the early 1950's.

It is perhaps valid to distinguish three motives in the musical writing and publishing of the period. The object of some authors was to provide textbooks giving a survey of the history of music for courses in liberal arts colleges. The second group aimed at providing the professional musicologist, both teacher and student, with the basic handbooks of his discipline. The most remarkable achievement here, and one of permanent value to musicology in all English speaking countries, was Gustave Reese's volume on *Music in the Middle Ages* (1940), which presents a masterly digest of the whole of accumulated scholarship about ancient and medieval music. This was later followed by Reese's equally comprehensive *Music in the Renaissance* (1954). Other works in this category are Strunk's *Source Readings in Musical History* (1950) and (as a guide rather than a companion) Glen Haydon's *Introduction to Musicology* (1941). A third kind of writing consisted of doctoral dissertations. These covered an admirably wide range of subjects, some potentially of interest to scholars in other disciplines, and the group included books by Barbour, Steinhardt, Cannon, Nelson, Waite, Myers, Rowen, Crosten, Rubsamen, Newlin, Oliver, and Carpenter and editions of music by Marrocco, Ellinwood, Hewitt, Cuyler, and Apel.

All the works mentioned in the previous paragraph were published by 1954. This, roughly speaking, seems to be the date at which the costs of production and the lack of adequate subsidies began seriously to interfere with publication in the field of musicology. Taking as the chief evidence of activity and communication in musicology since 1954 the amount of publication in America, the amount of publication by Americans abroad, and the number of doctoral dissertations, one's definite impression is of a rapid increase in activity and a disturbing decrease in communication. Only the textbook survey aimed at large undergraduate courses seems really to interest publishers. While the quality of recent works of this kind shows clearly the effects of developments in musicology at the higher level, most such books cannot be said to transcend their practical aims or to function well either as handbooks for the professional student and performer or as introductions for the interested amateur. On the level of musicological writing the decline in publication since about 1954 is very marked. Among the few distinguished works that have been able to find a publisher in the United States are Apel's *Gregorian Chant,* Kirkpatrick's *Domenico Scarlatti,* Newman's *The Sonata in the Baroque Era,* Kerman's *Opera as Drama,* and Parrish's *The Notation of Medieval Music.* The publishing of editions of music would be in no better case if it depended on normal avenues of publication. Most of the few existing series are brought out by the music departments of institutions such as Smith College, Yale University, and the New York Public Library. Presumably some of these depend on *ad hoc* subvention by the institution concerned or by private patrons. With respect both to books and to editions it does not seem an overstatement to say that there appears to be a near-breakdown of the dissemination of knowledge of one of the central arts of Western society. If this is due to what are termed "good" commercial reasons, then intervention by noncommercial bodies should take place with a minimum of delay.

The problem cannot lie in lack of material, for one of the starkest evidences of the failure in communication is the fate of the great majority of the doctoral dissertations in musicology completed in American universities. The third edition (1961) of Helen Hewitt's *Doctoral Dissertations in Mu-*

sicology lists the more than eight hundred theses then completed or in progress. Those actually completed number some three hundred and fifty. The total of eight hundred in 1961 compares with five hundred and fifty in the second edition in 1957 and two hundred and forty-five (excluding theses written in departments other than music) in the first edition in 1952. The widening gap between the proportion of valuable scholarly work that exists in theses and its communication to the world of humanistic scholarship seems no less than calamitous. It cannot begin to be bridged by partial publication in journals and selective reproduction on microfilm and microcard. Nor can it be regarded as a satisfactory situation that better possibilities for the publication of the work of American musicologists exist in Europe than in their own country. A degree of interchange between countries is a healthy feature of scholarship, especially in a subject of international concern, but the fact is indisputable that other countries are providing, often through public or private grants, more than a just proportion of media for the communication of American scholarship in musicology.

AMERICAN MUSICOLOGY AND AMERICAN MUSIC

American musicologists are in a special and perhaps unique position in relation to the musical history of their own country. This is partly, but not entirely, explained by the fact that American musical scholarship developed in close contact with the "official" musicological outlook of Europe, but without real involvement in the musical culture of either Europe or America. It has meant that the attention of American musical historians has been turned almost wholly away from the music of their own country and society. As a consequence some aspects of music in America during the past half century that are now seen to be important for American music as a whole, and for the understanding of the American arts abroad, have failed to be recorded, and none has been thoroughly studied by those most competent to do so. It has justly been held that the artistic expressions of a society need the closest study during the thirty years or so after they have taken place. After that time firsthand contacts with the artists and observation of their immediate and wider relations with the social milieu become increasingly difficult. Records become less precise and more scattered, until eventually reconstruction becomes a major historical and imaginative enterprise. A symptom rather than necessarily the most cogent case of this is the lack of serious study of the technical and social aspects of American jazz.

Jazz, though an indigenous North American music, has generally been more highly regarded and more seriously studied by musicologists abroad than at home. A French musicologist and critic, André Coeuroy, has said: "Improvised jazz is the most potent force in music at the present time: long may it remain so." Jazz in its authentic form is essentially a matter of improvisation on an agreed framework and is to that degree an art of instantaneous musical creation. In the identity of creation and execution it possesses a characteristic that was for centuries an integral part of European music at all levels of society. Extemporaneous creation and elaboration are a mark alike of the most primitive and the most sophisticated levels of the act of music making. Jazz was created in New Orleans about 1900 with elements from blues, ragtime, and the wind band. Helped as no musical art had been before by the resources of the twentieth century technology of dissemination, it evolved with spectacular rapidity from its folklorish beginnings to a subtle and resourceful art which its younger practitioners pursue to the frontiers of the avant-garde techniques of "serious" music. "Today," says a recent French encyclopedia of music (*Encyclopédie de la musique,* by F. Michel in collaboration with F. Lesure and V. Féderov, Paris, 1958-61), "jazz can be defined as music in free forms which in the course of its fifty years of history has appropriated most of the harmonic refinements of classical music, and which is characterized by the criteria that execution is creation, that this execution must be 'swinging,' and that a free play of sonorities is an expressive necessity." "A band swings," it has been said, "when its collective improvisation is rhythmically integrated." A purely American phenomenon in its origins and early development, jazz has become an international art, with a complex of traditions, schools, and styles. Nevertheless, American creators and performers have remained unmatched for their cultivation of the vitality and technical brilliance which are essential to this music.

What has jazz to do with musicology? The most obvious and immediate relevance on the level of technique is the use of improvised elaboration. The scope and significance of improvisation in Western music were first made a subject of comprehensive study by the Hungarian-born (now American-domiciled) scholar Ernst Ferand in his extended study *Die Improvisation in der Musik* (1939). This work is "the first serious attempt to view this practice as a whole and as a specifically artistic phenomenon, to consider its origin and its historical development, to discover its principles, and to establish its relations to all other aspects of musical art." It is interesting to observe that this is one of the few musical subjects that already crosses the boundaries of cultures and societies. Ferand draws upon the work of ethnomusicologists, musical historians and theorists, and upon indications in surviving music to demonstrate the continuing role of extemporization in musical practice. The time-scale of his history is indicated by the fact that the material ranges from primitive cultures, the East and antiquity, through instrumental elaboration and the techniques of fauxbourdon and descant in the Middle Ages and the ornamentation of choral part-music at the close of the sixteenth century to vocal and instrumental cadenzas and other modern manifestations. In a supplementary anthology of examples from plainsong to the nineteenth century (*Die Improvisation in Beispielen aus neun Jahrhunderten abendlandischer Musik*, 1956), Ferand gives evidence for the virtual certainty that the beginnings of polyphony were founded on practices of improvisation. From these were gradually evolved the changing rules and conventions of written counterpoint, which in turn became the framework of new methods of extemporaneous elaboration.

One of the most interesting aspects of this history is the interaction of improvisation and written composition in both Western and non-Western music. Until relatively modern times the demarcation between them was very narrow, and the early stages of composition were normally taught through improvisation. The ramifications of the most recent studies of this subject (which do not yet include jazz) may be indicated by the titles of a group of papers written for the Congress of the International Musicological Society held in New York in September 1961. The general title of the group was "The Role of Improvised and Written Ornamentation in the Evolution of Musical Language," and the individual papers were:

"Introduction," Geneviève Thibault, Neuilly-sur-Seine
"Note sur l'ornementation en Afrique Noire," Gilbert Rouget, Paris
"Note sur l'ornementation dans le plain-chant grégorien," Solange Corbin, Paris
"Remarques sur l'ornementation dans l'ethnomusicologie européenne," Claudie Marcel-Dubois, Paris
"Note sur l'ornementation au Vietnam," Trân Van Khê, Vietnam

FRANK LL. HARRISON

"L'Ornementation dans la musique profane au Moyen-Age,"
Geneviève Thibault, Neuilly-sur-Seine
"A History of Music Seen in the Light of Ornamentation,"
Ernest T. Ferand, New York

In the jazz era the history of ornamentation has gone
through numerous phases (for mainly social reasons) in a
relatively short time. The relation of its varied and changing
techniques to the art of musical creation lies, according to
A. Hodeir (*Jazz: Its Evolution and Essence,* trans. from the
French by D. Noakes, 1956), in the role of continuity of
musical thought in the act of creation. Allowing that in jazz
"any attempt at construction appears . . . only incidentally
and in a rudimentary form," this writer goes on to note that
"in jazz the act of creation can be performed almost as freely
in the simple exposition of a theme as in the invention of a
chorus. By the way he handles sound itself and by a kind of
rhythmic modelling of the theme being interpreted, the musician is able to renew it in its very essence without actually
getting very far away from it. When the instrumentalist is
improvising freely, this important role of creative performance is seconded by the resources of melodic invention
in the traditional sense. However, in both cases it is thought
that is behind creation." Hodeir goes on to analyze the
thought of the improviser as carried out in the interpretation
of existing melody, in the invention of new melody to replace
it, and in the technique of paraphrase, leading him to examine the nature of collective creation. Here his belief that our
conception of the difficulty of group improvisation is greatly
exaggerated is enlightening in view of the misunderstanding
by historians of collective improvisation in earlier periods. All
this is very pertinent to some stages in the history of Western
music. The importance of jazz techniques of improvisation to
the musical historian is that they provide almost the only
opportunity that Western music of the twentieth century

64

affords of observing the actual practice of collective improvisation at work.

MUSICOLOGY AND MUSICAL LIFE

Jazz has also a relevance to American musicology on the level of the history and place of music in American society. Its comparative neglect is a part of the inattention of native musical historians to the musical past of their own country, as well as of their abstraction from many aspects of its musical present. Again, the problem is in part one of lack of communication. Isolation of the parts of a musical life and artificial barriers between them do disservice to every part and to the healthy development of the whole. Earlier in this essay reference was made to the need for viewing American musicology in the context of the nation's musical culture and to the recent survey *One Hundred Years of Music in America* as an informative panorama of the recent history of that culture. To the European reader there are perhaps two points that emerge with particular force from this picture of a rapidly changing scene: the feeling of apprehension in some of the essays about the future of the particular part of American music that is being discussed, and the desirability of publishing deeper and wider studies of the history of music in American society than the historical essays there could accomplish in their space.

The dilemma of artistic cultures in a society based on freedom of enterprise is of the most direct concern to humanism in the West. It is a problem that has been posed in various fields, and its urgency for American music is confirmed by the titles of two of the chapters in *One Hundred Years of Music in America* ("The Dilemma of the Music Publishing Industry" and "Neither Quick nor Dead: The Music Book

Paradox") and by the conclusions reached by the authors of several others. What is particularly interesting to note is the realization of the comparative suddenness with which the problems have become critical, and the feeling that superficial nostrums will no longer provide viable solutions. On the state of book publication R. D. Darrell has this to say (and here one is aware of the dangers of quotation out of full context):

> The growth in musical scholarship and research facilities has been influential largely within institutional circles only; the best of its book manifestations have won relatively scant attention from even seriously musically interested laymen. . . . Steadily the eternal gap between scholar and layman widens; increasingly the latter seems content with whatever second- or third-hand scholarship may trickle down through the few popularized books he does read; more and more widespread becomes the miasmic delusion that "learning" comes to a dead stop with the end of one's formal education.

And the last paragraph of Richard F. French's essay on the publishing industry has this observation:

> The next century, indeed, will ask new standards of professionalism of the industry—a new sense of responsibility to music and to society, new techniques of market research, a renewed respect for tradition and technology, and an excited curiosity. The industry cannot survive merely by improvisation and compromise, merely by being canny, resourceful, and flexible. It can re-assert its position as a major cultural force only if it combines a sense of history with an adventurous estimate of technological possibilities to form an effective view of the present and the future. The opportunities were never more abundant, the hazards never greater, and the greatest risk will be assumed by the least venturous. "Merely to sound the alarm is of no use," wrote Clausetti. "The march of science is like the course of a river which

must inevitably rejoin the sea. We can give it as a motto the verse of Dante: Non impedir lo suo fatale andare."

It is not, one believes, an overestimate of the function of musicology in the musical life of a modern society to say that it should both help and be helped to bridge the gap between scholar and layman that disturbs Mr. Darrell, and should provide some of the sense of history and of responsibility to music and to society that Mr. French sees to be needed.

In the musical life of his own society the musical historian has a role to play similar to that he fulfills on the wider canvas of the history of the West: to be aware of the roots and branches of his country's musical history, to rewrite them and reinterpret them, as an essential contribution to the self-knowledge of his society and as a means to a historical continuity that may carry a living and evolving culture through its periodic crises. The volume from which I have quoted, though it is primarily concerned with the composing and making of music and contains no essay specifically on musicology, nevertheless has historical contributions of great interest by musicologists, which promise well for the point of view we have been advocating. There are chapters on opera, concerts, church music, band music, music in education, and popular music. Arnold Shaw's conclusion to the last of these suggests very cogently the mutual relation of musicology and musical life:

> An increasing number of colleges, universities, and conservatories are giving courses in the history of jazz. One would have to look far and wide to find a curriculum that includes a course in the history of popular music as such.
>
> Our popular music deserves better treatment, not only because it is a body of material that has a relevance, fitness, and richness of its own, but because its influence reaches far beyond our own shores. The tumultuous reception of *Porgy*

and Bess in Moscow, of Dizzy Gillespie in the Middle East, of The Platters in South America, all suggest the high esteem in which our popular music is held abroad. Moreover, the hit lists of many foreign countries constantly contain American records in the original English-language versions by American artists. In other words, it is not an exaggeration to say that the popular music of our country has become a significant part of the popular music of the world. Whatever our prestige as a political, military, or space-exploring nation, our standing in the field of popular song is at an all-time peak. Paradoxically, our popular music has still to attain a similar prestige in its own land.

The study by Americans of their own music in all its aspects is important not only to the institution of musicology and to the deepening of musical life as a whole but also to the understanding abroad of the American arts and their place in the pattern of American life.

MUSICOLOGY AND MUSICAL EDUCATION

The foregoing reflections on the relation of the American musicologist to the musical culture of his own society are intended to suggest a point of view on the relation of the musicologist everywhere to his materials, of whatever place or period. Insofar as these materials are technical in character, the qualifications of a musicologist are a compound of innate musicianship, thorough musical training, and a feeling for the language and syntax of musical sound. Inborn musicianship and feeling for the language of music depend for their fulfillment on early and continuous musical education, and on its philosophy and methods. To a very important degree the quality and range of American musicology are dependent on the role of schools and colleges in developing personalities with musical potential. Here one who has observed the methods and results of musical education in several countries on both sides of the Atlantic cannot but feel that school musical education in the United States is lamentably uneven, is bedeviled with proponents of so-called educational music of poor taste and deleterious aesthetic value, and is generally ineffective because of its unwillingness to use valid methods for the training of ear and body. In most nonspecialist high schools (with some notable exceptions) the attitude to the arts amounts to miseducation, because it fails to recognize in them an avenue to emotional maturity and control and a medium that every civilized culture has used to promote social coherence, individual independence, and personal distinctiveness.

Since musical activity fosters both individual development and group coordination it takes a high place among the arts as a means to personal growth within the social context. Too often in the United States this growth is hampered by inadequate musical training at one stage or another of the educational process. In order to function properly this process must be treated as a whole in relation to each individual subject. In this sense all musical education is a preparation for musicology, for its purpose is to create conditions for the greatest possible awareness of the character and relationships of musical events past and present, and this is the essence of the musicological outlook. The natural acquirement of the language of music must begin with the early training of ear, memory, and body movement. Continuing into the high-school stage it should educe the capabilities latent in the adolescent for conscious analysis and increasing realization of artistic styles in terms of social and historical context. At all stages the material may be every kind of music—whether "classical," "popular," or "folk"—in which the varieties of musical thought can be related to the needs and impulses of human communication. One of the unfortunate results of the disparity in aims between the successive stages of education in music is the creation of artificial barriers and "social distinctions" between what are misguidedly thought of as "serious" and "popular" music. The false disunity of our musical culture is imposed on the real unity of all musical expression.

A further serious consequence of the poor treatment of the arts in school education is the fact that musicians who have passed through a humanistic education in music in a graduate school do not normally seek posts in schools. Thus the circle of musical education is not completed, its parts are artificially cut off from each other, and fail to develop a creative relationship. This results in an uncomfortable gap between school music and undergraduate music, and again between undergraduate and graduate music. A formidable task in developing technical and historical knowledge is laid upon the undergraduate student and teacher. Inevitably the consolidation of this training must be continued into the graduate stage, so that the time at which independent research may safely be undertaken is correspondingly delayed.

If better opportunities for musical training and experience were available in schools to the potential musician, the undergraduate stage of humanistic training could be considerably more specialized than at present for those likely to profit from it. This should neither exclude nor be compromised by courses for nonspecialist students on the lines that departments of music in the United States have so successfully developed.

HISTORY AND THEORY

In the booklet on *The Place of Musicology in American Institutions of Higher Learning,* the late Professor Manfred Bukofzer included a section on "European and American Plans of Instruction." His comments are pertinent to any discussion of the content and philosophy of musical education:

The training of musicologists at American universities does not exactly correspond to that offered at European institutions, except perhaps at institutions in England. In Europe musicology belongs to the "Faculty of Philosophy" and comprises virtually no courses in "practical" music. Since university study in Europe starts at what corresponds to our graduate level, there exists no formalized curriculum in music comparable to our undergraduate instruction On the one hand, therefore, the preparatory training is more flexible; but, on the other hand, the grave danger exists that deficiencies in the basic musical education are discovered too late When entering the university the European student of musicology is expected to have received his practical training at a conservatory or with a private music teacher concurrently with his general education, but largely as an extracurricular activity He may also continue his practical studies while active at the university. In general, the European student concentrates on his special field later than the American student. This has the advantage that he is usually better prepared in the prerequisites such as languages, general history, and philosophy, but the disadvantage is that his knowledge of musical literature and his facility in theory may be inadequate As a result musicology has sometimes lost touch with music and has become a pursuit centering upon itself. A number of musicological dissertations give evidence of this danger by their tendency toward irrelevant abstractions.

The American system, on the other hand, suffers sometimes from the dangers, inherent in premature specialization, that manifest themselves in overdetailed descriptions that never reach general conclusions. The reluctance to proceed from details to broader principles is caused also by the fact that undergraduate students and sometimes even graduate students are spoon-fed too long.

If the "American Plan" indeed differs from the Continental in bringing specialization at an earlier stage, it differs even more from English practice, in which specialization may begin in the last year at school. Musical history is of more recent origin as a subject of university study in England than in either the Continent or America. At Oxford, for example, the institution of a full-time Faculty of Music and the granting of a B.A. degree with honors in music dates from 1944. However, degrees in composition (B.Mus. and D.Mus.) have existed since the late fifteenth century, and part-time professorships since early in the seventeenth century. This tradition of the recognition of musical composition in the university is still continued in the new plan of the faculty, alongside what may be termed without too invidious a distinction the humanistic approach to history and theory. The older degrees are affected by the new development since the B.A. degree is now prerequisite to the B.Mus. degree. Conversely, the tradition of theoretical studies and of composition inherent in the older degrees has taken an important place as a historically oriented study of theory and composition within the new curriculum. It is a constant concern of the faculty to keep a good balance between history and theory in the B.A. course; the study of the history of music is pursued in the closest possible relation to the music of history and the study of the theory of music takes the form of constant practice in composition in specific historical styles.

Training in performance has no direct place in this curriculum. Students who wish to pursue intensive studies in that direction must go to a conservatory. This is by no means to say that performances by members of the university are not of frequent occurrence. As in some American universities, the music clubs and societies of the university and the colleges at Oxford carry on an active musical life, and music outside the usual repertory of the professional concert hall and opera house is often heard and deliberately fostered. The high quality of the work in music in public (fee paying) and grammar schools is an important factor in making pos-

sible the specialization of the academic study and the cultivation of extracurricular music by specialists and nonspecial-
ists alike. The serious approach to specialist examinations and
to musical performance that has been adopted by many
English schools since early in the present century has had
notable effects on the level of university music and on the
level of young public taste in music, and may thus affect the
development of musical culture as a whole. University
trained musicians have played some part in this development of music in schools, which has in turn contributed
greatly to making the university musical community a place
where the potential scholar and the cultivated amateur meet
in the common cause of music making. (See Fig. 4.)

Given a curriculum of school and university music that
keeps a balance between the theoretical and historical sides,
early specialization loses most of its dangers. In contrast to
both the American and Continental systems the student in
music in a British university concentrates early. He specializes
in music through the undergraduate stage and is required
to pursue a course that prepares him equally for graduate
work in either composition or musicology. If he has obtained
a good degree (in Oxford a first- or second-class) and is
accepted for a higher degree in musicology (B.Litt. or D.
Phil.) he is assumed to be ready for independent research,
with the guidance, but not the formal teaching, of a super-
visor.

THE ANALYSIS OF STYLE

The danger of a musicology that has lost touch with music
arises chiefly from an unbalanced training and approach, one
in which writing, technical analysis, and performing have
not been made integral parts of a humanistic study. The

first task of the musicologist is to contribute to the understanding and re-creation of music by a close analysis of the composer's musical thought and style in the light of the technical and aesthetic principles of his day. For this task thorough preparatory studies in historically determined theory are as essential as those in the technically oriented study of the course of musical history. The language of music has to be studied in terms of its own medium of ordered sound. The nature of this order, however, which is what we call style in the larger sense, cannot reveal itself in the results of "pure" analysis. The style (in the particular sense) of each of its aspects—melody, harmony, rhythm, texture, form, tone-color—must be considered in relation to the historical situation of the work, and to the appropriate principles of composition and canons of expression.

It cannot be said that American musicology entirely escapes the charge of losing touch with music, in the sense of

Fig. 4.

(*left*) The concert ensemble of New York Pro Musica, Noah Greenberg, Musical Director. This ensemble, perhaps best known for its performances of the medieval *Play of Daniel,* both in the United States and in Europe, offered a special program of liturgical music at a recent Congress of the International Musicological Society. Photograph by George Ancona; reproduced by permission of New York Pro Musica.

(*right*) The young American musician Horace Fitzpatrick, who combines the musicological study of the history of the horn with professional performance on the Viennese hand horn.

showing a lack of concern with the basic technical problems that determine a style and its re-creation in performance. In part, this lack of concern may reflect a lack of balance between the historical and technical training of musicians—such as Ritter noticed in the nineteenth century—but it probably derives also from the influence of the Continental system of education in musicology, and to that extent the situation is a more general one that musicology in America shares with musicology elsewhere.

Western musicology is confronted with the pressing problem of evolving adequate and appropriate methods of technical and stylistic analysis. The analytical methods and criteria at the disposal of the musical historian seem to be considerably less sensitive than those of the art historian or archaeologist. In music there are no agreed criteria upon which comparative studies can be based, because there are as yet no techniques to facilitate the making of exhaustive analyses. In few cases, for example, are there terms other than the most general in which attributions of anonymous compositions can be justified. This is a matter in which the more objective distinctions and the more exact analytical techniques of the ethnomusicologists may provide new avenues of approach for Western musicology.

The directions in which progress in the techniques of stylistic analysis is greatly needed are the refinement of terms and the use of statistics. Musical historians have become accustomed to using the terms that have grown up with musical historiography without due regard to their historical limitations on the one hand or to their possible universal connotations on the other. Terms with a modern and limited currency and meaning are sometimes applied to earlier times and to other genres than those that observe their presuppositions. At the same time terms with a long history in Western music are used without regard to their changes of meaning, while those that are valid for certain features of the music of all cultures are used in limited and arbitrary senses. The first requirement for a meaningful analysis of the style of any music is a clear vocabulary for its technical features, based on adequate theoretical and practical knowledge.

The use of statistics in the analysis of musical styles has so far been applied only to stylistic features of an elementary kind. Their use can be misleading or meaningless when based, as is sometimes the case, on anachronistic criteria. Nevertheless, the raw material of any stylistic analysis consists of statistical information on the occurrences and recurrences of specific idioms, whether in a particular piece, in the complete works of a composer or school, or ultimately in the total output of a period. The process of compiling information of this kind by hand, so to speak, is so laborious and lengthy as to make it impractical on any extended scale. It seems likely that the use of computers could be of great value in reducing this process to practical terms. Since an electronic synthesizer can be used to produce a "performance" of music, there seems no reason why an electronic "analyzer" should not provide statistics on its technical elements. This is clearly a field for expert investigation. While statistical methods may provide quantitative information, the musicologist will always be needed to frame the appropriate questions and to interpret the answers in terms of historical style and genre.

THE RELATION OF STYLE AND FUNCTION

The era of musical historiography that began with Adler's article of 1885 was dominated by the concept of style and its metamorphoses in terms of the sum of the technical aspects of the music of each historical period. In accordance with the historical thinking of the time, the history of the West was viewed as an organic process of development, and the object of the musical historian was to determine the "laws" of the successive styles in which the musical expression of that process manifested itself. The main materials of this study were the musical "monuments" of the past (the focus of the new musical learning, Adler emphasized, was the musical work of art itself), and the period therefore saw the continuous accumulation of editions of music designed for the purposes of scholarly investigation in the library and in the graduate seminar. It also achieved a new periodization of musical history conforming to that of the art historians, formulations of the style characteristics of some of those periods, and a historical concept of the evolution of musical forms. It was again a reflection of the historical philosophies of the period that the histories of forms were seen as obeying "inner laws" of musical evolution and as having "organic" cycles of growth, maturity, and decay. Such was the international European tradition of musical scholarship when American musicology entered its formative period.

The provision of materials in the form of editions of the musical "monuments" of the past must continue to be an important function of the musicologist. Important works still remain to be published, earlier editions go out of print, and the editorial aims and methods of one generation do not satisfy the requirements of another. Though some editions of today continue the format that virtually confines the volumes to the library and precludes their use for performance, it is more characteristic of the present trend to combine in one edition the apparatus of scholarship with the practical requirements of performance.

It is in respect to its general philosophy and aims—which such things as "library" editions symbolize—that the "Adler period" of Western musicology is even less adequate to the new conformations of society, and in America to the changing relation of the United States with the Western and non-Western parts of the world. What I have tried to suggest about the place of the American musicologist in the musical life of his society is no less true of the role of the musicologist everywhere in relation to the music of whatever time or place. In the words of Jacques Handschin, one of the most original and far-sighted musicologists. "Le véritable objet de la musicologie n'est pas la musique en tant qu'un fait donné par lui-même, mais l'homme, pour autant qu'il s'exprime musicalement." Parallel to this statement is a recent observation of the ethnomusicologist John Blacking: "The most meticulous analysis of a song loses its value if it has been divorced from the reality of its social context." The material of the musicologist remains, as always, music; his task of style criticism and analysis becomes if anything more demanding in its requirements of exactitude and discrimination, but his aim becomes the study of men in society insofar as they express themselves through the medium of music.

One corollary of this shift in aim would be a widening of the range of musicological interest. For example, it has been considered "respectable" for a musicologist to be interested in the jongleurs and minstrels of the Middle Ages but not in modern music-hall and popular music. Similarly, he can properly take notice of the musical devotions of the sixteenth century Italian layman as expressed in the simple *laude* written especially for him, but not of the evangelical hymns of the nineteenth century churchgoer. (In this respect Robert Stevenson's chapter on church music in *One Hundred Years of Music in America* is an exemplary exception.) Logically, a musicologist should have reason to be as interested in and as observant of the activities of an amateur choral society today as of the organization and repertory of an early Lutheran *Kantorei*. If the subject of musical history is the history of musical man in society, then its province must include the musician and his audience at all levels of the social order.

A more significant corollary of a further social object for musicology is the need to consider the relation between all the circumstances of music making and the styles and forms of musical composition, rather than to regard musical forms as autonomous growths that come and go according to the inclinations of composers and the tastes of audiences. It becomes no less essential to re-create as far as possible the function, social meaning, and manner of performance of every type of musical work than to establish the notes of the musical texts that make the re-creation possible. With the further emphasis on the history of music as an aspect of the history of man in society, the traditional enterprises of musicology can no longer be pursued *in vacuo*. For their ultimate meaning and value rest on their contribution to restoring

79

silent music to the state of being once more a medium of human communication. Re-creation in any full sense cannot be divorced from the original function of the music, any more than a musical work from another society can be fully understood apart from its social context.

Looked at in this way, it is the function of all musicology to be in fact ethnomusicology, that is, to take its range of research to include material that is termed "sociological." This view would still assume the basic importance of analytical and stylistic studies, but would look further than has been customary in investigating the various aspects of music as an expression of an individual in his social context. For this the musicologist would deal, as some have done in particular studies, with the history, organization, and resources of musical institutions and those in which music has a function, with the changing relationship of the composer to the performer and of each to the audience, with the social or ritual function of the music, with the conditions of performance and the performing forces involved, with the precise quality and performance characteristics of the instruments or voices taking part, and with all such factors as have generally been regarded as subsidiary or optional studies in the work of the musicologist.

MUSICOLOGY AND THE HUMANITIES

In the article on *Musicologie* in the *Encyclopédie de la musique,* M. François Lesure reviews the scope and meaning of the term as defined by eminent musicologists. Commenting on Handschin's statement quoted above, he observes that it is among the humanities that musicology has its place and should seek out its path. He notes the almost negligible influence of sociology, though this is a direction that might have been suggested by ethnomusicology, and might have led musicologists to re-examine their methods. He points to several ways in which musicology may look for escape from its isolation: by striving for a more adequate appraisal of the relations between music and human problems; by establishing a new scale of values for the comparative study of the art of music and social life; by distinguishing in a musical work of art the respective roles of the composer, of technique, and of the social milieu. He suggests as a final aim of musicology to discover what musical thought teaches us about man that is different from what we learn about him from language, from religion, or from law.

M. Lesure enlarged on these views in a paper, "Pour une sociologie historique des faits musicaux," written for the Congress of the International Society for Musicology in New York in September 1961. One of his observations on the place of musicology among the humanities is particularly relevant here:

> The lack of solidarity between the humanities is indeed cause for surprise. For example, the renewal of certain methods in linguistics, and the considerable developments in sociology and ethnology have left musicology virtually untouched. Should one see in this fact, along with the lack of consciousness of the existence of such problems, the cause of the feeble repercussion of our studies on researches in the history of civilization? I can speak from my own knowledge only of France, but the example is particularly cogent; the great historical collections (Glotz, Halphen-Sagnac, *Clio, L'évolution de l'humanité*), which concern themselves markedly with painting and sculpture, are almost dumb when it is a question of music. Still more characteristic, it seems to me, is the case of a work, otherwise masterly, like that of Huizinga on *The Waning of the Middle Ages,* which would have been greatly increased in value by an interpreta-

tion of the musical life of the fifteenth century, or again the more recent work of W. K. Ferguson on *The Renaissance in Historical Thought.*

As examples of subjects which call for cooperative researches in the sociological aspects of musical history, M. Lesure cites the musical establishments of churches, minstrels and fiddlers whether vagrant or of a court or city, and the economics of music publishing. Relative to the first of these examples, he proposes a number of specific points on which researches in the choral foundations of France might profitably be done. As a complement to M. Lesure's paper, my own Second Paper, also presented at the Congress, consists of materials for discussion in the form of tables of the numbers and stipends of choir singers, notes on the movements of musicians, special payments and other entries from archives, all bearing on the social position of musicians in English choral foundations during the century before the Reformation. Such information as this must be sought in sources other than these which have hitherto been the almost exclusive concern of musicology. Research of this kind obviously involves special difficulties for musicologists in the United States. Even a large university library may not have a complete run of such a basic liturgical collection as the Henry Bradshaw Society series. The numerous series of historical records printed by city, county, and other local societies of Europe are seldom more than sparsely represented. The broadening of musicological research along the lines suggested here would require cooperative organization, sufficient provision for travel and maintenance grants, and a more ample view of the material that should be acquired by the musicological and historical sections of university and institutional libraries.

M. Lesure is not the only musical historian to have observed with some dismay the neglect of music and its place in history on the part of general historians. Manfred Bukofzer, in *The Place of Musicology in American Institutions of Higher Learning,* says: "That music forms an integral part of the history of culture is a truism, yet it will be found that some of the leading books on this subject pass over music with a few inconsequential remarks, if indeed they mention it at all."

It is possible, however, that the blame for this situation does not lie altogether on the side of the general historian. It may rather be due to the musical historians' neglect of their role of interpreters of the place of music in cultural history to the general historian and the general reader of history. It is arguable that most musical history has been written for a circle of colleagues and specialist students rather than for those who read and write general history. This is not to advocate the superficial kind of musical history which has a merely popularizing aim, or yet to ignore the better musical history textbooks for undergraduates, which have a useful function in the educational system. It is rather to suggest that every aspect of music as human expression and as a part of human history is a responsibility of the musicologist. It follows that an important part of his function is to communicate the results of those of his studies that have humanistic interest in terms that can be generally understood.

Bukofzer has this further comment:

> The [general] historian is interested in the history of music as part of general history. But he should not lose sight of the documentary importance of compositions for political and historical occasions, for dignitaries of church and state, songs of protest and censure, and music for propaganda, which are directly linked with political history. Church history and more especially the history of liturgy are obviously incomplete without a consideration of music.

The general historian might ask "Where shall I find the history of music treated in this way by a musical historian?" The answer would be that Paul Lang's *Music in Western Civilization* does this superbly on the broad canvas suggested by its title and purpose; that there are some special studies not easily to be found by the general historian; and that whole periods, notably but not only the Middle Ages and Renaissance, are almost untouched by any serious studies of "music as an integral part of the history of culture." Hence perhaps the neglect of music by general historians, and hence also the vague generalities and hoary misconceptions that too often characterize the attempts of musical historians to relate music to its cultural and social setting.

Many researchers will be needed to fill in the details of a fully humanistic content of musical history. Only the trained musicologist is likely to keep in proper focus the panorama of historical facts and social circumstances that are relevant to the life of music, for only he sees them from the viewpoint of the music itself. At one point in his inquiry Bukofzer is inclined to question the wisdom of a comprehensive approach to the social and cultural aspects of musical history, though he earlier pleads for a recognition of music as an integral element in social and cultural history. Music can be regarded "not as an art, but as a business and an industry. Indeed it offers an interesting history in labor relations; the results of such studies are important for social and cultural history, but care must be taken not to confuse the economic with the musicological approach." It is high time to ask whether the musicological approach does not properly involve also the economic and other social approaches, insofar as they are approached from the music and throw light on the history and development of musical forms and practices. The economic conditions of musicians are as relevant to the history of music as to the history of labor relations, and

84

the study of the life of cathedrals, opera houses, and music halls is just as much a part of the history of church music, opera, and popular music as both are of the history of human institutions.

Today the United States is probably richer than any other part of the world in the materials and events that make a living and growing culture. Its musical life represents in some respects an extension of the European patterns with the special characteristic that it is more fully international than that of any single European country. The traditional functions of musical scholarship are particularly germane to a society where most musical institutions are of relatively recent origin and others are still in the planning and formative stages. Alongside this continuing traditional culture America is germinating new forms of musical language and of musical institutions through the cross-fertilizing of music of different roots and of different elements in society. These are circumstances in which the functions and opportunities of musicology are as many-sided as the aspects of the musical life of the nation as a whole.

One of the special opportunities of American musicology is to look beyond the cautious fences of recent tradition and to range over the whole of musical culture with the same avid curiosity as did Praetorius or Burney. In these days, besides the sense of history and the experience of the practical and social requirements of music making, the awareness of unrealized possibilities is the most important of the values that musicology should bring to an expanding musical life.

AMERICAN SCHOLARSHIP
IN WESTERN MUSIC

◈

CLAUDE V. PALISCA

ASSOCIATE PROFESSOR OF
THE HISTORY OF MUSIC
YALE UNIVERSITY

THE SCOPE OF AMERICAN MUSICOLOGY

For American musicology to become retrospective in its present youthful stage may seem premature. Yet, in spite of its short life—less than a half-century—and the fact that many of its outstanding practitioners both were trained and formerly worked abroad, American scholarship in music has acquired a mode of operation, a style of presentation, and patterns of education setting it apart from that of countries boasting older traditions. To describe these characteristics and to trace the emergence of American musicology, as well as to note some of its achievements, is the purpose of this essay.

Musical scholarship, one might say, is a disciplined study of music. A "disciplined study of music," however, may be undertaken as a means to many different ends: to perform a recital, to conduct an orchestra, to become acquainted with the art of composition, to ascertain music's physical or psychological nature, or to measure its aesthetic, recreational, or entertainment value. Any of these kinds of musical study would probably occur to the average man—if not to the reader of this book—before the one that we are concerned with here.

This diffuseness of the field of music as a subject of serious study requires that boundaries be carefully drawn. The study of music was pursued in our conservatories and universities for many years before anything that deserves to be called musical scholarship emerged. First, a consciousness of the necessity and possibility of a scholarly approach to music had to be awakened. This consciousness may be summed up in the word *musicology,* which, like the spirit behind it, was an

importation from Europe. In America, as in England, it encountered resistance because it represented a new dimension
—a nonartistic, nonhedonistic attack upon a subject that
should have been in the view of many all pleasure, creativity,
and inspiration.

To be sure, not everything that has gone under the name of
musicology can be considered musical scholarship. Nor can
it be denied that distinguished musical scholarship was produced in this country before the concept of musicology was
planted here. But nearly all musical scholarship in America
has been a product of the musicological movement.

CHANGING VIEWS

What did musicology represent to its earliest American
advocates? Their conception of this discipline was derived
from the German and Austrian scholars who were its pioneers. The earliest American supporters of musicology were
persuaded that these foreign scholars had introduced scientific methods into a field that had previously been a happy
breeding ground for loose and fanciful speculation. Karl
Friedrich Chrysander is considered the first spokesman for
modern musical scholarship. He saw the need for a new standard for musical knowledge that would put it on the same
level of objective validity as the sciences. He turned away
from the rich poetic language of the critics and commentators on musical taste, from the embroideries of romantic
biographers, and from historiography based exclusively on
authority. He conceived a body of scientific knowledge acquired by researchers bound to the same requirements of
accuracy and methodology as the investigators who had
achieved in his time such impressive results in the exact
sciences. He recognized that the critical examination of docu-

mentary evidence was not unlike the controlled observation of the chemist, physicist, or botanist. Therefore, when he launched his yearbooks in 1863, he called the learned discipline of music a *musikalische Wissenschaft,* a term that had been used already by Lorenz Mizler in 1738. Only two issues of the journal appeared, in 1863 and 1867, but when Chrysander entered into collaboration with Philipp Spitta and Guido Adler, they inaugurated a new journal in 1885 that did take hold. the *Vierteljahrsschrift für Musikwissenschaft*—the "Quarterly for Musical Scholarship."

The term *Wissenschaft* had become current in other branches of learning. The belles-lettres were known as the *schöne Wissenschaften,* while the natural sciences were described as *Naturwissenschaften.* The earliest American advocates of musical scholarship perhaps mistakenly employed the word *science* to render *Wissenschaft,* when the significance of the German word was more nearly "learning." *Musical learning* would thus have been more faithful than *musical science,* but it was the latter that gained acceptance. *Musikwissenschaft* implied a dynamic truth-searching activity, as opposed to a static learned tradition. For the American followers of Adler, this was best evoked by the idea of musical science. Eventually the word *musicologie* was adopted in France and *musicology* became the equivalent of *Musikwissenschaft* in America, though in England *musical research* was preferred because it avoided the connotation of exact science.

Adler gave the classic definition of musical scholarship in his editorial, "The Scope, Method and Aim of *Musikwissenschaft,"* in the first issue of the *Vierteljahrsschrift* (1885). Musical facts, he recognized, could be organized in two ways —historically and systematically. The historical method arranged the facts concerning music of the past by epochs, peoples, empires, countries, provinces, towns, schools, and individual artists. It involved the study of systems of musical notation, the changing forms and types of musical composition, the principles of composition both as taught by theorists and as induced from written music of the various periods, the principles of musical performance, and musical instruments. From the systematic point of view the musical scholar aims to set down the laws that abide in various branches of musical study, both artistic and scientific. The most important branch is the theory of music, which is divided into harmonics, rhythmics, and melics. Here Adler adopted the classic Greek musical disciplines in which the fundamental laws of music were studied. These for Adler do not coincide with the didactic systems of harmony, counterpoint, and orchestration taught to students of composition. The latter, along with methods for training students in general musicianship and vocal and instrumental practice, constituted for him the branch of pedagogy and didactics. Another branch of systematic study is the aesthetics and psychology of music. Finally Adler considered the branch that deals with the music of primitives and non-Western peoples and that contributes to the broader fields of ethnography and folklore.

While Adler included in his system of musicology every conceivable aspect of the historical and systematic study of music, his own principal interest was history. Consequently he considered historical style criticism the highest task of the musicologist, one to which all the branches of the field contributed. Such criticism was concerned with the characterization of the musical output of individual composers, schools, epochs, and geographical areas. But it also comprehends the establishing of links, influences, and comparisons, the tracing of stylistic evolutions and decays, and the formulation of syntheses.

Another who proposed a classification of the musicological field was the prolific German scholar Hugo Riemann, Professor at Leipzig, in his *Grundriss der Musikwissenschaft* (1908). He conceived of it as containing five divisions: (1) acoustics, (2) tone-physiology and -psychology, (3) musical aesthetics, including speculative music theory, (4) theory of composition or performance, and (5) music history. While doing away with the historical-systematic dichotomy, Riemann preserved essentially the same content as Adler.

The definitions elaborated by Adler and Riemann received both sympathetic and critical comment in America. As early as 1890, Waldo Selden Pratt in an address to the Music Teachers National Association (MTNA) convention in Detroit, "The Scientific Study of Music," suggested a division of the field very similar to Riemann's (MTNA, *Official Report,* 1890). He later revised and developed this in a longer paper delivered also before the MTNA (*MQ,* 1915). Pratt was at this time Professor of Music and Hymnology at the Hartford Theological Seminary in Connecticut. During his college days at Williams he had been chapel organist, although his major field had been Greek, which he continued at Johns Hopkins for a year of graduate work before he became a Fellow in Aesthetics there. For two years he had been assistant director of the Metropolitan Museum in New York and in 1882 he went to the Hartford Theological Seminary. Pratt was one of the leaders of the MTNA, editing its *Proceedings* between 1906 and 1915. He also served as president between 1906 and 1908 and later as treasurer.

In his 1890 address Pratt called for an extension of scientific method to musical study in America:

> We ought to find a place in it not simply for what we call *"theory,"* meaning thereby musical construction and creation, not simply for *technique,* or musical reproduction and interpretation, not simply for *methods of teaching* this or that practical branch, but for musical *acoustics,* the science

93

of the physical material of music and the physical means by which music is produced, for musical *aesthetics,* the science of the perception, appreciation, criticism, and translation of music, for musical *pedagogics,* the science of teaching music so that music itself shall be taught, and not simply the phantasms of notation or technique, and for what may be called musical *practics,* the science of the relation of music to ends outside itself, to health, to social intercourse, to the great subject of education as now understood, to the growth of individual character, and above all, to the truths and the work of religion. Having found a fit place for these branches of musical science, we ought to conquer each of them by means of patient and minute analysis and classification. The advancement of each of the other arts and sciences is universally being sought at present through this kind of severe scientific scrutiny and systemization within its own field. Why should not the field of music be similarly treated, in order that it may be similarly extended, developed, and mastered in a scientific sense?

The system of musical knowledge outlined in this statement was developed more extensively in Pratt's paper of 1915, "On Behalf of Musicology," in which he criticized both the classifications of Adler and Riemann on certain points. He saw no need for Adler's systematic-historical dichotomy. Certain facts tend to be grouped chronologically and become history. Where the present state of things is the center of attention, the natural method is the systematic, in which logical definition and classification prevail. In other spheres a normative criticism is demanded, and here the science of music merges with philosophy. At other times the aim is to bring certain standards into practice, and the pedagogical method is needed. Thus Pratt would have replaced the systematic-historical axis with four methodological areas that overlap his subject divisions like aesthetics and practics: musical

94

history, musical encyclopedia, musical criticism, and musical pedagogy.

As for Riemann's classification, Pratt held that it was incomplete and that it confused logical categories by ranking music history as a coordinate of acoustics and physiology. Musicology, in Pratt's view, should contain all fields of music subject to scientific scrutiny, which together constitute a comprehensive "science of music." He saw the realm of music to be investigated as a great complex of subjective experiences, objective facts, principles and laws, processes, utensils, products, creators, organizations, institutions, ideals. These operate at various levels that can be studied under seven divisions: (1) musical physics or acoustics, which concerns the nature, transmission, and interrelations of tones; (2) musical psychics, which considers the effects of music; (3) musical poetics, containing the morphology, syntax, and rhetoric of music, including the theory of composition, analytical criticism, and the study of lives of composers; (4) musical aesthetics; (5) musical graphics—the notation, recording, and publishing of music; (6) musical technics—the method of playing instruments and singing, and the study of the instruments themselves; and (7) musical practics—the use of music in drama, dancing, hygiene, therapeutics, education, and social amusement. To all of these should be applied critical methods of observation sifting, verification, recording, codification, classification, definition, and elucidation. Finally, general laws are induced from a logical examination of the facts, and a body of collective opinion results that Pratt believed deserves to be called a science of music.

Continued skepticism of Adler's historical-systematic division is reflected in the writings of several other American scholars in the Twenties and Thirties, notably Charles Seeger, Oliver Strunk, Roy Dickinson Welch, and Curt Sachs. Most

95

of these tended to de-emphasize the role of acoustics, psychology of music, aesthetics, and pedagogy as components of musicology.

In "On the Principles of Musicology" (*MQ, 1924*), Seeger sees a danger in applying the vocabulary of psychology, history, and physics to music. To speak of sound waves, sense data, behavior types, manifestations of the sublime or beautiful, arithmetical relations, social values, tells us little about music. Musical aesthetics is frequently only a field for the elaboration of aesthetic theory, and as much may be said of musical acoustics, psychology, and physiology. Results in these fields as they touch music may contribute to knowledge in those subjects but are not pertinent to music until translated into technical musical terms. The musicologist's first task, before he invites foreign disciplines, is to clean his house. He must evolve a vocabulary through which he can speak about music itself and organize the knowledge thus expressed. The best sphere for such a reorientation is contemporary musical life. In an address to the AMS in 1935 (*Acta, 1939*), Seeger complained that musicologists dealt too much with parts and sections, inert categories instead of dynamic wholes. They should, he felt, become interested in the processes presently at work. These processes, once understood, could be discerned also in the musical cultures of the past. While the approach he favored was thus "systematic," Seeger urged a unified view of music. The division into systematic and historical was for him a symptom of an attachment to a linguistic convention that separated fixed categories and perniciously influenced our thought about music.

Oliver Strunk, also dissatisfied with the prevailing classifications, returned to comment upon Riemann's scheme in an address to the MTNA (*Proc., 1936*). He credited it with a simplicity that Pratt's division lacked, agreeing with Pratt, however, that history of music was not a field in a system of fields, but a way of looking at a subject, an aspect not a part of musicology. The other disciplines of Riemann's system, Strunk argued, all converge on the general task of determining the expressive value of the elements of musical creation. Through acoustics are formulated the physical characteristics of sounds and the mechanics of their production and propagation. Psychology studies their effects on the hearing, intellect, and emotions. Theory is concerned with the employment of musical elements in complex musical structures. But history is involved with all of these insofar as they operate in the music and thought of ages gone by. Strunk thus accepted Riemann's comprehensive definition of musicology but was inclined to see history as a more universal occupation than any of Riemann's component musicological disciplines, which both serve and are comprehended in history.

While the American scholars we have considered up to now tended to accept the broad definition of musicology promulgated by its European founders, Roy Dickinson Welch in an address to the MTNA (*Proc.*, 1936) aimed to concentrate musicology's sphere in the musical repertory itself. "Unless to the musicologist nothing musical is alien, we must assume that the musicologist's proper and central concern is for exact knowledge of his basic monuments and a clear perception of their relationships." Most of the disciplines contained in Riemann and Adler's view of musicology were to Welch either contributory to, or derivative from, this central core. Contributory subjects were knowledge of harmony, counterpoint, languages, history in general; derivative were aesthetics and criticism. Aesthetics is the business of the poet, philosopher, and psychologist. Criticism may be the function of a scholar but of one who is more than purely erudite.

Similarly, Curt Sachs in an address to a joint meeting of the AMS and MTNA in December 1940 (MTNA *Proc.*,

1940) expressed a wish to see the scope of musicology narrowed down to proper limits. "One of the confusions sur-
rounding the term Musicology is that it confounds two main
and entirely different fields, music history and music theory.
The theory of music is not in the domain of musicologists."
Music theory, he pointed out, has been mainly a pursuit of
composers, and he cited Rameau, Fux, Berlioz, Schoenberg,
and Hindemith. As for musical aesthetics, Sachs took the
view that there was no single aesthetics of music valid for all
times and places, but only regional and transitory aesthetic
theories. Wagner's aesthetic ideals were not valid for Brahms,
no more than those of the Occident are valid for the Orient.
One of the tasks of a music historian is to reveal precisely
these changing conditions and standards of musical taste.

In spite of changing views about musicology, the definition
of the field that has been most influential in America is that
contained in Glen Haydon's textbook, *Introduction to Musicology* (1941). Haydon revived the division into systematic
and historical and he justified the categories on the grounds
that "the concepts of space and time afford the most fundamental axes for the orientation of knowledge and experience."

> The understanding of a particular composition may be
> said to depend on a comprehension of what it is in itself and
> in relation to other similar and contrasting, contemporary
> style-types. This is systematic knowledge. But it can scarcely
> be separated from the complementary knowledge, that of
> understanding this particular composition in its historical
> perspective. Thus, we conceive of understanding as a knowl-
> edge of relations in a two-dimensional frame of reference.

More than two hundred pages of Haydon's book deal with the
subdivisions of systematic musicology. In several chapters
he outlines the principal concepts and theories in musical
acoustics, physiology, psychology, musical aesthetics, the

"theory of music theory," musical pedagogy, and comparative musicology (folk and non-European music). The remaining fifty pages deal with historical musicology, its philosophy, sources, and methods of research. As the author warns us in his introduction, it must not be assumed that the importance of the several subdivisions is proportionate to the size of the sections of the book. It is tempting, however, to make a different assumption: that Haydon addresses the reader principally interested in history, theory, and comparative musicology. For in the sections devoted to these subjects he is concerned with their theory, sources, and methodology, while in the sections on acoustics, physiology, psychology, and aesthetics, he is preoccupied with imparting elementary knowledge. In the former the text orients the future researcher; in the latter it introduces him to fields foreign to him. There is a tacit admission by the author that acoustics, physiology, psychology, and aesthetics may be preparatory to musicological work but are not really part of it.

If we turn from a consideration of expressed opinions about the boundaries of musicology to the scope of professional practice, we find in America an even more restrictive interpretation of the meaning of the field. Taking the years between 1950 and 1960 as a standard, we rarely encounter in the *Journal of the American Musicological Society* (*JAMS*) any contributions outside the fields of historical and ethnological musicology. The few in theory of music are not what I would call creative theory but analytical pieces. Since the founding of *Ethnomusicology* and the *Journal of Music Theory,* both in 1957, *JAMS* has become almost exclusively a journal of music history and analytical criticism.

The *Musical Quarterly* (*MQ*), this country's oldest musicological review, has gone in the same direction. Since its founding in 1915 by the publishing company of Gustave Schirmer, the *Quarterly* has always been edited by historical musicologists: Oscar Sonneck, Carl Engel, Gustave Reese, Paul Henry Lang. Until World War II, its contributors were mainly European musicologists and its pages reflected the conception of musicology and criticism prevailing in Europe. Articles on acoustics, psychology, physiology, aesthetics, ethnographic and folk music subjects appeared along with biographical, critical, theoretical, and historical contributions. In 1935 the *Quarterly* pledged a hundred pages each year to papers submitted through the Publications Committee of the AMS. From about 1937, the *Quarterly*'s pages have been in fact dominated by scholars living in the United States and its contents overwhelmingly comprised of historical and to a lesser degree ethnomusicological material. Since 1948 an important part of each issue has been the "Current Chronicle," a section devoted to analytical critiques by highly qualified composers, critics, and scholars of new music performed throughout the world. Only the book reviews in *JAMS* as well as in the *Quarterly* have tended to spill over into the branches no longer covered by articles: acoustics, psychology, philosophy of music, pedagogy, and instrumental technique. Such books are most often by authors not themselves musicologists.

The graduate programs in musicology in our universities show a similar trend. Specifications for subjects in which the Ph.D. may be taken typically state that it may be in theory, musicology, or music education. A closer look at a university catalog usually reveals that the courses in musicology are actually in the history of music, though occasional introductions crop up in the aesthetics of music, folk music, primitive music, or Asiatic music. Acoustics appears rarely, and the courses in psychology of music that are encountered seem to be destined for students in music education.

The evidence, whether it is the consensus among active musicologists, the material published by scholarly reviews, or the programs of university music departments, points to a conception of the field in America that is far more specific than that of its European founders. The acoustics, psychology, physiology, and pedagogy of music have become truly periphereal areas that musical scholars prefer to leave to specialists outside of music. Theory is usually left to composer-teachers and aesthetics to philosophers.

Whether this narrowing of musicology is a healthy trend remains to be discussed. But this is a question that cannot be separated from a consideration of the nature of musical scholarship itself.

SOME BROAD DEFINITIONS

Otto Kinkeldey has written: "In the widest sense musical scholarship may be fairly said to include any scholarly or scientific activity directed toward the investigation and understanding of the facts, the processes, the developments and the effects of the musical art" (*Journal of Renaissance and Baroque Music,* 1946). In another place he has stated: "Musicology denotes a rational, systematized, scientific formulation of what we know about music" (*Music Clubs Magazine,* 1934).

Glen Haydon has also offered two slightly varying definitions: "Musicology may be defined as systematized knowledge concerning music; and this, of course, carries with it the implication of research as a means of discovering, verifying, and formulating the statement of whatever we may think we can know about music" (MTNA *Proc.,* 1940). He begins his textbook with the statement "Musicology is that branch of learning which concerns the discovery and systematization of knowledge concerning music."

There is one apparent inconsistency in these statements.

Both authors at one time call musicology a system of knowledge and at another an activity or branch of learning. No one will deny that it is both a branch of learning and an activity of scholars. Nor shall we take issue with the general scope of musicology as defined in these statements.

We may accept these general definitions, however, without acknowledging the concept of musicology that these two scholars have elaborated in their publications.

Take, for example, the expression *scholarly or scientific activity* in Kinkeldey's statement. Kinkeldey has explained elsewhere how he understands *scientific* in this context (MTNA *Proc.,* 1940). He means it both in the German sense of *wissenschaftlich,* pertaining to "any body of organized knowledge which rests on a foundation of systematic observation, study and reasoning," and in the more specific sense it has in English usage. A musical investigator may be scientific in this narrower sense if he works in branches of the natural sciences, such as acoustics or psychology. Haydon in his textbook has also used the terms *science* and *scientific* in both of these senses. We shall see that this double usage is a source of ambiguity in our understanding of the field.

MUSICOLOGY AND RELATED FIELDS

If, as both of these definitions attest, the focus of inquiry is music or musical art, can there truly be a scientific investigation of this subject in the narrower sense? Music, understood as an artful organization of sounds, has no material existence outside the human mind. It may be caused by a complex of vibrations, but these are not themselves the musical scholar's subject of study. To study the property of vibrations is quite outside the scope of musicology as it has been defined. Moreover, information about vibrations tells us nothing about music until it is interpreted in terms of sensations. Now it may be argued that sensations are subject to scientific study by the psychologist. But here again what is studied scientifically is not music, but at best its effects, or more typically the effect of specific sound phenomena. Psychologists have told us very little about music, though their data on human and animal reactions to it have helped complete the picture of man's mental and emotional life. Rarely have psychological studies dealt with really significant problems about the effects of music as an art except in ways too tentative to be considered scientific. They have usually dwelt on elementary problems of pitch relationships and sound qualities. For example, to know the reason for our differentiated reactions to various consonances and dissonances—a fundamental problem psychologists have yet to solve—would interest musicologists very much and might even influence composers. Such knowledge, however, would not affect our understanding of music already in existence.

These are some categorical reasons for excluding acoustics, physiology, and psychology from the scope of musicology, even though these disciplines are obviously related and relevant to the work of the musicologist. There are also practical reasons.

Acoustics has progressed today far beyond the state in which a monochord was the researcher's principal tool and every learned musician could possess the entire field by manipulating a few pipes, strings, and ratios. As soon as vibrations rather than string lengths became the units of measurement in acoustics early in the seventeenth century, the field moved out of the musician's studio and the scholar's library into the mechanics laboratory. A few musicians could still contribute significantly to the field—Mersenne, Descartes, Christian Huyghens—but only because they were more than purely musicians.

Closer to our own day, the oscilloscope and oscillator have taken acoustics out of the mechanics laboratory into the electronics laboratory. To have some knowledge of music is certainly useful, but much more necessary is a thorough command of electronic circuits and the vast array of tubes, transistors, resistors, capacitators, filters, relays, and coils that make the circuits respond to the requirements of the investigator. A researcher who is not so equipped is unlikely to make a contribution to acoustics, musical or otherwise. A musicologist can consider himself an acoustician today if he is also an electronic engineer, but the combination is rarely attainable in our specialized graduate programs.

The musicologist who is acquainted with the principles of acoustics can, however, collaborate with an acoustician by presenting problems to him and interpreting his findings. This he must often do in his capacity as a student of music. Musicology and acoustics are better served by distinguishing than by confounding their separate functions. The scholar who is aware of his limitations will not be inclined to waste his time in leisurely speculations when what is demanded is a rigorous and exact technique. Similarly, the judicious acoustician will leave the musical interpretation and application of his discoveries to those who fully understand their artistic implications.

A similar set of circumstances excludes from musicology the psychology and physiology of music. Both of these fields demand a considerable knowledge of anatomy, physiology, and psychological theory. In addition the researcher must acquire a refined laboratory technique if he is to add to knowledge in any but a tentative way. It is obvious that these are beyond the reach of all but few musical scholars.

Aside from the technical nature of research in these fields, there are some other reasons for the dearth of acousticians and psychologists among our musicologists. In Europe a number of musicological institutes have been established in which the problems of music and sound are studied from a scientific standpoint, permitting musicologists to specialize in the psychological, physiological, or acoustical areas. In the United States there are no such institutes, and musicologists are normally employed in universities where their primary function is to teach the history and literature of music, methods of research, and sometimes the theory of music and related courses. The first requirement of such a teacher is that he know music, itself a subject demanding enough to justify the exclusion of a knowledge of mechanics, electronics, physiology, or psychology.

It might be asked, in view of these circumstances, why the founding fathers of musicology considered the fields I have excluded a part of their domain. Caught up in the enthusiasm for scientific discovery even historians in the middle of the nineteenth century embraced science and claimed to be engaged in it. Once history was part of science, it was easy to annex to musicology both true sciences like acoustics and pseudo-sciences like pedagogy, musical sociology, and anthropology, and to consider them all scientific disciplines. While we are ready to acknowledge the benefits of the methodological purge that the scientific movement incited, today we no longer deceive ourselves about the scientific status of history.

There remains the most cogent reason for eliminating scientific subdisciplines from musicology. If musicology is to have any standing among the liberal disciplines, it must meet the standards of humanistic scholarship. These standards are as rigorous as those of science, but are distinct from them. What the controlled experiment is to science, the authenticated document or artifact is to musical scholarship.

Just as science is not limited to evidence gathered from experiments, but exploits carefully measured and recorded observations of natural phenomena, so the musicologist uses living samples of music making faithfully recorded and observed. Written documents, including music; pictorial or sculptural representations; musical instruments; and other remains constitute the principal forms of evidence used by the historian. Live music making, data gathered from living informants, and musical instruments are types of evidence most fruitful for the ethnomusicologist. But both historical and ethnical musicologists use all of these types of evidence, and the two fields overlap at many points.

Ethnomusicology is now the accepted term for what was previously known as *comparative musicology*. The latter name derives from the fact that the approach to the study of music of various peoples, particularly of their folk songs, was in the earlier days of the field mainly comparative. Various forms of native music were compared with each other, and with Western art music as well. This approach has now been largely discarded in favor of investigating each musical culture in terms of its own society and geographical area. While the study of primitive and folk music was once an extension of scholarship in Western music, today it is a field for specialists. Few historians of music are now also ethnomusicologists as was once the case. Curt Sachs, Manfred Bukofzer, Marius Schneider, Otto Gombosi, Hans Nathan, and a number of others trained in the German tradition have been active in both fields. In America, on the other hand, until recently most of the researchers in this field have been anthropologists. Indeed, many American historians of music take the view that the study of primitive music belongs in the field of anthropology more than in musicology. This is not the view of the authors of this volume. Nor do the reasons here given for excluding the scientific subdisciplines from the musicological field apply to the study of primitive and folk music. Although an array of scientific instruments is necessary for a well-equipped center of ethnic musical studies, the scholar himself need not become involved in any laboratory experiments or scientific theories. The methods of gathering and analyzing evidence must be accurate and systematic, but these must fulfill the standards of humanistic scholarship rather than those of scientific research.

When we pass from folk and primitive music to the art music of certain non-Western cultures, such as those of China, Korea, Japan, Indonesia, or India, our categories become sorely inadequate. Neither *comparative* nor *ethnic-musicology* is a fitting label. The student of these musical cultures is in a position analogous to that of the student of Western music. If his interest is mainly in the art music practiced today—as has been the case with most scholars specializing in the musical culture of India, Japan, and Indonesia—he faces problems similar to those of the scholar who specializes in our contemporary musical scene. He studies a phase of a musical culture that has a written as well as an oral tradition, that has long possessed a notation and theoretical concepts. It is not enough for him to know what is the practice today; he must relate this knowledge to earlier practices. Such a scholar is a musicologist in the same sense as a historian of Western music is, except that he specializes in a foreign musical culture. *Foreign* as used here is only a relative term, since the connections between Syrian, Hebrew, Byzantine, ancient Greek, Arabic, and Indian music and the Western music of early Christian times and of the Middle Ages are important and numerous. More recent influences are also not negligible. Perhaps the most striking symptom of the inadequacy of our categories is the fact that ancient Hebrew and medieval Byzantine music have traditionally been provinces of the Western historical musicologist. Yet these musics have contemporary Asiatic counterparts that fall into the domain of the so-called ethnomusicologist who must take their ancient traditions into account.

The inevitable conclusion is that there is only one musicology and that its branches are primitive music, folk music, European, Asiatic, Oceanic, African, North and South American music, and their subgroups. (Charles Seeger has long endorsed this view; see "Music and Musicology" in *Encyclopedia of the Social Sciences,* vol. XI, pp. 243-50.) When we speak of musical scholarship, we comprehend all of these branches. Precisely what scholarly study in this subject implies we shall see later. My purpose here has been to show that there is a unity in the fields that belong in musicology. This unity bears the characteristics of humanistic scholarship and excludes the fields that have rather a community of methods with the sciences.

A study of methods of teaching composition, instrumental performance, singing, or musical literature may well benefit the musicologist-in-training who will have to face students in these fields. But such methods, aside from their history, are hardly subjects for scholarly inquiry. Methods should be derived from sound psychological principles and the accumulated experience of ages. Most of all, pedagogy demands mastery of the subject at hand and not a little native endowment. In the fields of composition and performance, pedagogy is better left to masters of these arts, who, if they are also teachers, should acquaint themselves with relevant psychological and physiological theory. The history and present state of music education, on the other hand, is a province for musicologists. It is to them that we turn for the facts. A conscientious scholar, as an informed citizen of the musical community, will also work for desirable goals and efficient means in music education, but this is a moral duty rather than a scholarly function.

The musicologist's relation to instrumental and vocal technique is similarly oriented. He is not interested in developing these or even in defining their "scientific" principles. Rather, as an acute observer, the musicologist describes performance techniques in relation to musical cultures. He shows how performance practices affect and are affected by musical styles and their social setting. He shows us why one keyboard technique is necessary for Couperin and another for Debussy; why the sixteenth century organ used a mean-tone tuning and the lute did not. With respect to music whose historical context may not be familiar to the musician, the musicologist does have the responsibility of suggesting to the musician the effect that an acceptable technique should achieve. For this and many other reasons the musicologist should be a musician who continually grapples with the problems of performance. But it is outside the scholar's sphere to theorize about the performer's digital, pharyngial, or mental mechanics.

The musical scholar's relation to aesthetics is much more complex. The writers who have had the greatest influence on philosophies of music have been philosophers; yet few philosophers have had sufficient command of music to say much that is significant and at the same time specific. Usually commentators versed in the techniques of music have extended the thought of influential philosophers to cover musical problems. This has happened in recent times, for example, to the aesthetic thought of John Dewey, Henri Bergson, Benedetto Croce, and George Santayana.

Through the ages, aesthetic theory has presented to philosophers a formidable challenge. To arrive at a statement of what constitutes beauty and art and to determine the values that should govern our judgments of them, the philosopher must jump hurdles that test all his powers. He must define the relation of sensation to material objects. He must penetrate the meaning of space and time so that he can show

how illusions of these operate in art. He has to understand the urge to express and represent, and to reconcile this with the urge to create beautiful forms. The accidents of language, moreover, create a problem which tends to lead him away from the things themselves into frozen concepts. So he must be a metaphysician, psychologist, and semanticist.

While a good musicologist, who should be all of these too, can contribute much to aesthetic theory, he depends on the philosopher to point the way through the maze of theories and countertheories that might serve as foundations for a musical aesthetics. Once a general aesthetic theory has been formulated, there is no person more qualified than the musicologist to show how it might operate in his sphere. He often has to modify certain concepts and broaden the meaning of others, since his job is as much to extend as to apply. For this reason not every musicologist, but only those gifted and trained in philosophical speculation, should venture into aesthetics. But given this equipment, the musicologist, because of his intimate acquaintance with the processes of the creation, performance, and consumption of music over the ages and lands, is in an excellent position to interpret the meaning of music of contemporary philosophies. We cannot forget, though, that musical aesthetics is not musical scholarship; it is musical experience and musical theory converging upon a philosophical problem. Aesthetics does not rest on documentary or similar evidence but on philosophical and psychological principles tested by experience.

MUSIC THEORY

Music theory, whose place in musicology has been contested, is a field that needs definition almost as badly as that of musicology itself. Adler distinguished the theory of music in a general sense from the didactic theory used to train musicians and composers, and he considered both kinds of theory within the domain of musicology. For Riemann the theory of music contained the theory of notation, of composition, and of musical performance. While Haydon included these in his concept of musicology, he singled out the "theory of theory" as the aspect most deserving the attention of the scholar. By this he meant the definition of terms and the formulation of problems and general principles that must underlie all theory. Some of the problems that Haydon considered under this heading are the nature of musical scales, melody, and rhythm; the concepts of harmony, counterpoint, and form. These are the same topics that Riemann comprehended under "musical aesthetics or speculative theory."

The distinctions made by these authors need to be modified to fit the contemporary state of music theory. For example, the theory of harmony that Riemann developed was to him a universal theory, the culmination of centuries of evolution. We now recognize it as a synthesis of the harmonic practice of the nineteenth century. The term "traditional harmony" has consequently been adopted by many authors to denote such a historically limited theory. New harmonic systems have been proposed to fill the vacuum left by the abandonment of nineteenth century harmony. Some of these have also laid claim to universal validity, as Paul Hindemith's. Other theories have described acknowledgedly limited contemporary modes of composition—the twelve-tone method of George Rochberg, for example. This is a prudent approach, for our present historical consciousness leads us to regard any theory as having limited applicability. This same consciousness of changing styles and standards has produced a retrospective analytical theory whose purpose is to illuminate a practice of the past rather than to train composers of the future. To these two types must be added two other classes of theory: that used for elementary instruction and that which Haydon called the theory of theory.

It is evident, then, that the theory of music has several branches. These branches may be called for the sake of this discussion *practical theory, creative theory, analytical theory,* and *pure theory.* These terms, of course, are not standard. Each needs to be defined and its relation to musicology shown. It also must be kept in mind that, since these are artificial classes, any one treatise may belong to more than one of them.

The training of musicians in theory and composition has become in the United States chiefly the responsibility of practicing composers. This is true both in universities and in conservatories. By contrast, in Germany the university teacher of theory is usually a musicologist who holds a Doctor of Philosophy degree. In England he may be a scholar, composer, or performer, but rarely is he a man who considers himself primarily a composer. Composers are more likely to be found teaching theory in the conservatories of Europe than in the universities. In our country, because the university music department often functions in place of the conservatory as the training ground for the practical musician and composer, theory in the more flourishing departments has become the province of the composer. It would be unfortunate if this became a monopoly, but few would deny that an active composer often makes this study vital and lively as few others can do.

The term *practical theory* seems appropriate for the systematizations of melodic, rhythmic, contrapuntal, and harmonic techniques that aim mainly at the training of musicians generally. Walter Piston's *Harmony* (1941) and *Counterpoint* (1947) are outstanding pedagogical books for the study of traditional styles through exercises in practical composition. *Harmonic Practice* (1951) by Roger Sessions and *Tonal Harmony in Concept and Practice* (1962) by Allen Forte are other notable examples of training manuals in traditional styles, while *Twentieth Century Harmony* (1961) by Vincent Persichetti fulfills a similar function for more recent idioms. It is no accident that all of these authors are composers, with one exception, Forte, who is a theorist.

Scholarly research and critical observation may be quite essential to the preparation of such textbooks. But the most important foundation for them is the author's experience in handling and teaching the resources of composition. Practical theory, then, must also be excluded from musicology.

What I want to call *creative theory* goes beyond the elementary training of music students to the training of composers. The need for a creative theory arises when the theoretical foundation taught young musicians is based on a traditional practice no longer respected by composers. Hindemith's *The Craft of Musical Composition,* Book II (1941), and Krenek's *Studies in Counterpoint* (1940) are among the works in this sphere. *The Hexachord and its Relation to the Twelve-Tone Row* (1955) by Rochberg cited above is another example. Treatises of this kind tend to steer the composer into the particular methods favored by the author. They are not peculiar to our own age. The *Ars cantus mensurabilis* (c. 1260) of Franco of Cologne, the *Pomerium in arte musicae mensuratae* (1319) of Marchettus of Padua, the *Ars nova* (1320) of Philip de Vitry, the *Musica practica* (1482) of Bartholomé Ramos de Pareja, the counterpoint treatise (1591) of Vincenzo Galilei—these are among the works that crusaded for new approaches to composition. Such theories are the most ephemeral, but in any age they are the most revealing of the creative thought of the time. To write them is truly the business of the composer; to read them is the duty of the musicologist who wants to know the period in which they were in vogue.

By *analytical theory* is meant a theoretical system that has been induced from a body of existing compositions. Such a theory establishes a terminology, a system of symbols and ciphers and basic principles for the analysis of the music of a particular period. Walter Piston, in his textbook on harmony mentioned above, evolved such a scheme for what he calls the "common practice period," extending from around 1720 to around 1900. Heinrich Schenker's *Der freie Satz* (1935) offers a parallel basis for analysis. Though Schenker's American interpreters claim greater universality for his theory, it operates most successfully within these chronological limits. Analytical theories are by their nature interpretations of a somehow homogeneous body of facts. Schenker emphasized the essential unity of tonality within a work and devised a scheme for showing the relatedness of sections of a long piece constructed in several key areas. Piston related such sections through the concept of modulation and concentrated on the interpretation of chordal functions within a narrower context. Similar theories have been evolved in other specific areas like melody and counterpoint. Dom Paolo Ferretti's *Estetica gregoriana* (1934) and Knud Jeppesen's *The Style of Palestrina and the Dissonance* (1927) deal with these two areas respectively, and always in reference to particular styles.

The musicologist, constantly faced with the task of analyzing musical structure in all its dimensions, exploits every analytical theory that he finds consistent with the facts, whether written by a composer, analyst, or musicologist. May he also contribute such a theory? This is assuredly one of the fields in which he may profitably work. More than the composer, the musicologist who specializes in a period is steeped in its melodic, harmonic, contrapuntal, and rhythmic language. It is his responsibility to discover the principles that were once at work in musical creation. A. Tillman Merritt has done this for the polyphonic music of the sixteenth century. Hugo Leichtentritt's *Musical Form* (1951) is another example of a book in general analytical theory by a scholar. In a broader vein, Leonard Meyer's *Emotion and Meaning in Music* (1957) sets forth a basis for the analysis of content applicable to a wide range of musical styles. Whether by musicologists or not, valid analytical theories are contributions to musicology that scholars must take into account.

The class of theory that might be called *pure theory* aims primarily neither at the training of musicians and composers nor at the understanding of the music of the past, though it may serve both these ends. It organizes the materials of music in some logical way that expresses the philosophy of its author, without regard to whether the theory is corroborated by past or present practice. Works that deserve to be placed in this category are rare in the history of music. The *Harmonics* of Aristoxenus, the *Harmonics* of Ptolemy, the *Micrologus* of Guido of Arezzo, *The Harmonic Institutions* of Gioseffo Zarlino, the collected theoretical work of Jean Philippe Rameau, the *Craft of Musical Composition,* Part I, of Paul Hindemith are outstanding examples of pure theory. After a long period of comparative stagnation in this field, it is today giving signs of restless and explosive activity. The widespread employment of the serial method and the electronic medium, added to the general breakdown of the traditional modes of composition, has created an atmosphere of freedom bordering on chaos that has been an invitation to those inclined to constructing new systems. Information theory, linguistics, formal logic, acoustics, psychology, probability theory, mathematical set theory—these are some of the foundations on which new theories are being constructed. No definitive system has yet emerged from these speculations, but when one does, if it has any validity at all, it will tell us something about the music of the past and present, as well as of future possibilities.

Where does the musicologist stand in relation to this area of endeavor? He may well be the author of such a theory, though not in his capacity as a scholar. Like the aesthetics of music, pure theory is an extension of the musicologist's work but not a division of musicology. Almost all the men who have been active in this field are, in fact, composers—for example, Milton Babbitt, Lejaren Hiller, and David Kraehenbuehl. But scholars have also been active; Grosvenor Cooper and Leonard Meyer, two University of Chicago professors, have recently issued a treatise on musical form that is in many ways a new departure, *The Rhythmic Structure of Music* (1960).

Only one of the four areas of theoretical activity that have been described belongs, then, properly to the musicologist—analytical theory. But a theory once written, whether analytical, practical, creative, or pure theory, immediately becomes material for the scholar. A truly successful theory is a tool in his hands, and even a partially valid theory in some significant way reflects and explains the musical practice within which it was written. Besides, theoretical works are among the most precious of historical documents. Therefore the history of every branch of theory is an eminently important subject, though a neglected one, for the musicologist.

MUSICOLOGY—A DEFINITION

The area of the musicologist is, then, distinct from the areas of the theorist, the acoustician, the aesthetician, the psychologist, and the pedagogue. *The musicologist is concerned with music that exists, whether as an oral or a written tradition, and with everything that can shed light on its human context.* This is his concrete subject, not sound in its abstraction, technical skill, theories of value, or theories of composition.

The musicologist, while recognizing that he can speak with only limited authority upon these related subjects, must nevertheless be conversant with them. He must have a basic knowledge of their principles, history, and current theories. How deeply a musical scholar goes into any of them depends on his specialty. An ethnomusicologist or historian of music theory will have greater use for acoustical knowledge than one specializing in plain chant. A researcher in the performance-practice of the seventeenth century must have as a background much of the material otherwise relegated to musical pedagogy—the technique of playing string, wind, and keyboard instruments, of singing, of ensemble and choral performance. One who investigates the aesthetic theories behind the music of any period will want to know the history of philosophy and psychology, and should be well grounded in theory to understand the technical issues discussed in his sources. So the fields that in today's practice of musicology in America are treated as related rather than component disciplines should be included in the training of a musicologist. The course of studies represented by Haydon's book remains, in spite of his overly broad definition of the field, a valid introduction to musicology.

In addition to the related fields that were once regarded as components of musicology, there are other related disciplines that may be even more essential to musical scholars working in certain areas. Liturgiology, church history, classical metrics, and philology are of greater value to the student of medieval tropes than any of the scientific disciplines. Philological method and a thorough knowledge of Latin syntax are essential for the scholar who edits medieval treatises Anthropological and sociological principles and methods are fundamental for the ethnomusicologist. Literature and poetry in particular are constant preoccupations for all musicologists—because so much music is either set to or inspired by verbal texts—and every musicologist must also be a historian and linguist.

Many of the tasks that the musicologist attacks today require profound scholarship in nonmusical fields. Once these tasks were performed by men who were specifically trained in them and happened besides to know music. Jean Beck, a Romance philologist, edited trobadour and trouvère chansonniers. Karl von Jan, classical philologist, edited the principal Greek theoretical treatises on music. George Herzog, an anthropologist, has been one of the leading scholars in the field of American Indian music. Professors of English have been the most active collectors of ballards. Scholarly clergymen with years of theological and liturgical study behind them were once the leading investigators in medieval and Renaissance church music. While aspects of musicology will continue to be investigated by some whose main business lies elsewhere, the bulk of the tasks once done by these specialists are now the projects of professional musical scholars. They must now venture deeply into neighboring regions. It is no wonder that today's musicologist fancies himself more a humanist than a scientist.

Since the title *musicologist* gained acceptance, it has been bestowed liberally on a variety of musical journalists and essayists, choral directors, lutanists, organists, harpsichordists, and other performers who specialize in the older repertory, folk song collectors and singers, biographers of musical personalities, "classical disc-jockeys," record-jacket authors, instrument builders, and others. A few of these may be musicologists, but not by virtue of their occupations. Not even all scholars who have worked in music should be called musicologists. A number of persons who are designated musicologists in *Baker's Biographical Dictionary of Musicians* do not fit the title, while very few true American musicologists can be found in any American musical dictionary, though more of their biographies may be read in *Riemanns Musiklexikon* or in *Die Musik in Geschichte und Gegenwart,* two large German encyclopedias.

If the title is to carry any significance, *musicologist* must imply that the person so described is a master of a broad area of learning. Someone who plays the lute and knows its particular literature, or a biographer of a celebrated composer, if his acquaintance with music is limited to this one interest, is no more a musicologist than a gamekeeper is a zoologist or a manicurist a physician. A manicurist may know the care of hands, but he is far from a physician, who must know the care of the entire body, although in practice he may specialize in a limited area. So the knowledge of the musicologist must range over the entire domain this book describes and through the entire history of music. In his research he naturally specializes in one or several areas. However, not every musicologist needs to be a researcher, though he should be one potentially. Some utilize the research of others in teaching, criticism, performance, or librarianship. Not all musicologists have Ph.D's, and all holders of the Ph.D. in music are not musicologists, since the degree is given also in theory, composition, and education. More and more the Ph.D. degree is becoming representative of mastery in the field—and as long as high standards are maintained this is all to the good. The doctorate is not the only path to professional recognition, however; many outstanding American scholars have achieved this by virtue of publication and teaching.

The musicologist is first and foremost a historian. If his domain is music that exists, all such music, even that first performed yesterday, is part of history. Unlike the newspaper critic, who is most concerned with the merits of the individual composition or performance, the musicologist wants to know the work's connections with what has occurred before in its genre and with previous efforts by its composer. The composer's aesthetic outlook, his theoretical orientation, his means of livelihood, even his political opinions are all subject to the musicologist's curiosity. He also is interested in what, outside the composer's inner life, occasioned and conditioned a work and for whom, where, and when it was written. To the musicologist a good musical work is, to be sure, a work of art, but it is one in a stream of works, good and bad. Just as the political and diplomatic historian does not neglect scandals, crimes, and corruption, the musicologist must scrutinize poor works as well as masterpieces, for the process of history is revealed in the humble as well as in the great.

In his capacity as historian, the musicologist writes histories—general, topical, regional—and period studies. The general and period histories usually take the form of textbooks Topical histories may be scholarly monographs. The musical historian also writes lives of musicians, composers, critics, and anyone who has made a mark on musical life. He writes studies of the styles of individual composers, or of groups of them. Forms and types of music, like the symphony or fugue, may be his subjects He also writes histories of aesthetic ideas affecting music and of technical theories and performance practices In all these genres of work, he is the musical counterpart of the literary historian.

Why not simply call musicology history of music? Because there is much in the discipline that is not properly history. There is criticism and analysis, lexicography, bibliography, paleography, philology, archaeology, and sociology The relevance of the first five of these disciplines is self-evident. By musical philology I refer to the important task of making available legible and authentic texts of music that exists only in manuscripts and rare editions. A large part of musicological effort all over the world is concentrated on this task at the present time. The musical scholar functions as an archaeologist when he studies the remains of music of the past that are in the shape of instruments, artistic representations of instruments and performances, and the like. Classification and description of instrument collections constitute a part of his work. The social functions and organization of music, are also scrutinized the role of musicians' guilds, of choir schools, universities, religious associations, the drama, dance, public ceremony. All of these activities of the musicologist contribute to history of music, of course, but it is misleading to think of the musicologist only as a historian, because often his emphasis is not on the chronicle, but on some aspect of the thing being chronicled.

❧ 2 ❧

A BRIEF HISTORY

The earliest scholarly work on music by Americans antedates
the concepts of musicology that have been considered up
to now. It was accomplished by men who could devote only
their spare time to this occupation. Alexander Wheelock
Thayer (1817-97), the American author of *The Life of
Ludwig van Beethoven,* which remains after nearly a century the most definitive biography, worked as a librarian and
diplomat. Although this biography was written in English,
it was first published in German, the first three volumes
(Berlin, 1866, 1872, 1879), covering the years of the composer's life up to 1816, in a translation by Hermann Deiters.
The remainder of the work was in the form of notes when
Thayer died and these were the basis for the fourth volume,
completed by Deiters before he died in 1907 and edited and
published by Riemann the same year. Riemann, still using
Thayer's material, was responsible for the final volume
(1908) and for a revised edition of the earlier volumes
(II, 1910; III, 1911; I, 1917). Not until 1921 was Thayer's
English version of the earlier volumes restored and edited,
together with a translation of the rest, in Henry Krehbiel's
three-volume English edition published by the Beethoven
Association of New York. A thoroughly revised edition of
the Thayer-Deiters-Riemann-Krehbiel life, aiming to restore
as much as possible Thayer's own version and to bring the
facts up-to-date, has been prepared by Elliot Forbes for the
Princeton University Press.

The greatest of the older school of American scholars was
Oscar George Sonneck (1873-1928). Although he was born

in Lafayette, New Jersey, now part of Jersey City, Sonneck received most of his education in Germany. There he spent six years in elementary school, four in gymnasium, and four at the universities of Heidelberg and Munich between 1893 and 1897. At Munich he studied musicology with Adolph Sandberger. From 1902 to 1917 he was chief of the music division of the Library of Congress, a post created with remarkable foresight by Herbert Putnam, then Librarian of Congress. During his tenure, Sonneck built a collection that ranked among the best in the world. The collection of opera librettos, the largest anywhere, is covered by Sonneck's *Catalogue of Opera Librettos Printed before 1800,* issued by the library in 1914. This and his *Catalogue of Full Scores* (1908) are fundamental bibliographical tools, and more, for they are enriched with annotations that are the fruits of Sonneck's constant research into the history of opera, one of his favorite subjects. Another of his interests, eighteenth century American concert and opera life, is represented in three other important books: *A Bibliography of Early Secular American Music,* published at the author's expense in 1905 and later revised by W. T. Upton (1945), *Early Concert Life in America,* published by Breitkopf and Hartel in Leipzig in 1907, and *Early Opera in America* (Schirmer, 1915). In 1915 Sonneck became editor of the *Musical Quarterly,* which he founded under the auspices of Rudolph Schirmer, head of the G. Schirmer publishing house. Three years later he became director of publications for the firm, leaving the Library of Congress job, which went to Carl Engel.

In the prospectus distributed before the magazine made its appearance, Sonneck stated· "The appeal of the magazine will be to cultured music lovers and musicians who take an interest in more or less scholarly discussions of problems that affect the past, present and future of the art of music." Presenting essays by the best English and Continental au-

123

thors, most of whom could otherwise be read only in foreign languages, the *Quarterly* set distinguished and readable examples of musical scholarship before Americans inclined toward research. For these patrons it also provided a ready forum. Although European authors dominated the periodical until around 1937, American contributions appeared sporadically in its early years: essays by Daniel Gregory Mason, Henry F. Gilbert, Edwin Hughes, Henry Krehbiel, Arthur Ware Locke, Carl Engel, Ernest C. Krohn.

Engel, the *Quarterly's* second editor, from 1929 to his death in 1944, continued the policy of his predecessor. Engel's career, indeed, parallels Sonneck's in many ways. He too was educated in Europe, having been born in Paris in 1883. He studied at the universities of Strasbourg and Munich. He also held the job of Chief of the Music Division of the Library of Congress and eventually forsook this for full-time duties as president of the Schirmer house in 1934 In his sagacious and sparkling editorials called "Views and Reviews," Engel propagandized subtly for a more scholarly approach to musical subjects in America. The announcement by the new International Society of Musicology in 1927 that its executive board would always include representatives of the four countries "most actively engaged in musical research," namely Germany, England, France, and Italy, pricked Engel's patriotic pride. The United States was not among these most active nations, although in most sciences it was either equal to, or ahead of other countries. Talent was not lacking and newly acquired rich library resources awaited readers. "What we have still in insufficient numbers are trained music critics, music historians, and music librarians— or, in one word, musicologists—that is, musicians equipped with critical acumen, historical vision, and bibliographical knowledge" (*MQ,* 1928). Sonneck, Theodore Baker, Kinkeldey, and Engel himself had acquired this equipment in

Europe. Where in America could a musicologist be similarly trained? And what would he do after he was educated? True, the pages of the *Quarterly* were open to him, but there was no ready place for the musical scholar in our universities; there were no national research organizations that sponsored monumental series publications of music, and no society of musical scholars to recognize his work and gain recognition for it internationally.

As long as scholars worked in isolation, without institutional or organizational support, musicology in America was doomed to remain an avocation. Traditional marks of professional status—recognition as a field for graduate study and degrees, a journal and a society, a pursuit that advances a teacher's standing in a faculty—these musicology lacked. Until it acquired them there was little chance that musical scholarship would be recognized or that it would mature and grow.

The first important seal of recognition came on January 26, 1929, when the incipient American Council of Learned Societies (ACLS) "believing that the history and science of music constitute an important branch of learning," requested its Executive Committee to appoint a standing Committee on Musicology "and to take such other measures as may be calculated to promote research and education in that field" (ACLS Bulletin No. 11, 1929). The inspiration for this move came from a "valediction" to Sonneck that Engel wrote in the *Quarterly,* in which he made his usual strong stand for musicology. Dr. Waldo Leland of the ACLS read it and went to Engel at the Library of Congress to propose the creation of the committee. "With one stroke," said Engel later, " 'musicology' had come of age, the word had acquired a meaning, and was officially invested with the dignity to which it was born" ("An Address," AMS *Papers,* 1937).

The committee's first step was to study the state of musicological instruction and research in the country as a whole. The report was compiled by Oliver Strunk, then on the staff of the Library of Congress, and published in December 1932 as Bulletin No. 19 of the ACLS. It revealed a surprising potential of resources that invited exploitation and direction. The first part of the study examined the resources of musicology in American universities and colleges, the field being understood in the broadest possible terms. Few institutions, it was evident, recognized an independent field of musical scholarship and even fewer under the name of musicology. But an encouraging number of serious courses in research, aesthetics, history, acoustics, psychology, and theory of music were available in the fifty representative institutions surveyed. Moreover in twenty-one universities work in musicology was accepted toward advanced degrees. In a few of these it had recently become itself a field for an advanced degree. A fuller discussion of this academic aspect of the report will come in a later section of this essay.

The second part of the report concentrated on the resources at university, city, and other libraries. Here again the results were heartening: basic research libraries existed in about fifteen institutions and cities and numerous special collections of instruments were located in the East and Middle West. However, very few university libraries showed consistent strength in all the essential categories: periodicals, standard historical works and bibliographies, and monumental editions of music. Several distinguished university libraries reported that no funds at all were available for the development of music collections. The combined impression of the two parts of the report was that more institutions probably were attempting advanced training in scholarly aspects of music than were equipped to do so. As still prevails today, there was an excess of human resources over material resources, of ambition over direction.

Meanwhile the United States still lacked a society of musicologists. American musicologists were slow in organizing one partly because there already existed a forum for the exchange of ideas on musical questions, the Music Teachers National Association. Organized in 1876 by Theodore Presser and a small group of teachers, most of them connected with normal schools in Ohio and neighboring states, it grew to include many of those engaged in college and university teaching. It issued a report each year, with some exceptions, and in 1906 began a volume of papers and proceedings which was entitled "Studies in Musical Education, History and Aesthetics" in 1915. Among MTNA's presidents were two early champions of American musicology, Albert A. Stanley, in 1886, and Waldo Selden Pratt, between 1906 and 1908. The first volume of the *Proceedings* included papers by Edward Dickinson of Oberlin College on teaching music history, by Sonneck on European musical associations, by Stanley on Cesti's *Il Pomo d'oro,* and two papers on aesthetic theories. Hardly an issue went by without some distinguished piece of research or criticism. Inventories of research materials in the Library of Congress, the Newberry, Boston Public, and New York Public libraries appeared from time to time which were at once bibliographic aids and invitations to research. Beginning with the 1907 issue, the volumes included reports on the meetings of the North American Section of the International Music Society (Internationale Musik Gesellschaft).

This group was the true forerunner of the American Musicological Society. As the AMS was later to do, the International Music Society section met annually along with the MTNA and often had joint sessions with it. Some of the papers were printed in the *Proceedings* of the MTNA, others in the *Musical Quarterly,* the monthly *Zeitschrift* or the quarterly *Sammelbande* of the international group. Through the three latter organs a scholar could put the results of his research on view before the international fraternity, a fact that compensated somewhat for the absence of a strong national organization. The approximately twenty contributions by Oscar Sonneck to these two international journals, and others by Richard Aldrich, Franz Arens, Bruno Hirzel, Otto Kinkeldey, and Albert Stanley gave evidence to the international community of a growing activity. But in reality there were few real scholars amidst a larger group of well-wishers and amateurs.

The International Music Society had been founded in Leipzig in 1899 "to promote advanced musical scholarship." It fostered local and national associations and sponsored congresses at intervals. Eventually it secured thirty members from the United States, who formed a national section in 1907 under Albert A. Stanley as president. From 1911 it was headed by Waldo Selden Pratt. The American section was officially represented at the congresses of Vienna, 1909, London, 1911, and Paris, 1914. One of the American participants usually reported on a congress and communicated to the others some of the excitement of the gatherings, with their informal fellowship, excursions, concerts of both old and new music, and reports on the latest historical and scientific discoveries. Before the International Music Society was dissolved during World War I, American membership had risen to 120.

It was not until 1927 that a new international association, the Société Internationale de Musicologie, was organized. An American foundation, that of Elizabeth Sprague Coolidge, joined the governments of Germany, France, and the city of Basel to provide financial support for the establishment of a permanent seat and for the publication of a periodical. Carl Engel was elected to the executive council in anticipation of official American participation. Engel made an attempt to institute a national chapter in Washington in the spring of 1928 during a festival of music, but few in the heterogeneous attendance were aware of what musicology stood for. In Engel's words, "Although the company included not a few persons whose intelligence and learning were of a high order, that dubious word 'musicology' just made them shake their heads incredulously and turn away as from some dread abomination" ("An Address," AMS *Papers* 1937). Only ten from the United States were among the 170 members of the international society when it was founded, and their contributions to its journal, *Acta musicologica,* launched in 1931, were rare at first.

Meanwhile the MTNA continued to gather into its fold a number whose primary interest in music was scholarship. A standing Committee on History and Libraries began in 1925 to compile for the *Proceedings* an annual list of books on music. But aside from the retrospective 1928 volume, full of material for the history of American music during the previous fifty years, little space was given to matters of scholarly interest. The present character of MTNA as an association of private, college, and conservatory teachers of practical music was by this time becoming established. The time was ripe for a specialized group devoted to research.

Such a specialized but local group was formed in 1931 by Henry Cowell, Otto Kinkeldey, Charles Seeger, Joseph Schillinger, and Joseph Yasser. Known as the New York Musicological Society, it was interested chiefly in the systematic approach. During its four years of existence it held thirty-five meetings and published three numbers of a *Bulletin,* the first of which, in November 1931, proclaimed as the objective of the group the formation of a national society.

It was the New York Musicological Society that sponsored the foundation of the American Musicological Society in 1934. The New York Society's last meeting on June 3, 1934, at the home of Mrs. Ernest F. Walton at 25 Washington Square North was called by Seeger, Chairman of the Executive Committee, to dissolve itself in preparation for the foundation of the national association. This it proceeded to do. Then the one woman and eight men present, which included some not in the New York group, declared themselves "The American Musicological Association." They were. George Dickinson, Carl Engel, Gustave Reese, Helen Heffron Roberts, Joseph Schillinger, Charles Louis Seeger, Harold Spivacke, Oliver Strunk, and Joseph Yasser. They elected as president an absent colleague, Otto Kinkeldey, who had accepted the nomination by letter. An Organizing Committee was also elected. It chose Dickinson as chairman and prepared a constitution, by-laws, and a slate of officers, and on November 14 issued invitations to prospective members to attend a general meeting on December 1 in the rehearsal room of the Beethoven Association clubhouse at 30 West 56th Street. Meanwhile on September 15 the name of the association was changed to American Musicological Society. As someone quipped, it would not do to have the association become known as "AMUSA." The officers elected at the December 1 meeting were: Otto Kinkeldey, president, Charles Seeger and Oliver Strunk, vice presidents, Gustave Reese, secretary, Paul Henry Lang, treasurer, and Jean Beck, Archibald T. Davison, Carl Engel, and Carleton Sprague Smith, members-at-large. In 1935 the first chapters were established: Greater New York, Washington-Baltimore, and Western New York. The number of chapters has since grown to fourteen and the membership of the society to about 1,500, including student-members.

It would be wrong to assume that there are today more than a thousand practicing musicologists. Perhaps not one in four is an active researcher or teacher in the field. Membership is open to anyone who wishes to support the organization and has the sponsorship of one member. Subscription to the society's *Journal* is included in the membership fee, so that many belong only to receive the journal and to attend occasional meetings. Among these people are many composers, performing musicians and conductors, professors and teachers of music, music dealers, music critics, psychologists, anthropologists, instrument makers, and amateurs. The great interest that the meetings of the society and the journal have elicited are nevertheless a sign of its vitality in its twenty-seventh year. In 1961, subscribers to the *Journal* included 449 libraries in forty-eight states and twenty-nine foreign countries.

American participation in the International Society has grown apace. Today there are 272 American members, and eighty-one institutions and libraries in this country who subscribe to *Acta musicologica.* Two of the society's presidents have been Americans: Paul H. Lang and Donald Grout.

The tardy arrival of musicology on American campuses is not to be blamed so much on the lack of a musical tradition in our institutions of higher learning as on the absence of a scholarly musical tradition. The teaching of music in our colleges and universities was probably as widespread in the United States at the turn of the twentieth century as it was anywhere. But the instruction was at the undergraduate level, if not actually at the secondary school level, while in Germany and Austria, where musicology had made the greatest progress by this time, it was aimed at preparing students to write specialized doctoral dissertations.

The characteristic direction musical training took in the United States, by contrast with that in Germany and Austria, was determined by our particular pattern of education. Since few students continued beyond the bachelor's degree, the best that could be given them was a grounding in music theory and an acquaintance with the standard repertory, supplemented perhaps with instruction in singing or playing some instrument. Historical research, philosophical inquiries into the aesthetics of music, scientific studies in musical acoustics, psychology and physiology, such as were carried on in German universities, could find no place in our nineteenth century curriculums. Whereas the German music student was expected to meet the same standards of scholarship that were required in such fields as literature, languages, and philosophy, which, indeed, constituted the core of his work, the American student worked on an elementary though technical level that had little in common with advanced work in the other humanistic disciplines.

Apart from this fundamental cleavage, the development of music in the two systems of advanced education ran nearly parallel in intensity. Neither continent can boast a continuous tradition in music teaching that other disciplines have enjoyed. It is true that music was included in the curriculums of the *studia* of Paris, Cambridge, Oxford, Bologna, Salamanca, and other cities early in their history. It was usually taught as one of the mathematical disciplines of the quadrivium alongside arithmetic, geometry, and astronomy. In the thirteenth and fourteenth centuries, music contributed, as one of the liberal arts, to the basic curriculum that preceded intensive studies in theology, medicine, or law. There were lectureships in music at Prague, Heidelberg, Salamanca, Oxford, and Cambridge in the fifteenth century. However, by the end of the sixteenth century most of the chairs in music had ceased to exist outside of England, where they continued to flourish. Music study had to be developed afresh in the German, Austrian, and Swiss universities in the nineteenth century and subsequently in France and Italy. Heinrich Karl Breidenstein in Bonn and Adolf Bernhard Marx in Berlin were among the pioneer lecturers on music in the 1820's and

1830's. In due course Basel, Vienna, and other universities followed suit.

American colleges and universities did not remain far behind. In 1835 Elihu Parsons Ingersoll was appointed Professor of Sacred Music at Oberlin College, but he taught for only a year and was not replaced until 1837. Then George Nelson Allen, while still a student, took up the thread and upon graduation in 1841 was made professor. A presentation of $5,000 to Yale College in 1854 for "a teacher of the science of music" resulted in the appointment the following year of Gustave Jacob Stoeckel to give instruction in singing and choral music. The year Eduard Hanslick inaugurated musical lectures at Vienna—1861—saw Karl Merz initiate his courses at Oxford College for Women in Ohio. The following year John Knowles Paine began a series of lectures on musical forms without compensation at Harvard, but only a few attended. The catalog of 1870-71 lists a course of eighteen lectures on the history of music by Paine. In 1873, he was appointed assistant professor and promoted to professor two years later. "Honors in music" were established at Harvard at about this time. A true music historian, Frederic Louis Ritter (1834-91) became Professor of Music at Vassar in 1867, and by 1872 he had around him a staff of seven instructors in music. In 1875 a chair in music was established at the University of Pennsylvania, where Hugh Archibald Clark became Professor of the Science of Music. By 1880 courses in music were being taught also at Carleton, Elmira, Grinnell, Hillsdale (Michigan), Hollins (Virginia), University of Michigan, Mills, Ripon, Smith, and Wellesley.

In 1906 a survey showed that fifty-eight colleges granted credit for music toward the B.A. degree, among them Amherst, Barnard, Beloit, Columbia, Cornell, Dartmouth, Harvard, Oberlin, Radcliffe, Smith, Syracuse, Tufts, Vassar, and

Yale (MTNA *Proc.,* 1907). The branches of music in which credit was given were: music appreciation in forty-two colleges, harmony in forty-seven, counterpoint in thirty-three, composition in eighteen, practical music in twenty-one.

College music enjoyed a remarkable growth in the first quarter of this century. In a survey prepared by the Research Council of the Music Supervisors National Conference in cooperation with the National Bureau for the Advancement of Music (1930), it was discovered that three-fourths of the 594 institutions investigated offered some instruction in music and 170 allowed it to count as a major for the B.A. degree. There was a corresponding growth in graduate study, though the share of musicology in this expansion was very small. The course given by Charles Seeger at the University of California in 1917-18 was an isolated example. It was an "Introduction to Musicology," and Glen Haydon, who was later to establish musicology at the University of North Carolina, was in the class.

Cornell was another pioneering institution. Back in 1894 the administration was interested in establishing a scholarly department and the president sought the counsel of Waldo S. Pratt. In an address delivered at Cornell on May 14, 1894 (*Music Magazine,* 1894), Pratt advocated appointing a professor of music with the same dignity and rights of assistance from associates and instructors as those who taught English literature or Greek. After a provisional period during which a certain amount of practical instruction and nontechnical lectures in music would be provided, he envisioned a three-fold program of studies: (1) general classes and concerts; (2) technical courses for highly selected students of performance and composition, leading to suitable degrees up to Doctor of Music; (3) strictly intellectual courses in all the leading aspects of musical science, psychology, physics, vocal physiology, musical poetics, aesthetics and criticism, history, pedagogy, and sociology. The aim of the last group of studies was to stimulate investigation and publication, and the highest degree given would be the Doctor of Philosophy. Pratt called his program a "daring ideal." It was indeed, for only in 1930 was a professorship such as he had in mind established at Cornell, when the first chair of musicology in the United States was created for Otto Kinkeldey. Kinkeldey had been head of the department between 1923 and the spring of 1926, when he returned to the New York Public Library. In 1928, W. G. Whittaker, Reader in Music at Durham University in England, collaborated in a study of musical conditions at Cornell, and the report submitted to the president was the basis of a reorganization that led to Kinkeldey's appointment.

Instruction in musicology under Kinkeldey at Cornell was carried on through a seminar. Usually a central topic was chosen for the year, and students worked and reported on special aspects of it according to their particular interests and preparation. The approach was largely historical but the acoustics, psychology, aesthetics, and theory of music were not neglected. This method of instruction Kinkeldey brought with him from Germany, where he had held the position of Royal Professor of Musicology at the University of Breslau between 1910 and 1914, having received his Doctor of Philosophy degree at Berlin in 1909. In an address to the MTNA in 1915, soon after his return, he had described in detail how a musicological seminar in a German or Austrian university operated, but he appreciated at that time that such a thing was still far from realization here. Many of the students at Cornell who attended Kinkeldey's seminars during the early years later established similar seminars elsewhere. Fortunately Kinkeldey's teaching was not confined to the Ithaca campus. In summer sessions at Harvard, as visiting professor there and subsequently at Texas, Princeton,

North Texas State, Illinois, California in Berkeley, Boston University, and Washington in Seattle, he gave generously of his wisdom and counsel to a multitude of graduate students. His introductions to bibliography and research methods were models for this type of course, now given almost everywhere. As George S. Dickinson stated, "There is no serious American musical scholar of this generation who does not consciously reflect some sort of contact with the ideal of scholarship which Dr. Kinkeldey personally embodies" (*MQ*, 1938). Thanks to Kinkeldey's activity since retirement in 1946, this is true also of the succeeding generation.

In his ACLS report, Oliver Strunk listed only three courses, besides the seminar at Cornell, that were expressly designated *musicology* in 1932: a course in musicological method taught by Dickinson at Vassar, a seminar in medieval musicology by Jean Beck at Pennsylvania, and a history of music taught under the heading "musicology" by Harold Gleason at the Eastman School of Music, Rochester. A number of other seminars and advanced courses in musical research and history were available at New York University, University of Kansas, Michigan, Missouri, Northwestern, Ohio State, Smith, Wellesley, and Wisconsin. Other institutions offered individual guidance in the field. Only a few universities at this time accepted music toward the Ph.D. degree—Harvard (and Radcliffe), Teachers College of Columbia, State University of Iowa, the universities of Missouri, Michigan, Indiana, Rochester, Cornell. Altogether thirty-six institutions offered advanced degrees for work in music, or accepted work in music toward advanced degrees. Fewer, however, recognized musicology. Strunk concluded, "In short, if our distinction between instruction in music and instruction in musicology be granted, and the offering of graduate instruction in musicology be accepted as the criterion, there appear to be in all twenty-one American universities offering advanced degrees for work in musicology (or accepting work in musicology toward the advanced degrees)." The study lists 167 dissertations, among which were 135 master's essays and thirty-two doctoral dissertations, but not one was specifically in the field of musicology. The first degree so designated was that awarded at Cornell in 1932 to J. Murray Barbour, whose thesis was "Equal Temperament: Its History from Ramis (1482) to Rameau (1737)."

The ACLS report in some ways presented an encouraging picture. Considerable gains in graduate work had accompanied the enormous expansion of undergraduate teaching. Almost everywhere some introductory course in the history of music could be found. Most of the fifty institutions studied offered also some advanced lecture courses, and several had seminars. The advanced courses tended to be concentrated in the eighteenth and nineteenth century, and courses in medieval or Renaissance music were the exceptions. The emphasis was cultural rather than scholarly, and more often on specific masterpieces than history. In general, graduate study in music in the United States continued to emphasize vocational ends—public school teaching, practical music teaching, or professional musicianship.

The growth of music in colleges and universities was a mixed blessing for musicology. While it laid the foundation for graduate study by preparing undergraduates, it also built vested interests into the established music departments and schools. It might have been easier for musicology in the 1930's had there been fewer flourishing music departments in the great universities. For now musicology had to fight not only indifference on the part of university administrations but also prejudice within the music departments.

In musicology's struggle for academic recognition, the

principal hurdle has not been lack of books or money, but this prejudice. The resistance to musical scholarship has several explanations.

First the character of musical personnel in American universities must be understood. Music entered the university picture not as a learned discipline but as an accessory to academic education. The earliest manifestations were bands, glee clubs, choruses, and chapel choirs that grew up on campuses despite, at times, the lack of any faculty leadership. In most institutions the musical directors and chapel organists were faculty members with teaching duties. The men who held these positions were rarely people of scholarly inclinations. They were practical musicians trained in conservatories, though they often possessed baccalaureate degrees. The courses they taught reflected this background. These were courses in "appreciation," sacred music, and basic musical theory such as harmony, counterpoint, and analysis. Around the conductors and organists grew the music departments that flourished in the first quarter of the present century. When a faculty member was chosen, more thought was given to his potentials as a conductor or player who could enhance the musical life of the campus than to his scholastic achievements. Occasionally composers were appointed.

However distinguished these men may have been in their musicianship or creative work, they failed to impress the academic community with their credentials as learned men. They did not speak the language or follow the patterns of work of their academic colleagues. Their noisy activities were tolerated only because they could provide occasional entertainment and add pomp, festiveness, or gaiety to campus ceremonies and celebrations.

This pattern of growth is characteristic particularly of the music departments in liberal arts colleges and in the universities that evolved around them. Another pattern took shape in the state universities, where often a school of music or conservatory already in existence was joined to the university, or formed within it. These conservatories had and still have a high degree of autonomy. They granted their own degrees, usually the Bachelor or Master of Music or the Bachelor of Science in Music or of Fine Arts in Music. The academic subject matter taught was usually slight, and the goal of education was the production of performers or composers who could enter the musical profession or train others in their specialties. While history of music was usually one of the subjects of the curriculum, it was rarely taught by a historian of music or scholar. Often when a man was no longer effective as a conductor, player, singer, or composer, he was given the course in the history of music because there his shortcomings were least exposed. Even when scholarly musicians became available for these positions in the Twenties and Thirties, they were rarely hired. It was assumed that the candidates had taken the road of scholarship because they had failed as musicians or composers. They substituted talking about music for making music, which was the professed business of a school of this kind. Moreover they acquired a reputation of being difficult to get along with. They insisted that libraries acquire basic reference and scholarly books and critical editions of music; they expected students to devote some time to historical studies and not merely to listen to lectures; and they almost invariably advocated "diluting" the musical training with liberal education. Many of the university schools of music, sometimes under pressure from the university administration, began to admit musical scholars to their faculties in the 1940's, some not until the 1950's. In one southwestern university the administration backed the appointment in 1956 of several musicologists in a department staffed by nonscholars. Within two years all of them had resigned because the opposition of other musicians had made their situation intolerable and the pursuit of their programs impossible. As recently as 1959 Paul H. Lang complained: "When a college is in the market for a professor for its music department, a practicing musician is preferred to a university man. Very few of our leading colleges have these days a painter or sculptor as head of their fine arts department, but in music the scholar is still the exception" (College Music Society, *Proceedings,* 1959).

Still a different pattern obtained in the teachers colleges. Here again practical musicians were in control until the state requirements for methods courses became so demanding that progressively larger proportions of former public school teachers and holders of doctorates in education invaded the faculties of the teachers colleges. While administrations were not opposed to scholarship in principle and often sought persons with academic achievements, the requirement that the candidate have some experience conducting musical groups or in public school teaching excluded most aspirants with musicological training. The demand for Ph.D.'s and other doctoral degrees that the accrediting associations and state boards created with their requirements stimulated graduate study. But most of this momentum was soon channeled into the production of more Doctors of Music Education. In practice, the teachers colleges offered their music majors only the most rudimentary instruction in music history or literature because of the demanding schedule in practical music and methodology necessitated by teacher certification requirements. It is not unusual to find graduates in music education who do not know the form of a sonata, have never examined a fugue, and are uncertain about the centuries in which Mozart or Beethoven lived, not to mention Monteverdi or Rameau.

The prejudice against musicology thus acted on two fronts: from the side of the academic community, which failed to recognize the musician as a fullfledged colleague, and from the members of music departments, who insisted on judging the scholar strictly by standards of practical musicianship. The first was more easily overcome than the second. Among the earliest supporters of musicology in the universities were the humanities faculties. The impetus for the reorganization of the Cornell department came from outside the music faculty. At Harvard the emphasis in the Department of Music was for long on training in composition, and the earliest Ph.D.'s were granted in recognition of distinguished achievement in creative work. Musicology was somewhat suspect because of its pseudo-scientific connotations and because it was feared that to insist on scholarship would stifle creativity. When President Lowell first heard the word *musicology* he is said to have exploded, "Nonsense—the word doesn't exist. You might as well speak of grandmotherology." Willi Apel and Hugo Leichtentritt both lectured at Harvard for a time, and Otto Kinkeldey taught summer sessions and as visiting professor in 1946-48. A musicologist of international reputation, Otto Gombosi, was finally appointed to a tenure position in 1951. Scholars now dominate the department and hold most of the endowed chairs, as befits Harvard's exceptional research facilities. The late arrival of music at Princeton University, where no music courses were taught before 1931-32, favored the establishment of a scholarly program. Since graduate study in musicology was inaugurated by Oliver Strunk in 1940-41, Princeton has been one of the most stable and most productive training centers in the field. Similar conditions hastened the advance of musicology at the two main branches of the University of California.

University schools of music, in an advantageous position because of their ability to support faculties of specialists, were among the earliest sponsors of musicology. The Eastman School of Music of the University of Rochester, home of the famous Sibley Music Library, already in 1932 had a professor of musicology, Harold Gleason, and in 1934 he was joined by Charles Warren Fox, who had been a student of Kinkeldey at Cornell. At Yale, David Stanley Smith, Dean of the School of Music, recommended the appointment of Leo Schrade as lecturer in musicology in 1938. In 1940 the degree of Ph.D. in musicology (the designation was changed to *history of music* in 1946) was first offered through the Graduate School. Other consistent supporters of musicological studies have been the schools of music of Northwestern, Indiana, Michigan, Illinois, Southern California, and Ohio State. There is a growing recognition of the benefits gained by both sides from the close association of a conservatory's practical music instruction and its active musical life with the scholarly activities of a musicological department. There is nothing that young American musicians need more than the critical attitude and stylistic consciousness that the musicologist's command of the music of the past can contribute to their training. On the other hand, musicologists could not find better stimulants for a realistic and aesthetically oriented approach to the editing of forgotten music than close communion with open minded musicians of good taste. Practical demonstrations of this can be heard in the distinguished work of the *collegia musica* at Illinois, Yale, Boston, Southern California, and Northwestern.

A few recent facts about the progress of musicological training in our universities will be sufficient to bring this account to a close. A survey compiled by Catherine Brooks for the Pan American Union (1943) showed that in the academic year 1941-42, graduate seminars or introductions to musicology and research were available at the following twenty-seven institutions: Arizona, California, UCLA, Chicago Musical College, Cincinnati, Columbia, Cornell, Drake,

Fisk, Harvard, Hunter, Michigan, Michigan State, New York University, North Carolina, North Texas, Oregon, Pennsylvania, Redlands, Rochester, Smith, Southern California, Texas State, Vassar, Washington (state), Wisconsin, and Yale. Eight universities offered courses restricted to ancient and medieval music, while twenty-four had such courses in music of the seventeenth and eighteenth century. A survey by Frederick W. Sternfeld covering the academic year 1949-50 (AMS *Journal,* 1950) disclosed that musicological courses leading to the master's or doctor's degree were offered at the following institutions in addition to those already named: Baylor, Boston, Carnegie, Catholic, Florida State, Hamline, Idaho, Iowa (Iowa City), Ithaca, Kansas, Miami (Ohio), Minnesota, Missouri, New Mexico, Northwestern, Oberlin, Queens (New York), George Peabody, Pittsburgh, Roosevelt, Stanford, Syracuse, Texas Christian, Tulane, Union Theological, Wayne, and Western Reserve. The third edition of *Doctoral Dissertations in Musicology* (1961), compiled by Helen Hewitt, shows that thirty-one universities in the United States are awarding or have awarded the Ph.D. degree in musicology or history of music.

If the academic gates have been effectively swung open, hostility to scholarship in music among musically cultivated people remains. America has been a land where the doer has been more respected than the thinker. In the public's esteem, only achievement as a composer or musician has conferred authority. Scholarship, it tends to believe, kills the artist's feeling and the critic's insight. It is content to regard musicians as specially gifted people whose eccentricities and economic unproductivity are excused by their genius. In the absence of this quality, which is measured by virtuosity of performance or prodigality of composition, a musician is considered a failure. And nothing is less prized than the artistic failure. Such a romantic conception of the musical artist has died slowly here, perhaps because until recently so few great musicians and composers grew up among us.

Many of our best scholars have been, still are, or are at least potentially musical artists, though not virtuosos. But few outside the academic world recognize their authority. Rarely have newspapers hired scholars as music critics or asked them to review books on music or records, although this is standard practice in literature or history. A book on music has had greater chance of success if authored by a composer, musician, or critic, or even a radio announcer, than if written by a musicologist. Some of our most distinguished presses have launched presumptuous books on music that are counterfeits of musical scholarship. They either failed to seek counsel among the many qualified scholars available, or, having received negative criticisms, chose to dismiss them as the rantings of cranky academicians. Record-jacket scriptwriters daily perpetuate falsehoods that have been known as such to scholars for half a century. Although thousands of dollars are lavished on art work, fancy printing, and high-fidelity engineering, the little it might cost to have a scholar as editorial consultant is perhaps considered too much to ensure a minimum of historical fidelity and honest criticism. But these are growing pains of a not yet mature musical culture. The distinguished services to musicology of publishers like Norton, Princeton, Harvard, Columbia, Oxford, of the *Saturday Review of Literature,* the *New York Times* and the *Herald Tribune,* and of the numerous recording companies far outweigh the blunders that have been committed.

The recognition of musicology by book and music publishers in the United States has lagged behind its academic growth. While this is understandable on several grounds, the inhibiting effect it has had and continues to have on the progress of scholarship cannot be ignored.

Scholars and publishers share responsibility for this slowness of recognition. Musicologists, with few exceptions, have failed to enter into and maintain good relations with domestic publishers. They have not been bold enough in proposing publication projects and few have cared to invest their energies in fund raising and promotional activities. The publishers, in an age of expanding education and burgeoning of new scientific areas, have been too busy keeping pace with the requirements and potentials of these fields to nurture a small discipline promising little profit. While many general publishers have employed music editors or consultants, these have tended to be public school music men, who as a group have not been sympathetic to musicology. General editors shy away from music as too technical a subject and tend to regard the musical public as one that prefers easy reading. They have been hardly aware of a growing segment of this public that is ready for scholarly books or at least books based on honest scholarship. Bookdealers, who ultimately decide the fate of books, have been wary of stocking any but the most popular music books. Even in university towns they tend to refer customers to the musicdealer, who in turn finds it more profitable to cater to the instrumental and vocal teacher and performer, and most recently to the record collector. Scholars have tended to weaken further the local potential by resorting to mail-order purchasing, though it must be said that they buy fewer books than their European counterparts and so do not sufficiently support their colleagues' efforts.

The principal reason for the weak appeal of the musicological book to publishers has been the size of the market, which has not warranted the costly production processes often required. In addition to the musical examples usually necessary to a scholarly study, there are normally many quotations in foreign languages, abundant footnotes, numerous symbols, charts, and diagrams, all of which make production expensive. The number of copies that must be sold before the publisher can break even, let alone realize a profit, is consequently larger than in most other fields. These financial reasons for the neglect of scholarly music books, however, have been more valid in the past than they are now. A publisher can now count upon several thousand potential purchasers in the United States and many abroad for an important scholarly book. Specialized studies, on the other hand, may always require some kind of subsidy.

The resistance experienced by musicological books at commercial presses is shared to a degree by books in the other humanities, but the boundary line between what is considered financially feasible by commercial presses and by university presses has been more confining in music than in most other fields. The contribution of commercial presses in music has been generally limited to reference works, basic handbooks, textbooks, general histories, and biographies of well-known composers. There have been only occasional reprints, such as Dover's of Burney's *History,* or translations of important documents. Notable examples are C.P.E. Bach's *Essay on the True Art of Playing Keyboard Instruments,* translated and edited by William J. Mitchell and published by Norton in 1949, and *The Bach Reader* (1945) by Hans David and Arthur Mendel, also a Norton book.

More particular studies have almost all come from the university presses, but even these deal with large areas such as the history of Gregorian chant, the baroque sonata, primitive music, and the like. The book on an individual composer of the period before 1700 is rare and one concerning a particular problem—the University of California Press's *Tonality and Atonality in Sixteenth Century Music* (1961) by Edward Lowinsky, for example—is rarer still. Documents, editions, and translations of historically important treatises, or books derived from dissertations of limited scope, are usually turned down by university presses. Biographies or collections of papers pertaining to local political figures with some national importance but no international renown are considered better money-losing prestige items for a university press than documents or monographs on musical subjects of international and key historical importance. Such an attitude undoubtedly reflects the prejudices of the editors and advisory boards as well as the difficulties and expense of production involved.

The scarcity of domestic outlets has led scholars to place manuscripts with publishers abroad who often manage to distribute their books outside the normal bookselling channels. For example, between 1959 and 1962 as many important scholarly books by American musicologists were issued by presses in Europe as in the United States. Among these were Robert Stevenson's *Spanish Music in the Age of Columbus* (1960), which one reviewer has called "a milestone in Hispanic musical scholarship," and Curt Sachs's *The Wellsprings of Music* (1962), both published by Martinus Nijhoff in The Hague. Also printed mainly in Holland —though issued under the imprint of the American Institute of Musicology, which has a business office in Dallas, Texas—were several of the recent volumes by Americans in the series of "Musicological Studies and Documents," including editions, translations, and studies of important documents of the fifteenth, sixteenth, and seventeenth centuries. To these must be added H. C. Robbins Landon's *The Collected Correspondence and London Notebooks of Joseph Haydn* (1959), which was published in England by Barrie and Rockliff, though it was distributed also by Essential Books of Fairlawn, New Jersey, and Barry S. Brook's *La Symphonie française dans la seconde moitié du XVIIIe siècle* (Paris, 1962). A notable example on the ethnomusicological side is William P. Malm's *Japanese Music and Musical Instru-*

ments (1959), luxuriously produced with copious illustrations, many in color, by the Charles E. Tuttle Company of Tokyo.

In the field of music publishing the United States is far behind Europe. A single publisher in Kassel, Germany, has set a pace for quality and quantity of scholarly music publishing since World War II that all American music publishers combined could not approach for many years to come, even if they aimed to do so. A more ambitious program for the publication of historically important music in critical editions is under way in war-ravaged Poland than exists in the United States.

The cost of labor is undoubtedly the main factor that favors the European printer, but part of the reluctance of the New York houses to venture into scholarly music publishing must be their conservative adherence to the traditional function of serving the domestic market, whereas international distribution is essential if a scholarly edition of music is to subsist or fulfill its function. Most of the trade in America lies in music used for instructional purposes. When the big American music publishers have been able to afford the luxury of gratifying altruistic motives, they have tended to fulfill first their moral obligation to the contemporary American composer. Few musicologists would argue against this emphasis on contemporary music. What they would like to see added is not deficit publication of old music, but profitable publication of old music for educational needs that are now satisfied by unartistic pot-boilers and old-fashioned, over-edited choral and orchestral arrangements. There is no reason why editions of scholarly merit cannot be used in schools and colleges if a flexible method is adopted for their publication. Once a firm possesses the plates, it can print individual pieces from a set and provide performance instructions for little extra cost. Needed is less intransigence on the part of musicologists and greater boldness on the part of music publishers.

Another pattern of modern publishing, one that has been strengthened since the last war, inhibits participation of American scholars in the publication of old music. This is the network of relationships established between American and foreign publishers and between New York agents and their parent firms. Both New York and Wiesbaden, Kassel, Paris, Milan, or London are cited in the imprint of many scholarly editions, but the editorial work and printing are almost always done abroad. Often an American musicologist may be better qualified or may even have already completed a transcription, when a scholar nearer the overseas home office is commissioned to do the edition or initiates negotiations for it. From the American musicologist's point of view it is therefore important for established domestic firms to enter into competition with foreign publishers in this field rather than take the easier road of marketing the latter's products. If a system of private enterprise music publishing is to prove its vitality, it ought to fulfill its responsibility to the scholarly community at least as well as the subsidized state presses of eastern Europe.

The limited communication that publication difficulties have imposed upon American musicology weakens its international impact and makes an appraisal of its total contribution in recent times tentative. A truly comprehensive critical survey of American achievements in this field would take into consideration the many unpublished dissertations that it has been possible to review only spottily. The remarks that follow are therefore confined, with a few exceptions, to material in print.

◄§ 3 ß►

NOTABLE ACHIEVEMENTS

It is often stated that musicology's first task is to furnish the student, scholar, and performer with readable and reliable editions of otherwise unavailable music. This may be the most fundamental need, but it cannot be the beginning in a country that has neither experience nor tradition in musical scholarship. The first necessity is some orientation in the field, such as can be provided by handbooks in the general history of music, national history, bibliography, and research. The most significant early works published in America in fact do fall into these categories.

GENERAL HISTORIES

Frederic L. Ritter (1834-91) of Vassar College wrote several histories. In eleven lectures published from 1870 to 1874 Ritter made an earnest attempt to sum up current knowledge in the history of music gained by such men as Ambros, Winterfeld, and Chrysander. He did not fail to add his own appraisals of some of the music, which he shows he knew at first hand. His avowed principle was never to accept "any judgment, any opinion, of an important historical fact, or aesthetic appreciation of important works, that marked or prepared an era in music, until after a conscientious, careful examination, comparison, and study of the most reliable sources which were at my disposal, and most of which are in my own possession." This is surely an unassailable principle. Ritter's *Music in England* (1883), while it perpetuates the idea of English insularity and makes only a nod at the Middle Ages, is distinguished by a section of about seventy pages devoted to the aesthetic ideas of the principal English writers on music from Christopher Simpson, through Malcolm, Avison, Brown, Harris, Webb, and others, up to Burke. Ritter considered this book a preparation for his *Music in America* (1883, 1895), a work far more original than its predecessor. Probably forced into a sociological approach by the inaccessibility of the music of American composers, Ritter communicated to his readers much painstakingly gathered information about the musical societies of Dartmouth College, New York, and Boston, the three centers he knew most intimately. He found New York and Boston healthy in their musical lives and gaining each year a more solid basis of musical culture. But he characterized the rural areas and towns as "fat pastures on which an army of musical charlatans, ignoramuses, and cunning adventurers feed, under the names of convention conductors, leaders, organizers, lecturers, teachers, performers, etc."

The most distinguished of the early professors was Waldo Selden Pratt (1857-1939). His *History of Music,* first published in 1907 and several times revised, is not so much a history as a handbook. Within a mixed chronological, systematic, and geographical organization, it compiles short biographies of composers, theorists, and musicians. Some attention is given to listing their main contributions, but one gets hardly any idea of their music. For its time it was both a thorough and reliable reference book but not a work that could inspire much interest in the music of the past. Pratt's encyclopedic tendencies found a more satisfactory channel in the *American Supplement* of *Grove's Dictionary of Music and Musicians* (1920), in which he was assisted by Charles N. Boyd. This was a work that could stand comparison with the best examples of European lexicography. Pratt's life-long interest in psalmody moreover bore fruit in two distinguished pieces of original research.

These men were among the earliest Americans to attempt general histories of music. However, the first such history that may be said to represent an American contribution to international scholarship is Paul Henry Lang's *Music in Western Civilization* (1941). A publication of the farsighted Norton Company, it has been translated into several European languages. No one before Lang had attempted such a vast canvas of the cultures in which Western music developed. The important histories of music up to this time had concentrated on the evolution of musical techniques and forms, the social and intellectual habitat being kept in the background. Lang, whose book contains not a single musical example, is interested in music as an expression of the spirit of time and place. The music itself is described, sometimes most vividly, and it is obvious that the author has digested it, but familiarity with it is to a degree also presumed in the reader. Needless to say, few of its first American readers, particularly the students who used this book as a text, could appreciate the truth and significance of the symbolic values Lang attached to the music he described and placed in its setting. Today many possess the necessary background, and have the further advantage of being able to draw on the expanded knowledge gained by musicology since 1941. Yet after twenty years very few of Lang's penetrating conclusions need revision.

Another full-length history was not published until 1960, again by Norton, Donald Jay Grout's *A History of Western Music*. While this is truly a textbook, it is imbued throughout with the profound scholarship of its author and can serve even advanced musicology students as a handbook for quick factual reference and bibliography, because it gathers together the most recent information. Grout's emphasis contrasts both with Pratt's, which was on biographical facts, and with Lang's, on intellectual and cultural background, for Grout places it on history of style. In focusing attention on style Grout reflects a current preoccupation among American historians, who feel that, with much of the important music published, the time has arrived to make careful and justifiable generalizations about it. Another recent textbook, addressed mainly to the general college student, is *The Art of Music* (1960) by Beekman Cannon, Alvin Johnson, and William Waite. While it is not a comprehensive history of music, it deserves mention here because it offers models of a kind of many-sided analysis, particularly of medieval, Renaissance, and baroque works, that is rare in our scholarly literature. It also attempts for the first time in a textbook of this kind to link up currents of philosophic and aesthetic thought with musical styles.

PERIOD HISTORIES AND HANDBOOKS

Enter Taruskin

No one-volume history, however scholarly, can provide the detailed analysis, source material, and bibliographical references essential to the advanced student or researcher. This can at best be achieved in period histories. Until the Norton Company began to issue its volumes of period studies in 1940, there existed two such scholarly works. *The Oxford History of Music,* first published between 1901 and 1905, was quite outdated by 1940 in spite of the new edition with supplementary volumes issued between 1929 and 1938. The *Handbuch der Musikwissenschaft* edited by Ernst Bücken between 1928 and 1931 contains individual volumes dedicated respectively to ancient music, the Middle Ages and the Renaissance, the classic period, the baroque, the nineteenth century, and modern. It had the obvious disadvantages of being out of print and in a foreign language. So the Norton series was a boon to all English speaking researchers and teachers.

While no series was contemplated when the first book, *Music in the Middle Ages* (1940) by Gustave Reese, was published, and no stylistic uniformity is present among the volumes, all the periods of music history have been covered except the classic period. Each author has approached the problem of writing a history limited to the music of one period in his own way. Even the two books by Reese, that on the Middle Ages and *Music in the Renaissance* (1954), do not follow the same policy. The two books are consistent, however, in that they are addressed to advanced students and uncompromisingly attack difficult problems in all the depth and detail that the scope of the books allows. The Renaissance book goes beyond the usual idea of a period history, and approaches the character of a research manual. It is, of course, first a history, in that its plan is to trace the development of the Renaissance style in France, the low countries and Italy, and then to show its diffusion in the Iberian peninsula, Germany, eastern Europe, and England. It is not only a chronological narrative that gives essential facts, but a history of styles in the broadest sense—styles of groups of composers and nations, as well as individuals. It contains, besides, a great many analyses of individual works. Primarily, however, it is a scholar's source-book, for it compiles information scattered among more than two thousand articles, studies, books, editions, and numerous manuscripts, all of which are carefully identified. It thus serves as a descriptive, classified, and chronological Renaissance bibliography.

That a source-book whose usefulness is greatest to the advanced graduate student and professional musicologist should have been published by a commercial press, and that this book should have been successful enough to reach a second edition six years later is an indication of the large number of people who are eager to be informed in an area that not long ago was considered quite esoteric. It was published as a textbook, and it has certainly been used as such, but its importance for the advancement of scholarship in the Renaissance far exceeds that of textbooks in other fields. One of the ironies of publishing in musicology is that if a book of this quality is not capable of fulfilling a classroom role its publication is often considerably delayed.

The other volumes in the Norton series are also significant contributions to scholarship, though they are of more modest scope. Perhaps the most successful of these is *Music in the Baroque Era* (1947) by Manfred F. Bukofzer. The author is concerned with demonstrating the application of certain fundamental stylistic principles in the music of this period. Although there is a wealth of detail, including analysis of individual works, the author has been highly selective and critical. Rather than present the views of a number of scholars as Reese does, Bukofzer, after considering their opinions, has expressed his own conclusions. Moreover, when Bukofzer is specific it is in order to relate the specific to trends that have broad application.

Curt Sachs in *The Rise of Music in the Ancient World East and West* (1943) and Alfred Einstein in *Music in the Romantic Era* (1947) are even more personal in their approach than Bukofzer. (The remaining volume of the series, *Music in Our Time,* is not relevant to this discussion. Its author, Spanish scholar Adolfo Salazar, is now resident in Mexico.) Sachs develops from the outset his own theses about ancient music, a field in which hypotheses must often replace conclusions. His theories have been and will continue to be contested. But no other scholar has had the unique experience of dividing his efforts so equally over both Eastern and Western music. Therefore his brilliant insights into their interrelationships will continue to command attention even after the intense investigation that the East is now undergoing proves him wrong on many counts. Sachs gives little documentation and no bibliography to guide further readings. Einstein's book is even more extreme in this respect, containing only about eighty footnotes in 360 pages, and no bibliography. His particular approach is to characterize the romantic movement through its musical expression. It is not a history in the traditional sense but a series of essays on various aspects of the nineteenth century· the rise of romanticism, Schubert, opera, symphonic and chamber music, church music, nationalism, and so on. However, what it lacks in completeness and objectivity, it gains in richness of interpretation. This work is history distilled through the keen mind of a man of authority —a man, furthermore, who was during a long part of his career a critic and who has here written a book of criticism rather than scholarship.

Where, one may ask, does this leave us in the field of period histories? We still do not have a set of suitable textbooks in the different periods—a real need considering that almost every university now has undergraduate courses covering specific periods of music history. These manuals must be written by reputable specialists, the same scholars who are reluctant to drop their research long enough to write them. Moreover, in all fields but the Renaissance, research handbooks are needed. These should not be mere annotated bibliographies, but, like Reese's *Renaissance,* objective, studious historical works that interpret as well as inform, correlate as well as catalog, stimulate appreciation as well as dissect. Works in this category are fundamental to progress in the field and deserve the same support from foundations and universities that original research projects are granted.

More specifically related to the training of scholars are the two manuals of early notation: Willi Apel's *The Nota-*

tion of Polyphonic Music (1942) and Carl Parrish's *The Notation of Medieval Music* (1957). Apel's book, an outgrowth of his pioneering courses taught at Harvard from 1937 to 1941, begins with the later more standardized stages of Renaissance notation, and proceeds from these to the more difficult problems of medieval notation. Parrish begins with plainchant notation, and continues in chronological order to analyze the notation used in secular monophonic songs and polyphonic music up to the early fifteenth century, focusing his discussion always on particular manuscripts.

A book in a category by itself is Oliver Strunk's *Source Readings in Music History* (1950), which presents carefully selected literary documents as a background for the study of music history. Some of them are milestones in musical theory and aesthetics; others are guides to performance, critical pieces, prefaces, letters, excerpts from books and polemic pamphlets. They are presented in the original, when this is in English, in an early English translation if available, or otherwise in a modern English translation. Each item is painstakingly annotated and provided with an introductory and biographical note about its author. Comprised of more than 900 pages, Strunk's anthology is the most comprehensive in any language.

Also unique among American music books is Bukofzer's *Studies in Medieval and Renaissance Music* (1950), like Strunk's anthology a Norton publication. These scholarly essays on problems in the fourteenth and fifteenth centuries were intended, in the author's words, "not only as contributions to the ever growing research material of musicology, but also as object lessons of a point of method, namely that specialized topics can be fruitfully discussed only against the background of a broad perspective." It was precisely Bukofzer's own rich experience and knowledge that permitted him to reveal here the full significance of several

157

newly discovered sources, as well as of some already well
known, and to unravel one of the knottiest puzzles in early
Renaissance music, the origin of the *Caput* melody used in
masses by three leading composers—Dufay, Ockeghem, and
Obrecht. The essays together provided a method and stimulus for what has become a major preoccupation of scholars
everywhere, the identification and use of borrowed melodies,
particularly by composers in the Middle Ages and the Renaissance.

BIBLIOGRAPHIES

Besides period histories and handbooks, another logical
field for American scholars has been bibliography. This is
an area in which they have long continued to distinguish
themselves. Sonneck's bibliographies of American secular
music of the eighteenth century (1905; 2nd ed., 1945), his
catalogs of the Library of Congress opera librettos (1914)
and dramatic music (1908; 2nd ed., 1917) have been mentioned. Another early work is Albert A. Stanley's *Catalogue of
the Stearns Collection of Music Instruments* (1918), donated
to the University of Michigan by the drug manufacturer
Frederick Stearns. In addition to accurate descriptions and
measurements of the items, Stanley gave historical notes and
brief characterizations of the manners of performance, which
made his catalog practically a textbook in the study of primitive Eastern and Western musical instruments. The Crosby
Brown collection of instruments of the Metropolitan Museum
of Art also received printed catalogs between 1903 and 1907.

Several other important instrument collections have been
described in published catalogs. N. Bessaraboff made a monumental catalog of the Mason collection in the Boston Museum of Fine Arts (1941) and a luxurious catalog by the

158

owner describes the Belle Skinner collection (1933), mostly keyboard instruments, many of them now at Yale University. In another catalog Erich Lachmann describes his own collection of string instruments. The National Museum's collection, mainly anthropological in character, is described in Frances Densmore's handbook (1927).

Periodical indexing has top priority in the field of bibliography in almost any musicologist's requirements. Ernest C. Krohn, one of the most active musical bibliographers, in 1919 published in the *Musical Quarterly* a twenty-three page historical survey of musical bibliography, with particular emphasis on national resources. His most important work is an index of periodical literature in the history of music (1952) covering forty periodicals dated 1863 to 1951.

A short-lived periodical index of musicology and allied fields was sponsored by the ACLS and compiled by D. S. Daugherty, Leonard Ellinwood, and Richard S. Hill. It covered the years 1938 to 1940 before the project was abandoned because of wartime difficulties in obtaining foreign periodicals.

The most ambitious periodical indexing service in music was begun in 1949 by Florence Kretschmar for Information Service Inc. of Detroit, Michigan, under the title *The Music Index.* Each year more musicological periodicals in all languages were covered. One of its shortcomings, however, from the point of view of scholarly use, was that many scholarly articles on music appear in nonmusical periodicals, such as *Speculum, Journal of the History of Ideas,* in *Festschriften,* and the like. A German indexing service includes such publications but it is usually at least three years behind. Meanwhile the New York Public Library has had to continue its valuable periodical indexing on cards for its own readers. Recently a cooperating agreement was reached between *Music Index* and the New York Public Library, whereby the library would concentrate on technical and scholarly material, especially in foreign languages, while the Detroit staff would cover mainly English language and popular periodicals. The combined items would be united in *Music Index*. The recent introduction of an Acme Visible Records system in combination with International Business Machines equipment will permit faster and extended service by *Music Index*.

These advances still leave one large gap to be filled—the proper indexing of musical material in periodicals before 1949, only a small part of which has ever been covered. The present emphasis on speedy current indexing, because this is most pressing in the natural sciences, does not always work in favor of the musicologist, since for him an article published in 1900 may be as important as one published in 1962.

Professional musical organizations have been active in sponsoring current indexes of various kinds. The Music Library Association has since July 1934 published *Notes,* a quarterly of current bibliography, notes, and articles of interest particularly to music librarians. The expanding services this periodical has given to scholars owe a great deal to the initiative of its first editor, Richard S. Hill (1901-61). In each issue there are lists of new books about music in all languages as well as new musical scores and an index of reviews of recordings. Critics' ratings of records are summarized through an ingenious system of symbols. This index has been cumulated as of 1956 and issued in a single volume as *Record Ratings*. Another important scholarly contribution of *Notes* was the publication between 1945 and 1948 of Einstein's supplement to Emil Vogel's famous bibliography of printed Italian secular vocal music of the sixteenth and seventeenth centuries. A further service of the MLA was the sponsorship of a committee under Helen Joy Sleeper to prepare a guide to thematic catalogs of music, which was published in 1954.

The Music Teachers National Association and the AMS

cooperated in 1952 in bringing out the first list of doctoral dissertations in musicology. This has been supplemented periodically, and a second edition was compiled by Helen Hewitt in 1958, under joint sponsorship of the two groups. A third edition, also compiled by Miss Hewitt, was published by the AMS alone in 1961.

Numerous publications of the U.S. government provide invaluable assistance to scholars. Two Library of Congress publications, *Catalogue of Early Books on Music (Before 1800)* by Julia Gregory (1913), together with its *Supplement* of books acquired from 1913 to 1942, by Hazel Bartlett (1944), constitute the most reliable bibliography of printed writings about music within the period covered in existence, though of course it is incomplete, as any one library's collection must be. Gilbert Chase's *Guide to Latin American Music* (1945), a classified and geographical directory, is another publication of the national library. Since 1953 the Library of Congress has issued under the title *Music and Phono-records* semiannual and cumulative annual lists of music, musical scores, books on music, records, and tapes currently received by the library and cooperating institutions. A subject index, using the standard Library of Congress classifications, makes this list a handy annual subject guide to books and music, one that is finding in this expanding field a growing number of scholarly users. Another important government publication is the musical section of the *Catalog of Copyright Entries.* Since 1947 this catalog has been the most complete guide to published music available, for almost all music published in other countries is copyrighted in this country as well as the place of publication.

Music before 1800 is a vast area for indexing and classification. Some essential projects now being attacked by international and American organizations have figured prominently in these. The largest of these programs is the "International Inventory of Musical Sources," undertaken jointly by the International Musicological Society and the International Association of Music Libraries, with the support of UNESCO through the International Council for Philosophy and Humanistic Studies.

The foreword of the first volume of the "Inventory"—a chronological list of sixteenth and seventeenth century printed collections of music (1960)—describes the plan of the project.

> [The "Inventory" is] intended to provide a catalogue of all available bibliographical music works, writings about music and textbooks on music from all countries of the world, including monodic music, liturgical sources, song-books, treatises and methods, books and periodicals on music, from the earliest times to the year 1800. The sources should be indicated exactly as far as bibliography is concerned (manuscripts also described), and collections should be analysed. By "sources" will be understood written and printed indications . . . The location of all sources will be indicated by a system of sigla. The work as a whole will be divided into two series, one alphabetic and the other systematic.

The work of cataloging and compiling the numerous items owned by libraries in the United States is directed by a national committee formed by the American Musicological Society and the Music Library Association. It consisted at first of Manfred Bukofzer, Gustave Reese, and R. S. Hill; Lang replaced Bukofzer after his death. The music division of the Library of Congress, with Harold Spivacke and Hill at its center, served as a clearing house for information. Before Hill was stricken by a heart attack in 1960 he was working to establish an American office of the "Inventory," for which he had obtained financing from an American foundation. Such an office was recently established, with Nathan Broder in charge and Donald Mintz as full-time assistant.

162

While the alphabetical, chronological, and classified lists of printed sources can be compiled through the cooperation of trained music librarians, the best of whom in the United States have also had musicological training, the breakdown of collections and the description of manuscripts requires the participation of specialized musicologists. Americans figure prominently in this current work of the "Inventory." John Ward and Howard Brown have analyzed the contents of printed collections of instrumental music of the sixteenth century. Dragan Plamenac has contributed to the task of analyzing early polyphonic sources. Carol MacClintock and Joel Newman are contributing to the analysis of the contents of manuscript lute books. Miloš Velimirović and Kenneth Levy are doing similar work in the field of Byzantine chant, a job being coordinated by Oliver Strunk.

Eventually the period after 1800 will also need extensive bibliographical exploration. A significant work by an American scholar is Anna H. Heyer's guide to the contents of historical and monumental collections and collected works of individual composers published up to 1956.

Bibliographic aids of the kind described above are minimum needs for efficient scholarly work. In most humanistic fields such aids have long existed and are kept up-to-date on a continuing basis. More specific aids to research, such as thematic catalogs, catalogs of sacred text settings, secular settings, and so forth should receive a larger part of our attention than they have up to now if duplication of effort is to be avoided.

The compilation of thematic catalogs is particularly intense today in two fields: the chanson of the fifteenth and sixteenth centuries and the symphony of the eighteenth. The reason for this is that attribution problems are acute in these areas. When a single work is assigned to diverse composers in different sources, a thematic index permits these sources to be efficiently tracked down and the dependability of the attribution evaluated. Only through a thematic catalog can listings of a composer's works be purged of false attributions and filled out with works that might otherwise remain anonymous. The principle behind the thematic index involves the use of pitches or musical intervals in the way letters are used in an alphabetical system. Numbers or letters usually take the place of conventional notes. A rising melody that goes CDEF would precede one that goes CEFG, or otherwise indicated, $0 + 2 + 4 + 5$ precedes $0 + 4 + 5 + 7$. Rhythm is usually ignored for this purpose.

The eighteenth century symphony is fertile territory for this kind of indexing. Collections of symphonies can be found in almost every European library and in many American libraries. Many of the symphonies are anonymous, but some composers are identified, particularly in printed sources, if not always correctly. Only by a systematic search of all sources and libraries, and by the arrangement of the melodic incipits of the works in some systematic order, can the mass of material be put in any order. Jan LaRue began in 1954 to compile a thematic catalog of symphonies. He personally searched through eighty libraries, and utilized printed and manuscript catalogs, both modern and eighteenth century. He also was fortunate in being able to incorporate the material of several scholars including the noted American Haydn scholar, H. C. Robbins Landon. As of 1959 he had 7,000 entries for a "Union Thematic Catalogue of 18th Century Symphonies." More than 400 works with conflicting attributions emerged from this file. The degree to which a thematic index may upset past attributions is demonstrated by the case of one composer, Franz Xaver Pokorny (1729-94). Fifty-seven symphonies that can probably be assigned to him have been attributed to thirty-six different composers including

Abel, Gretry, Michael Haydn, Monn, Piccinni, and Sammartini.

Other catalogs of this kind are being prepared for chamber music and concertos from about 1740 to 1810, both to be supported by grants from the American Philosophical Society. Gwynn McPeek of Tulane University has been at work on a thematic concordance of sources of fifteenth century polyphonic songs. Not only does correct and efficient attribution and location of settings and tunes depend on the availability of such an index, but the very nature of chanson tunes will not be fully understood until this preliminary work is accomplished. Nanie Bridgman, a member of the staff of the music department of the Bibliothèque Nationale in Paris, has since 1949 been compiling a thematic catalog of fifteenth and sixteenth century polyphonic music. Periodically she has urged the cooperation of other scholars, but with little success. Some guard their own lists of concordances jealously; others prefer a different system. Libraries have also taken little interest, since it is a specialized problem. But through the index she has been able to identify for example Leonhard Kleber organ tablature under the title "Philephos aves" as being none other than the French song "Fille vous avez mal gardé" of Isaac, and to discover that Isaac's "Gaude virgo" is the same as his "Je ne puis vivre," and to note that Agricola's song "Ai je rien fait contre vous" became in an Italian manuscript "Ayuyenes set conver nous." Because of the absence of a central index, a large number of Renaissance scholars have had to compile for their own use or in preparation of master's and doctoral dissertations thematic indexes and concordances covering particular manuscripts. Except for a few published in periodicals like *Musica disciplina,* thematic lists are rarely published because of the difficulty of typesetting. Since those who possess them will not likely

165

part with them unless there is a coordinated program, specialists should be commissioned to do parts of a general indexing
project through grants and the publication of the results
guaranteed. The same kind of work needs to be done also in
the field of the medieval monophonic chant and song. Many
unsuspected relationships between secular and sacred music
will probably emerge from such thematic indexes.

DICTIONARIES

Musical lexicography has not been neglected in the United
States, but large-scale works like *Grove's Dictionary of Music
and Musicians, Die Musik in Geschichte und Gegenwart,* or
the current edition of *Riemanns Musiklexikon* have not yet
been attempted. A special committee of the ACLS in 1958
proposed a plan for the publication of a universal musical
encyclopedia. The view of the committee, under the chairman-
ship of Edward N. Waters, was that neither *Grove's* nor the
German encyclopedia do justice to American musical life
or to sociological, popular, and ethnic aspects of music. The
plan was given a lukewarm reception by the council of the
AMS in December 1958 and there were good reasons for
withholding wholehearted support. *Die Musik in Geschichte
und Gegenwart,* which has reached the letter *R* after thirteen
years of publication, is still engaging the efforts of many of
the world's specialists, the very same people who would have
to be invited to participate in a new enterprise. Many Americans are among the contributors. A recent volume (IX,
Mel-Onslow, 1961), for example, contains contributions by
seventeen Americans, covering, among others, several of the
most important topics in this alphabetical section: polyphonic notation up to 1600 (Luther Dittmer), Mendelssohn
(Eric Werner), Luis Milán (John Ward), Cristobal Morales

(Robert Stevenson), Mussorgsky (Alfred Swan), and Ockeghem (Dragan Plamenac). To begin another large-scale encyclopedia now would mean much unnecessary duplication and competition. Many of the goals of the committee would be fulfilled by the compilation of a truly scholarly encyclopedia of American musical history and contemporary life. This would give a very desirable impetus to research in our national artistic history, which has lagged behind the study of European music.

On a smaller scale, this country has produced two indispensable and authoritative dictionaries respected throughout the world. These are Nicolas Slonimsky's fifth edition of *Baker's Biographical Dictionary of Musicians* (1958) and Willi Apel's *Harvard Dictionary of Music* (1944). Slonimsky's dictionary is a completely rewritten version of the dictionary published in 1900 by Theodore Baker. Baker (1851-1934) was one of the first Americans to undergo musicological training in Germany, where he spent the years between 1874 and 1890 and received a doctorate at Leipzig. His thesis was a trail-blazing study of North American Indian music. Between 1892 and 1926 he was literary editor and translator for the G. Schirmer publishing house. Baker's dictionary included many American biographies not represented in other reference works, and this has continued to be a feature of *Baker's* through the editions of Alfred Remy (1919), Carl Engel (1940), and Slonimsky (1949 and 1958). Slonimsky's diligence in tracking down and double-checking facts, particularly birth and death dates, has made this book the English speaking scholar's best friend.

Apel's dictionary of terms, although now in need of revision, remains the most reliable such dictionary in any language. The lucid and systematic presentation of meanings, historical background, and bibliography has made it a book of first recourse for the musicology or music history student.

For the scholar it has been the most complete subject bibliography available for quick reference, and for the teacher a perpetual refresher course in musical history. A popular and revised abridged version of the dictionary was recently published by Apel in collaboration with Ralph Daniel.

MONOGRAPHS

Much more useful to the scholar than general histories or one-volume dictionaries are histories and studies of narrower scope. The shelf of basic studies written by Americans is lengthening every year.

The survey of music written for a particular medium or within a genre of composition offers the scholar an exceptional opportunity to combine stylistic criticism with systematic description and analysis of sources. Not only is such a book a happy project for the author but is usually pleasant to read. Early in this century a series of fourteen such books was published in Leipzig under the general editorship of Hermann Kretzschmar (1905-22) and called "Small Handbooks of Music History According to Categories." The histories of the concerto, motet, oratorio, German Lied, cantata, and overture included in this series have still not been superseded, although most of them are quite obsolete. Why, one might ask, have not Americans, who could write these books without extended research trips, hastened to fill up such a shelf? The reasons will be obvious if we consider four such studies published in this country. Alfred Einstein's monumental *The Italian Madrigal* (3 vols., 1949) would be a difficult model to live up to in any case, but it illustrates the problems involved in writing a history of a type of musical composition. Einstein spent about forty years gathering material for this work in musical libraries throughout the world.

Meanwhile, to be sure, he was busy with many other projects. Almost all the music on which he based his conclusions had to be transcribed from the original sources. Without this preliminary work, he could not have spoken with authority about the music. But there were many other unknown areas into which his personal investigations had to extend—the social setting of Italian secular music, the taste of the time, the life at the princely courts, the relations of musicians to each other and to their patrons. This was a lifetime task or one for a team of scholars. Today the time would be much riper for a book like Einstein's, since many smaller studies have laid the foundation. On the other hand few would have been written had not his book come first.

A similar situation was faced by William S. Newman, who many years ago embarked on a survey of the "sonata idea." Having finished in 1939 a Ph.D. dissertation at Western Reserve University on "The Present Trend of the Sonata Idea," Newman decided to extend his investigation into the earlier history of his topic. He saw that he would have to find out what sort of sonata concept existed in the eighteenth century, where the origin of the sonata-allegro form is usually placed. When he saw that the word was much older than the formal concept he decided on a nonevolutionary approach to analysis of early sonatas. Another problem was that only a few of the composers responsible for the development of the keyboard or violin sonata were at all known and represented in modern printed collections. As with Einstein, transcription was to occupy many of the twenty years that preceded publication of *The Sonata in the Baroque Era* (1959), the first volume of a projected series. Much of the space the author would probably have liked to spend on stylistic and formal analysis and the tracing of influences and changing forms had to go into bibliographical description of collections of printed and manuscript music never before mentioned, classified, or put in any chronological order. Many of the composers, totally unknown, had to be located in time and place. Here again was a study for which the way was not adequately prepared by many smaller contributions.

Opera, on the other hand, is a field in which a mass of particularized studies is not lacking, as may be seen by inspecting the bibliography given by Donald Grout at the end of his *A Short History of Opera* (2 vols., 1947). Still his was the first systematic survey of the field since Hermann Kretzschmar's *Geschichte der Oper* (1919). Because little can be learned by reading about opera, the author could not profit much by others' descriptions. He had to bring the silent scores to life in his own mind if his descriptions were to evoke any conception of them in the reader. The most important scores were in the United States, but many were not, and only by limiting his scope was Grout able to get his "short" survey completed in a reasonable number of years. Had he wished to write a definitive history of seventeenth century opera instead, a lifetime would not have sufficed, for few of the operas have been studied and fewer still have been transcribed or printed. Now doing pioneering work in this almost virgin territory are several American scholars, among them Nino Pirrotta and Stuart Reiner.

Abundant also was the legacy inherited by Willi Apel when he began work on *Gregorian Chant* (1958) around 1954. Unlike Einstein, Newman, and Grout, who cultivated their familiar gardens, Apel trespassed on a field already well-plowed by others. Because plainchant is an area honeycombed by conflicting theories, to start out with a fresh, unbiased curiosity was an advantage for an author who aimed to set before the reader, as Apel stated was his purpose, the "'unleavened bread of sincerity and truth,' cleansed from, or at least clearly separated from, the 'sour dough' of conjecture and imagination." The great virtue of Apel's book is that it invited the nonspecialist to wander in what is otherwise forbidding if not forbidden territory. It is written from the point of view of musicology rather than liturgical history or church practice, as is often the case with chant, though it becomes involved with both when necessary. It demonstrates, moreover, that more may be accomplished by clear and organized exposition than by the obscure and pedantic over-classification that has plagued studies of medieval music in the past.

Of the four books briefly described here, only two are products of American-trained scholars. The older generation of Europeans ventured more easily than young Americans into large projects, although many of the latter possess the qualifications for writing histories of this kind. Some begin, it is true, only to become bogged down in narrower investigations where they find the ground not sufficiently prepared. This is certainly the principal reason for the dearth of such books in America, but it is not a valid excuse in many areas. Several factors seem to be inhibiting American scholars. A fear persists that it is difficult to find publishers for manuscripts of this kind It is true that none of the four described was issued by a commercial publisher but by the university presses of Princeton, North Carolina, Columbia, and Indiana and it is also true that three of them were supported through foundation subsidies for publication in addition to research grants. Nevertheless, the fact that they found their way should be proof that others will do likewise and that the author who knows he can write a strong manuscript may proceed with confidence.

Another deterrent seems to be operating. A university teacher constantly needs publications to bolster his candidacy for promotion, tenure, or a better job. A few articles a year possess greater leverage than several unpublished chapters. Such articles, though often hopefully written with a book in mind, rarely can function later as chapters. It would be wrong to charge security seeking and lack of courage against bright men who spend four years earning doctorates only to accept clerks' salaries, however, too many who begin adventurously when installed on a campus seem either to avoid tasks that do not bear early fruits or to allow their academic duties to overwhelm them. Then, there is the reluctance, possibly instilled during graduate study, of attacking projects in which every fact and source cannot be controlled. With this goes the horror of making small blunders that reviewers will pounce upon, a justifiable feeling, when one considers how often the reviewer of a musicological publication descends to compiling a catalog of errors instead of coming to terms with its principal contributions. Yet everyone knows that books without occasional misinterpretations, conclusions that further research will reverse, or lapses from recognizing the latest findings, do not exist.

The output of monographs in musicology, the staples of scholarly publication, has been meager in this country. At best we see printed only about one volume to every four in Germany. No one would like to see quantity replace quality, but whoever has read theses in musicology submitted to American universities knows that a great deal of worthwhile, useful, and often essential material remains buried in university archives and microfilm files. A way must be found to produce many more short books at prices within the reach of budgetbound American scholars and of financially limited foreign purchasers.

An excellent example of the kind of book that should be encountered often is J. Murray Barbour's *Tuning and Temperament: A Historical Survey*. Although highly technical and full of difficult composition, the Michigan State College Press was able to produce it in 1951 in a lithographic edition priced at $5 00. It reached a second edition within two years. By considerably revising and reorganizing his 350-page Cornell dissertation of 1932, Barbour compressed it into 200 printed pages, yet retained all the essential discussion and tables. The same year the Michigan State Press published another dissertation by a faculty member, a study of the sixteenth century composer Jacobus Vaet, Milton Steinhardt's New York University thesis of 1950.

An ideal solution would be for each university to publish its own series, even if only paperbound, of selected dissertations and studies. An early example was set by the Yale University Press. At the instigation of Leo Schrade, it inaugurated in 1947 a series of publications by young musical historians. So far two outstanding dissertations have been published. The first was Beekman C. Cannon's thesis of 1939, *Johann Mattheson: Spectator in Music* (1947). In addition to a valuable 141-page essay on Mattheson's life and work and its setting in Hamburg, there is a 70-page descriptive bibliography of the works of Mattheson, all based principally on material that has since been lost in the destruction of the Hamburg archives. The same combination of concise exposition and source-material characterizes the second volume of the series, William Waite's *The Rhythm of Twelfth Century Polyphony* (1954). The dissertation of 1951 was reduced by publishing only one-third of the transcriptions, which nevertheless occupy 254 pages and present a unified whole, the *Magnus liber organi* by Leonin.

Monograph series in music are also sponsored by the University of California and Columbia University, neither of which exists primarily for the sake of printing doctoral dissertations. "The University of California Publications in Music," a paperback series, includes five volumes, of which two are based on doctoral dissertations: Volume 3 (1948), Robert U. Nelson's Harvard dissertation of 1944 on the history of the variation, and Volume 5 (1954), W. Thomas

Marrocco's *The Music of Jacopo da Bologna,* an introduction to an edition of the extant music of this fourteenth century composer (UCLA dissertation of 1952). The series also contains Walter H. Rubsamen's *Literary Sources of Secular Music in Italy (ca. 1500)* (1943) as Volume 1, and Manfred Bukofzer's *'Sumer is icumen in' a Revision* (1944) as Volume 2, Number 2. "The Columbia University Studies in Musicology," begun in 1935, has run to seven volumes. It includes *John Milton the Elder and his Music* by the literary scholar Ernest Brennecke (II, 1938); W. S. Pratt's edition and study of the French Psalter of 1562 (III, 1939); William Treat Upton's portrait of Anthony Philip Heinrich, the Bohemian-born composer and violinist who was a prominent figure in mid-nineteenth century American music (IV, 1939); a book on Boston's musical life between 1795 and 1830 by Harold Earle Johnson (V, 1943); Edward Lowinsky's provocative exposition of his theory of the secret chromatic art in the Netherlands motet (VI, 1946), and *Serbo-Croatian Folk Songs* (VII, 1951), a collection edited by Béla Bartók and Albert B. Lord.

During the period Columbia University required publication of dissertations, a number of worthwhile volumes appeared, mostly under Crown imprint. Robert M. Myers on Handel's *Messiah* (1948); Ruth H. Rowen on early chamber music (1949); William L. Crosten on French grand opera (1948); Dika Newlin's *Bruckner, Mahler, Schonberg* (1947), and Alfred R. Oliver's *The Encyclopedists as Critics of Music* (1947).

Because series of this kind are the exception or too exclusive, most dissertations that have been published were done so under auspices other than the degree-granting university. Those of Barbour, Steinhardt, and Nelson have been cited. Louise Cuyler's Rochester dissertation of 1948 saw publication as "University of Michigan Publications, Fine Arts," Volume II, in 1950. It contains Book III of Heinrich Isaac's setting of the propers of the mass in his *Choralis Constantinus* (1555). This completes the cycle begun in the *Denkmaler der Tonkunst in Oesterreich* (1898, 1909). Nan Cooke Carpenter's Yale dissertation of 1948 was published very much abridged and revised, though not really brought up-to-date, ten years later as *Music in the Medieval and Renaissance Universities* by the Oklahoma Press. Helen M. Hewitt's Radcliffe dissertation of 1938, an extensive commentary upon and a transcription of the earliest printed collection of partmusic, the *Odhecaton* (1501), was published by the Mediaeval Academy of America (1942; 2nd ed, 1946). This academy also issued in 1939 Leonard W. Ellinwood's Rochester dissertation of 1936, the collected works of the fourteenth century composer Francesco Landini, with a commentary.

A number of dissertations by Americans have been published abroad, including, of course, those submitted to foreign universities. The most distinguished item on this list is Otto Kinkeldey's revealing study of keyboard music in the sixteenth century. Based almost entirely on material neglected up to that time, it was submitted to the University of Berlin in 1909 and published a year later in Leipzig. A recent example is Robert Tusler's Utrecht dissertation (1958) on the organ music of Jan Pieterszoon Sweelinck, the first volume of a new series of Utrecht studies in musicology. A part of Luther Dittmer's Basel dissertation is available in the American Institute of Musicology's series "Studies and Documents" under the title *The Worcester Fragments*. Barry S. Brook's *La Symphonie française dans la seconde moitié du XVIIIᵉ siecle,* whose publication was sponsored by the French Centre Nationale de la Recherche Scientifique, is mainly the fruit of his doctoral work at the University of Paris. The second of its three volumes contains a thematic index of more than 1,200 symphonies and symphonies concertantes by 130 French composers.

The AMS recently inaugurated a plan for sponsoring the publication of outstanding dissertations. The three chosen so far in the probable order of publication are: Joseph Kerman's Princeton thesis *The Elizabethan Madrigal: A Comparative Study* (1950), which is already in print; Putnam Aldrich's *A Study in Musical Ornamentation*, derived from his Harvard dissertation of 1942; and John Ward's *The Vihuela de Mano and Its Music* (New York University, 1953).

Although this is a selected list, it is nearly complete. Out of about 550 completed dissertations, the number of those published aside from microfilm and microcard is small. Of course, many of these not published have been represented in print by articles or editions of music.

Aside from dissertations, published scholarly monographs in the United States are almost nonexistent. Scholars who cannot publish their theses are usually too discouraged to attempt another book of the same kind, while those who have succeeded know too well the difficulties involved. Consequently to see what American musicologists are doing today, one must examine the scholarly periodicals, a discussion of which follows in a later section.

BIOGRAPHIES

The field of biographical and critical studies of individual composers presents a much different picture. The musical public will buy books on composers whose names are familiar, even if the book is relatively technical, so publishers will risk producing them, and the public library sale will usually allow them to break even, no matter how bad the book may be from a musicological standpoint. America has produced a large quantity of books in this category. Even if we include only those of positive scholarly value, they are too numerous to list. The total contribution to scholarship in this area has been a substantial one, when one considers that Americans are responsible for definitive biographies, source-books, or critical studies of the following composers: Bach, Bartók, Beethoven, Berg, Berlioz, Bizet, Haydn, Monteverdi, Mozart, Mussorgsky, Purcell, Domenico Scarlatti, Scriabin, Sibelius. To these should be added a host of American composers like Barber, Copland, Mason, Ives, and lesser-known figures from Bermudo to Ugolino of Orvieto. Three outstanding contributions should be singled out: Kirkpatrick's *Domenico Scarlatti,* Jacques Barzun's *Berlioz,* and Karl Geiringer's *The Bach Family*

Still, the field of biography is an underdeveloped one in America. The lives of most of the composers of the eighteenth and nineteenth century could bear rewriting in English, particularly if justice were done to their musical output and its historical significance. Commercial publishers could take the initiative in this field by commissioning young musicologists to write new, evaluative biographies. Publication of such studies, rather than translation of existing biographies, would not only be a probably successful commercial venture but would also be a service to scholarship.

CRITICAL TEXTS

At the present stage in the development of musicology, the most urgent task remains to make available through modern editions the vast quantity of music and primary literary sources of the period before 1800 that still exist only in manuscript and early printed editions. Some scholars have gone so far as to say that other musicological activity concerning this period has little meaning until this primary task is finished. However, periodic evaluation of material already known, even if it cannot be definitive, lays the foundation for further work by cultivating a sense of what is important and developing essential criteria for authenticating sources, deciding on methods of transcription, and editing. Nevertheless it is agreed that the editing and collating of manuscripts and rare editions have top priority, since decay, dispersion, and destruction work on the side of delay.

The desirable forms through which the several types of documents available to musicologists may be preserved and transmitted deserve consideration. The most important documents are those which contain musical compositions or fragments of them; these are found in autograph versions, contemporary copies, other copies, and printed editions more or less contemporary with the composer. Next in importance are treatises, including, as well as speculative works, all technical instructional writings relating to composition and performance. Then come letters of composers, musicians, or others that furnish descriptions of musical performances or organizations or that discuss music and musicians in some substantial way. Contemporary critical, aesthetic, and biographical writings and archival records are other documents that musicologists want to make accessible.

Whether the presentation of the document is to be a facsimile, a critical edition of the text, a transcription for performance, or a translation, the first step is to locate all manuscript copies or early editions of the text. With autograph letters and archival documents, the material is ready for transcription as soon as its authenticity is established. The job of locating all extant copies of most documents is a complicated process in itself and only international inventories of rare materials will ever make this much simpler. Such inventories of printed material are in sight, but really complete inventories of manuscripts are far in the future, because local cataloging of manuscripts and their contents is as yet inadequate. Meanwhile the musicologist usually starts with Robert Eitner's famous *Biographisch-bibliographisches Quellenlexikon* published between 1900 and 1904, and otherwise depends on the specialized literature, encyclopedia articles, and printed library catalogs to supplement and correct the information Eitner gives. If the document the scholar is interested in is an opera of Cavalli, for example, he has a good chance of locating all but unknown or anonymous copies this way. If his text is a motet by Alexander Agricola (1446-1506), he has an aid in another work of Eitner's, the *Bibliographie der Musik-Sammelwerke des XVI. und XVII. Jahrhunderts.* This was published in 1877, before many sources became known. Moreover it provides no guide to manuscripts. For these the scholar depends on his direct knowledge of them and of the widely scattered literature about manuscripts. Copies of a motet wrongly attributed or anonymous have only a slight chance of being identified without thematic indexes.

The situation facing the editor of a treatise is not much more favorable. Since catalogs usually record verbal incipits, such an editor has this resource not available to the musical editor. But aside from handwritten catalogs which can be consulted only in the libraries to which they apply, few published inventories of manuscripts are complete enough to be dependable. For example, when Albert Seay made his edition of the *Declaratio musicae disciplinae* of the fifteenth century writer Ugolino of Orvieto as part of his Ph D. dissertation at Yale (1954), he did so on the basis of five manuscripts, and a sixth he rejected as corrupt. Two of these are listed in printed catalogs, those of the British Museum and of the Bodleian Library of Oxford. The others have been known only through the specialized literature on early theory and on Ugolino himself. However, when Seay had the opportunity through a Fulbright grant to tour libraries in Italy, he found four additional manuscripts as well as much interesting biographical material. One of the manuscripts, at the Vatican, was only the third complete one known. Being fortunately of a different tradition from the first two, it provided a check against the others when Seay came to prepare the published edition of his treatise (American Institute of Musicology, 1959-60).

Once lists of all known manuscripts and printed editions of a work have been compiled and microfilms or photostats have been gathered, the work of sorting out the authentic and usable sources begins. The age and provenance of each source must be ascertained, the hand or printer identified. Handy as films are, they may turn out to be inadequate during this critical stage. The determination of dates, owners and history, and the proper order of items often depends upon watermarks, bindings, and the precise way gatherings are arranged and sewn together. Once the manuscripts have been analyzed, a family tree or stemma of traditions is derived. Finally the editor decides upon his principal source or sources and on those that are to be referred to in the *Revisionsbericht*—the revisions-report—or footnotes, as the case may be Usually the editor will have produced a transcription from a single source early in his work with a given text. Often, after better acquaintance with all the sources, this may turn out to be less reliable than another. It is then usually less toil to begin again than to modify the first text. It should be obvious from this description of how a musicologist proceeds that he operates in the same manner as a philologist producing a critical text of a classical work of prose or poetry.

An example of the difficulties encountered in collating musical texts is offered by the work of Arthur Mendel on his forthcoming edition of the full score of the *St. John Passion* for the *New Bach Edition* being published in Germany. He has himself described the state of the manuscripts of the *Passion:*

> It survives in a score partly autograph and partly in a copyist's hand, on three different types of paper; and in three sets of parts: one complete set all on the same paper, one set of duplicates of some parts on a different kind of paper, and a third set of triplicates of some parts on a still different kind of paper. [*MQ,* 1960.]

Mendel recently put his seminar at Princeton to work sorting out the approximately five hundred pages of parts. Twenty-one different handwritings were discovered. These results were compared with those of teams of investigators in Gottingen and Tubingen, who had classified the handwritings in all Bach manuscripts. Some modifications in the seminar's conclusions resulted. The Princeton group also went to work on the problem of relating the parts to particular known performances and of determining the earliest version. The seminar spent most of a year on these questions. After further consultation with the leader of the team in Gottingen, Alfred Durr, it became evident that the parts that seemed at first quite reasonably to be duplicates were really the earliest known set.

This kind of teamwork is rare in musicological efforts, not only because musical scholars shun cooperation, but because in most areas there are no organizations like the Johann-Sebastian-Bach Institut of Gottingen or the Bach-Archiv of Leipzig. A man will publish his conclusions about the dating of a manuscript and only years later will someone challenge them; then, after another delay the first or a third will offer still another opinion. The prolonged controversy over the dating of the famous "Sumer is icumen in," involving scholars on both sides of the ocean, is an example of the usual process.

Once the editor of a musical work has dated and established connections between his sources, and has arrived at a basic transcription, a host of new problems faces him. A number of these are peculiar to musical editing. The editor of a classical Latin literary text will often decide to use modern punctuation and spelling, because he may be aiming at other readers besides scholars. But in any case the edition is for reading. With music, the edition may be only for reading —that is, silent study—or it may be suitable for performance as well. Any edition, of course, can be used for performance, but certain techniques of presentation facilitate it. The current controversies on editing medieval, Renaissance, and baroque music center on the problem of making a compromise between historical accuracy and modern methods of notation.

Not long ago it was the practice to use as many as five clefs when scoring a five-part sixteenth century composition, because the original parts were written in this way. The original note-values were also preserved, even though they suggested a very slow tempo when the composer really intended a moderately fast one. Now the trend is toward making a score of an older work look as much as possible like a contemporary one, without misrepresenting the original notation. Those familiar with the appearance of music published since the nineteenth century are accustomed to seeing pitch, tempo, meter, rhythm, accentuation, dynamic force and gradations, phrasing, instrumentation, and other details explicitly indicated by the composer. Some early notations give only pitch, as in plainchant or the earliest organum; others give pitch and suggest the meter. In the thirteenth century the relative time-value of the notes became definitive, but the tempo was not precisely indicated. Still later, in the fifteenth century, ratios were given to show changes of tempo and meter, but no basic rate of pulsation was defined. Bar lines were generally absent in music written only in parts before about 1600, and often afterward; indications of instrumentation and "expression" were also rare at this time. Consequently, the musical editor who aims his publication at performers as well as scholars must reconstruct the probable performance and, at the same time, allow the scholar and the scholarly performer to see the original state through the reconstruction. To give expression marks, tempo indications, phrasing, and instrumentation, when the composer has not indicated them, is now considered poor editorial practice and remarks about these points are often relegated to a foreword. Present day editions of older music have thus achieved a "modern," yet clean appearance.

American musicologists have been very active transcribers and editors of old music. The proportion of their work that has seen print is relatively small, however, and the proportion of it printed in this country is even smaller. This is not to be blamed on lack of initiative on the part of scholars. If printing costs for books are high, those for music are altogether beyond the range of scholarly enterprises. American commercial music publishers have participated only negligibly in the printing of critical editions, even of well-known music. University presses are not equipped to publish music. This leaves the field to college and university music departments and *ad hoc* organizations that sponsor limited projects.

Some accomplishments should be credited to our commercial publishers nevertheless. A few examples must suffice. In 1958 G. Schirmer brought out the critical text of sixty sonatas by Domenico Scarlatti edited by Ralph Kirkpatrick, complete with preface, several pages of facsimiles, and revisions-report. It is a model edition that could be the beginning

183

of a new Scarlatti collected works. Theodore Presser in 1956 published a new edition of Mozart's sonatas and fantasias for the piano prepared from autographs and earliest printed sources by Nathan Broder. This is accompanied by a valuable preface that contains notes on ornamentation, several portraits, and a facsimile. It constitutes the only definitive edition of these piano works. Both of these editions have been greeted enthusiastically by musicologists in reviews and, to judge by the number of copies seen in circulation among performers, have probably been best sellers. Other notable achievements are the many sacred masterpieces owed to the Concordia firm of St. Louis and the Antonio Soler piano works being published by Mills Music Corporation.

The practice of issuing reprints became a flourishing activity during World War II and immediately afterward. The Kalmus Company lithographed a large number of so-called *Urtext* (original text) editions when these became unavailable during the war, but this operation stopped when the original publishers revived in postwar West Germany and set up their own agencies in New York. The Edwards Company of Ann Arbor, Michigan, made a distinctive contribution in reprinting standard series—e.g., the complete works of Bach and some of the complete Mozart—that were out of print and greatly needed by expanding university and college libraries. New complete editions are now being issued abroad, however, and the continuation of these projects has become unprofitable as well as unnecessary.

Because of the absence of initiative on the part of American commercial publishers, scholarly editions have been mainly a field for nonprofit organizations. Several important college and university series have been sustained with only a minimum of subsidy, thanks to inexpensive reproduction and binding methods. Three series of editions should be mentioned in particular: the *Smith College Music Archives,* the

Wellesley Edition, and the Yale Collegium Musicum series.

The oldest and longest series, founded at Smith College by Ross Lee Finney, has issued fourteen volumes to date. It includes modern editions of Andrea Antico's collection of part songs published first in 1517 (IV, Einstein, 1941); the chansons of Arcadelt (V, Everett B. Helm, 1942); the madrigals of de Rore for three and four voices (VI, Gertrude P. Smith, 1945); Galilei's *Contrapunti* (VIII, Louise Rood, 1947); a dramatic ballet by Francesca Caccini (VII, Doris Silbert, 1945); chamber music for strings by Geminiani (I, Finney, 1935), Boccherini (III, Marion DeRonde, 1937), Tartini (IX, Gilbert Ross, 1947), and Tommaso Antonio Vitali (XII, Silbert, Smith, and Rood, 1954); vocal works by Steffani (XI, Smith, 1951), Quagliati (XIII, Vernon Gotwals and Philip Keppler, 1957), and Fux (II, Smith, 1936); and Symphony No. 87 by Haydn (X, Einstein, 1949). Several of these editions were prepared with the help of transcriptions made by Alfred Einstein and left by him to Smith College.

The *Wellesley Edition,* which began under the direction of Jan LaRue, has published so far two musicological editions: *Fancies and Ayres* by John Jenkins (I, Helen Joy Sleeper, 1950) and *The Dublin Virginal Manuscript* (III, John Ward, 1954). In the Yale Collegium Musicum series, begun by Leo Schrade and now under the general editorship of Miloš Velimirović, there have been three volumes, containing Alessandro Scarlatti's *St. John Passion* (I, Edwin Hanley, 1955), thirty chansons for three and four voices from collections published in the sixteenth century by Attaingnant (II, Albert Seay, 1960), and a *Te Deum* by Michael Haydn (III, Reinhard G. Pauly, 1961).

University presses, scholarly associations, and private organizations have been responsible for the largest share of critical musical texts and other documentary material published in this country. One of the earliest university presses to venture into this field was that of the University of Pennsylvania, which issued Jean Beck's editions of medieval songbooks of the troubadours and trouvères—the first volume in 1927 and the second in 1938. Both were aided by donations from Mary Louise Curtis Bok, and the second by the ACLS. The Harvard University Press has contributed the now famous anthology of historical music in two volumes by Archibald Davison and Willi Apel (1946-50) and an anthology of works of the Bach family edited by Karl Geiringer (1955). Louise Cuyler's transcriptions of works by Heinrich Isaac, the *Choralis Constantinus* Book III (1950) and five polyphonic masses (1956), were both published with the help of the Rackham School of Graduate Studies by the University of Michigan Press. The Oxford Press recently issued a reconstruction by Noah Greenberg of *The Play of Daniel* based on a transcription by Rev. Rembert Weakland (1959). One of the most precious Bach manuscripts in the United States, the *Clavier-Buchlein vor Wilhelm Friedemann Bach,* acquired by Yale in 1932, was issued by the university's press in a facsimile in 1959, edited and introduced by Ralph Kirkpatrick.

The New York Public Library has contributed significantly with publications of some of its rare items. Particularly noteworthy are *Music of the Moravians* (1938-39), in twelve volumes edited by Hans David, and the recent edition and reconstruction by Sydney Beck of Morley's *The First Book of Consort Lessons* (1959).

The Mediaeval Academy of America, which has been a loyal supporter of musicology through its *Speculum,* has published several volumes pertaining to the fourteenth century: the complete works of Landini (1939), edited by Ellinwood, which was subsidized by the Carnegie Corporation, ACLS, and the Eastman School; a collection of fourteenth century French secular music (1950), edited by Willi Apel, and a group of fourteenth century cacce (1942), edited by Marrocco.

The American Musicological Society has been less active in this field than might be expected, considering the need for leadership, organization, and backing. It has published two volumes of a projected complete edition of the works of Johannes Ockeghem edited by Dragan Plamenac. In cooperation with the Royal Musical Association of Great Britain, a volume containing all the extant music of John Dunstable, edited by Manfred Bukofzer, was issued in 1953. No further plans have otherwise been made for continued participation in the music publishing field.

Among the private organizations in the United States devoted to publications of musical source material, the youngest and most energetic is the Institute of Medieval Music, founded by Luther Dittmer in Brooklyn, New York. Since it began publication in 1957, this institute has issued seven volumes of facsimiles, all but one edited by Dittmer. It has also published translations of two medieval theorists, the collected works of Faugues edited by George Schuetze, and three studies dealing with medieval music. The manuscripts published in facsimile are among the most important in the study of early polyphony, and their availability at moderate cost is of inestimable value for researchers and students working in this area. The output of the institute unfortunately is marred by some of the weaknesses of one-man enterprises, but it is a bold and promising undertaking.

Another organization, called Alpeg Editions, recently made its debut with a distinguished edition by Albert Fuller of Gaspard Le Roux's *Pieces for Harpsichord,* accompanied by an extensive discussion of seventeenth century French keyboard music. Alpeg Editions has announced several other volumes of unavailable baroque music.

The most important outlet for American editors of medieval and Renaissance music and literary sources on music has been the American Institute of Musicology. It began in 1944 as the Institute of Renaissance and Baroque Music, with headquarters at Cambridge, Massachusetts, an American advisory board, and Armen Carapetyan as director. Carapetyan, a musicologist, received the Ph.D. from Harvard in 1945, where his thesis was "The *Musica Nova* of Adriano Willaert." In 1946 the institute founded a periodical, *Journal of Renaissance and Baroque Music,* of which Carapetyan and Leo Schrade were joint editors. In 1947 the organization's name was changed to American Institute of Musicology in Rome, the journal became *Musica disciplina,* with Carapetyan as sole editor, and a European advisory board was asked to serve beside the American board. Summer sessions were held in Rome and Florence in 1947 and 1948 that offered advanced courses in history of music by both European and American professors. In 1949 the institute dropped Rome from its name, though not from its address, and reorganized without advisory boards as a private organization, supported partly by anonymous patrons and by subscribers.

The immediate postwar political, financial, legal, and intellectual conditions, which bred obstacles, scarcities, delays, disagreements, and poor communication, must be blamed in large measure for the failure of the institute to continue as an American-sponsored international center for scholarly exchange. There is great need today for such an organization, which, besides publishing editions, could sponsor seminars in Europe, where now so many graduate students, thanks to Fulbright grants, do their most fruitful research—despite the remoteness of academic advisors and often of adequate musicological libraries and film archives. Italy would still be a desirable location, and Bologna, with its rich store of primary sources, an ideal place for a complementary collection of films and secondary sources. A precedent for such a center exists in the American Academy in Rome, with its excellent library of art history and classics. Now that the conditions for international exchanges are favorable, every effort should be made to revive the concept the organizers of the American Institute had in mind.

Meanwhile the American Institute of Musicology, since it began publishing editions of music with its first volumes of the works of Dufay in 1947, has compiled the most impressive list of publications of any organization devoted to musicological sources active today. The institute has published three volumes of the works of Dufay (about half his complete works), six of Willaert (also about half), ten of Clemens non Papa (a little over half), a volume of Antoine Brumel, four of Nicolas Gombert, two of Franchino Gaffurio, three of Giovanni Gabrieli, and four of Loyset Compere. Other volumes have been devoted to the music of Jacobus Barbireau, Johannes Regis, Cipriano de Rore, Robert Carver, Robert Fayrfax, Johannes Tinctoris, Walter Frye, Alexander Agricola, Johannes Ghiselin, and Giaches Wert. Among the miscellaneous volumes are two of the music of fourteenth century Italy, two of the early fifteenth century, and one of the Cypriot-French repertory. These constitute parts of twenty-four separate series of "opera omnia." The editors are highly qualified specialists; the printing, paper, and well-designed format are of high quality.

Native American scholars and those who have settled here are prominent among the editors: Nino Pirrotta, who is editing fourteenth century Italian music; Gilbert Reaney, editing early fifteenth century music; Richard H. Hoppin, the Cypriot-French repertory; Edwin B. Warren, doing the works of Fayrfax, Sylvia Kenney, the works of Walter Frye;

Albert Seay, transcriptions of Pierre Attaingnant; Edward Lerner, the works of Agricola; Carol MacClintock, the works of Giaches Wert. Others are at work on volumes not yet published: Henry W. Kaufmann is preparing the works of Nicola Vicentino, and Alexander Main those of Costanzo Festa. A new multi-volume series just announced, *Corpus of Early Keyboard Music,* is to be under the general editorship of Willi Apel.

Besides the editions of early music, Carapetyan's institute has sponsored two other series of documents: the "Corpus scriptorum de musica," containing critical texts so far of seven important medieval and Renaissance treatises, and a series of "Studies and Documents," containing miscellaneous documents and translations.

The majority of editors involved in the series published by Carapetyan remains European. This is consistent with his avowed and justifiable policy of employing the best qualified personnel, regardless of nationality or politics. It is significant, however, that Americans, particularly of the younger generation, have been in the majority among the editors of series begun in the last few years.

Increased American participation has been evident in several other international enterprises. The *New Bach Edition* has among its American participants, besides Arthur Mendel, two of his Princeton collaborators, Leo Treitler, responsible for Cantata 187, and Robert Freeman, for Cantata 176.

A recent attempt to realize an edition of the collected works of Joseph Haydn was an American enterprise. The most unfortunate of the great composers from this point of view, Haydn has not yet been honored by a complete critical edition of his works. One begun in 1907 by Breitkopf and Hartel reached only eleven volumes by 1933, when publication ceased. After the war a Haydn Society was formed in Boston, with a branch in Vienna and publishers in Leipzig and Wiesbaden. Its founder and secretary-general was H. C. Robbins Landon, a native of Boston, educated at Swarthmore College and at Boston University, where he studied musicology with Karl Geiringer. In 1950 the society began to publish Haydn's symphonies, continuing where the older series had left off, with Symphonies No. 50 to No. 57. These were followed by 82 to 87 and 88 to 92, all edited by Landon. A thematic catalog of the symphonies, compiled by him and Larsen, was issued with the first volume. A monumental critical and bibliographic study of the symphonies was published by Landon in 1955, complementing the edition. Before failing financially, the Haydn Society published also a volume of masses and a large number of historical recordings of excellent quality. A new Haydn edition is now being published by the Joseph-Haydn-Institut founded in Cologne in 1955 under the direction of Jens Peter Larsen. Among the collaborators are Landon and Geiringer. One of the volumes in Landon's charge is an edition of the opera *Das abgebrannte Haus,* also known as *Die Feuerbrunst,* the only known manuscript of which is owned by Yale University, having been acquired by Eva J. O'Meara, music librarian there in 1935, and only recently authenticated by Landon.

The new edition of the works of Gesualdo, now being published in Kassel, is partly edited by a young American, Glenn Watkins, who is responsible for the sacred music.

Aside from the collected works of individual composers, other so-called monumental editions of music have enlisted the help of Americans. More than half the volume *Anthologie de la chanson parisienne au seizième siècle,* published by Louise Dyer in Paris, comprises editions by Kenneth Levy and Isabelle Cazeaux. The same publisher's series, *Poly-*

phonic Music of the Fourteenth Century, begun in 1956, contains four volumes prepared by Leo Schrade, who until recently was in the United States. The series *Treize livres de motets parus chez Pierre Attaingnant,* once edited by the late A. Smijers of Holland, is being continued by A. Tillman Merritt and its publication has been taken over by the Harvard University Press. *Monumenta musicae Byzantinae,* now headed by Oliver Strunk, includes in its series a volume by Miloš Velimirović.

One of the principal reasons why Americans have in the past been left out of large publication projects is that such projects have usually been national enterprises. The series of national music published in Austria, Belgium, England, France, Germany, Italy, the Netherlands, Poland, Spain, Sweden, among others, have usually been subsidized by the governments or by some national organization with official standing. The editors have normally been scholars close to the regional sources. Occasionally Americans working abroad, or recognized as authorities on a particular phase of a project, have been invited to participate in a national series. Otto Kinkeldey was in Germany when he edited Volumes 46 and 47 of the *Denkmaler deutscher Tonkunst,* containing Erlebach's *Harmonische Freude musikalischer Freunde.* Stephen Tuttle supplied the volume of keyboard music of Thomas Tomkins for the Royal Musical Association's series, *Musica Britannica.* The *Monumenta musica Neerlandica* will soon have among its volumes three edited by Alan Curtis, who recently spent two years in Holland—*Dutch Keyboard Music of the Seventeenth Century,* the music of Leningrad QN 124, and the Camphuysen and Gresse manuscripts.

Until recently no such enterprises have existed in this country, although there is here too a musical heritage to preserve—one not so ancient or glorious as the European, but substantial nevertheless. The formation of the Moravian Music Foundation has therefore been a particularly welcome development. Led by an enterprising director, Donald Mc-Corkle, the foundation now has at Winston-Salem, North Carolina, an archive of more than 10,000 manuscripts, sponsors a series of publications and recordings, and has established extensive links to performance organizations and festivals. It has also printed a quarterly *Bulletin* since 1957.

Perhaps the most significant contribution of the Moravian communities, or Unitas Fratrum, to American culture was their musical tradition. A large quantity of music by composers within the American communities and by European Moravians has been found, principally in the towns settled by them in the eighteenth century, Bethlehem, Lititz, and Nazareth, Pennsylvania, and Winston-Salem, North Carolina. The foundation has contracted with three music publishers to print music edited for performance from manuscripts in its archive: Brodt Music Company of Charlotte, North Carolina, and Boosey and Hawkes and the H. W. Gray Company of New York. A good number of items have already seen print, mostly short choral works. Columbia Records has initiated a series of recordings of Moravian music. Two research consultants, Jan LaRue and Irving Lowens, are attached to the foundation, and Marilyn P. Gombosi is its assistant director and chief of research.

Still in the planning stage, on the other hand, is the "American Recordings Project," which embraces a broader scheme than its name suggests. A committee of which Irving Lowens is chairman and Victor Yellin secretary, and which includes also John Edmunds and H. Wiley Hitchcock, has announced a program of publications, monographs, and recordings for which it is now seeking funds. About twenty scholars have so far been invited to collaborate in the series, which will cover not only the music of the past, but of recent times as well.

PERIODICAL LITERATURE

No satisfactory picture of American achievements in musicology can be obtained without looking into the learned journals, which have been the characteristic medium for communicating a discovery or a new interpretation. The principal periodicals have been mentioned many times in this essay. The *Bulletin* of the American Musicological Society began in 1936 to print abstracts of papers read at regional chapter meetings, and these continued to appear until 1944. Papers presented at annual meetings of the society were printed in the annual volumes of *Papers* from 1936 to 1941. These functions were mainly absorbed by the *Journal* of the society, which began publication in 1948, with Oliver Strunk as editor-in-chief. Other editors-in-chief have been Donald Grout, 1949-51; Charles W. Fox, 1952-58; and David Hughes, 1959 to the present. The *Musical Quarterly* has aimed at a wider reading public but from the beginning has held to a high scholarly standard, remaining today one of the most favored outlets for scholars throughout the world. *Notes,* the organ of the Music Library Association, prints articles particularly in the field of American music and on subjects of bibliographic interest.

Musica disciplina, which specializes in articles in English on the Middle Ages and the Renaissance, has published some lengthy studies by Americans requiring complex typesetting, facsimiles, and extended musical examples. This has also been true of the multilingual *Annales musicologiques.* This began under a joint French and American editorial committee. Sponsored at first by the Société de Musique d'Autrefois led by Geneviève Thibault of Paris, it is now supported also by the Centre Nationale de la Recherche Scientifique. *Acta musicologica,* the organ of the International Musicological Society, has printed in recent years a fair proportion of articles by American members. Of the other periodicals published abroad, *Music and Letters, Music Review,* both English, the recently founded *Organo* of Bologna, Italy, and the *Revue belge de musicologie* have been particularly hospitable to American contributions. The 1960 volume of *Revue belge* had no less than four articles by Americans, covering more than half the space available.

Of the journals in related fields, those that often contain musicological material are *Journal of Music Theory, Renaissance News, Speculum,* the *Journal of Aesthetics and Art Criticism,* and the *Journal of the History of Ideas.*

Not every musicological article of suitable length can find a publisher. But well-written studies that present significant new material are not being refused, though delays of more than a year are common. Purely interpretative, analytical, or critical articles meet much more resistance.

AREAS OF RESEARCH

No aspect of musicological publishing reveals so well the favored and neglected areas of research as the periodical literature. The Renaissance has received by far the greatest attention. Interest in other periods seems to fall in proportion to a period's distance from this central point: the Middle Ages and the baroque era are the next most popular periods; the classic and romantic periods are comparatively neglected; and antiquity and the twentieth century have attracted almost no interest from professional American musicologists. The reasons for the unequal distribution of interest are many, some deeply ingrained in the patterns of scholarship established by the early European musicologists. To the nineteenth and early twentieth century founders, the basic problem areas were the Middle Ages and the Renaissance; the romantic period was too recent; the classic period seemed well known —though what was known was the so-called Viennese classic period; the baroque excited some interest, but not in proportion to its problems. Friedrich Ludwig (Gottingen), Johannes Wolf (Berlin), Adolph Sandberger (Munich), Theodor Kroyer (Leipzig), André Pirro (Paris), early twentieth century scholars whose pupils have had a direct influence in the United States, all specialized in music before 1600.

There are some special reasons for the popularity of the Renaissance among American scholars. The spread of musical scholarship coincided with the recognition of the Renaissance as the golden age of choral music by those who worked to broaden the repertory of college choral groups. This movement was led by Archibald T. Davison, conductor of the

Harvard Glee Club and University Choir between 1912 and 1934, and mentor to two generations of musical scholars. Throughout the country editions by him and others of Palestrina, Vittoria, Morales, Lassus, Hassler, and other sixteenth century masters were put before choir singers. The results, while not always authentic in sound, stirred great enthusiasm. Counterpoint teachers began to look upon the polyphony of the sixteenth century masters as models for instruction in place of Bach.

Harvard consequently became a center of Renaissance studies. A. Tillman Merrit subjected a wide chronological range of sixteenth century choir music to analysis and arrived at a concise statement of the technical resources in *Sixteenth Century Polyphony* (1939). The majority who earned their doctorates at Harvard during the years when the choral movement was at its height wrote dissertations on Renaissance subjects and continued to devote their later efforts to the same period. Among these scholars were Helen Hewitt, Armen Carapetyan, Scott Goldthwaite, Everett B. Helm, Lloyd Hibberd, Richard H. Hoppin, Hugh Miller, Gordon Sutherland, and Stephen Tuttle. Interest in the period spread with them to other places.

Other early centers of Renaissance studies were the Eastman School of Music in Rochester and New York University. Charles Warren Fox of Rochester, a psychologist by training, early turned to sixteenth century music. As one of his first contributions he applied experimental methods to comparative style analysis by taking fifty polyphonic settings of a single German song as his subject, the song serving as a constant controlled condition. He has also contributed articles on Morales, the vihuela tablature, and the harmonic practice of the sixteenth century in general. Among his many students at Rochester, several have specialized in the Renaissance: Louise Cuyler, Ruth Watanabe, and Glenn Watkins.

Gustave Reese, who has taught almost continuously at New York University since 1927, established his reputation as a Renaissance scholar with an important article in 1934 (*MQ*), a probing review of the contents of the *Odhecaton,* the first printed part-music collection, which had just been published in facsimile two years earlier in Milan. While engaged in his monumental book on the Renaissance, he interested numerous students at the university in individual topics that needed wholesale researches. The chansons of Busnois, the psalm motets of Goudimel, the Latin sacred music of Peter Philips, the motets of Mouton, the vihuela repertory, the music of Robert White, Jacobus Vaet, Costanzo Festa, Antoine de Fevin, Philippe de Monte, Philippe Caron—all became dissertation subjects. A large number of important published contributions have come from this school: Steinhardt's book on Vaet, Ward's articles on instrumental arrangements of polyphonic music, and articles on Busnois by Catherine Brooks and on Goudimel by Eleanor Lawry, to cite a few examples.

Although Oliver Strunk's research has for many years been focused on Byzantine chant, several of his early articles were on the Renaissance, and three distinguished graduates of Princeton, where he teaches, have been Renaissance men: Joseph Kerman, Kenneth Levy, and Lewis Lockwood. Kerman's articles on the relationships between the Italian and English madrigal, Levy's on the Parisian chanson and court air, and Lockwood's on Vincenzo Ruffo and on the parody mass are fundamental studies. Two of these scholars have since turned in other directions, Kerman toward the history of opera, in which he has published a brilliant critical book, *Opera as Drama,* and Levy to Byzantine music.

Meanwhile a number of European scholars who had concentrated on the Renaissance immigrated to the United States: Willi Apel, Manfred Bukofzer, Alfred Einstein, Ernst Ferand, Otto Gombosi, Erich Hertzmann, Ernst Krenek, Edward Lowinsky, Dragan Plamenac, Leo Schrade. Some settled almost immediately in academic centers where they were in a position to influence graduate study: Schrade at Yale, Einstein at Smith, Bukofzer at the University of California in Berkeley, and Hertzmann at Columbia. Apel lectured at Harvard for a while before settling in Indiana; Lowinsky taught at Black Mountain and Queens colleges for many years before going to California, and then to Chicago. Gombosi taught at Washington in Seattle, Michigan State, and Chicago before going to Harvard. Plamenac was active in New York and St. Louis until he established himself at Illinois.

Of the "schools" founded by the emigré scholars the most productive have been those around Gombosi at Harvard and Schrade at Yale. Gombosi's own publications dwelt particularly on several problematic areas: the nature of the Greek and medieval modes; schemes of rhythmic and metrical organizations in medieval and Renaissance music; early dance music and its stock tunes and harmonic patterns. The last was certainly his greatest passion. Many fascinating riddles awaited solution. Where did the mysterious tunes used to improvise dance music in the Middle Ages and the Renaissance originate? What was the relation of the song literature to the dance? By what process did the particular style of harmony used in the dances evolve? What was the effect of learned counterpoint on this process? He realized that these questions were not to be answered by a single researcher, since most of the music is found in lute, guitar, vihuela, and keyboard tablatures. These are finger notations like the modern guitar chord symbols which must be laboriously transcribed into pitch notation before revealing their contents. Hours may go into the transcription of a piece that occupies one page of piano score. Gombosi saw the opportunity of creating a team out of a group of doctoral students he found when he arrived at Harvard in 1951 Howard Brown, Joseph

Burns, Daniel Heartz, Imogene Horsley, and Lawrence Moe. A glance at the publications of these scholars reveals that the problems, far from being solved, are only now being understood. What is equally important, the sources and their interrelations are being thoroughly described and analyzed. An index of the recognition these young Americans have achieved in the international sphere is the fact that two of them, Heartz and Moe, as well as an earlier Gombosi pupil, John Ward, were invited to participate in the International Conference on the Lute and its Music organized by the Centre National de la Recherche Scientifique at Neuilly-sur-Seine in 1957.

Although Schrade's interests during his stay in the United States ranged over a wide chronological area, the emphasis in his graduate teaching at Yale was on the Middle Ages and the Renaissance. Among his pupils who have made distinguished contributions in articles and reviews on the Renaissance are Alvin Johnson, a specialist on Cipriano de Rore, Edward Lerner, who has written on Agricola, and Sylvia Kenney, who has edited the works of Walter Frye and has made substantial steps toward a solution to the ancient fauxbourdon problem centering around the choral improvisatory style that was so fundamental in the evolution of Renaissance harmony. Even more important has been the output of studies stemming from Yale in the medieval sphere. The work of Carpenter, Seay, and Waite has been mentioned. The numerous articles of Hans Tischler on early French polyphony constitute another important corpus of writings, and the articles and reviews of Richard Crocker, Janet Knapp, and Sylvia Kenney in the medieval field all bear witness to the vitality and critical acumen cultivated in Schrade's "school."

The influence of Einstein, Apel, Plamenac, Bukofzer, Hertzmann and others of European origin has also been strongly felt both in choice of topics for investigation and in manner of approach. Concentration on problems related to these professors' own research has been less marked than in the cases just cited. A healthy variety, indeed, has been characteristic of graduate work at most universities. As departments have expanded and foreign influences have been assimilated, the framework for advanced graduate study has passed almost everywhere from the professor-disciple pattern typical of many European universities to one characterized by a multiplicity of loyalties and relationships and more generous opportunities for the student to choose both topic and mentor. This change has been particularly notable at the universities singled out earlier as centers of concentration in the Middle Ages and the Renaissance.

The past decade has witnessed a deepening involvement of American scholars with the search for new sources in Europe. American musicologists were mainly limited in the years before, during, and immediately after World War II to printed sources and manuscripts in the United States. But even these were not exploited in depth because readers of American journals and books were unprepared for pieces of minute research. The trend was therefore toward comprehensive views, comparative style and form analyses, and introductory surveys. This type of contribution occurs most frequently among the papers delivered in the first years of the AMS: surveys of the chanson, villancico, early choral music, motet types, early keyboard music, tablature notations. Through these, music history was acquiring a foundation in this country rather than materially adding to the fund of knowledge already available in European publications.

After World War II, scholars went abroad in large numbers to canvass the collections of manuscripts and rare books for unknown or neglected material. Grants from the Guggenheim Foundation, the Fulbright program of the Department of State, and foundations within universities have provided the indispensable material base for these forays. Several of the first to make the odyssey returned with accounts of precious holdings neglected for lack of funds and suitable buildings, particularly in Italy and Spain. Scholars brought back quantities of microfilm that would have been unthinkable earlier. Reports soon appeared of collections and manuscripts previously unknown or temporarily lost or forgotten. These were paraded before the musicological world with unprecedented brilliance and thoroughness. The manuscripts' owners, the owners' pedigrees and crests, the scribes, the ceremonial and political circumstances of the texts, the historical significance of the repertories—nothing was overlooked in the scholarly onslaught, except sometimes the music itself. Hardly a year has gone by since the early 1950's without our attention being focused upon some important new or neglected source. In 1950 it was a sixteenth century motet manuscript in the Vallicelliana in Rome described by Lowinsky (AMS *Journal*). In 1951 Bukofzer described some flyleaves in Coventry that constituted the only English source to contain a Dufay composition (AMS *Journal*). In the same year Plamenac published the first analysis of the Codex Faenza 117, a large repertory of early Italian keyboard music, some going back to the fourteenth century. He also reconstructed from two manuscripts, one in Seville and the other in Paris, a large book of polyphonic songs that had belonged to Ferdinand Columbus, natural son of the explorer (*MQ*, 1951, 1952). Walter H. Rubsamen indexed several important manuscripts in Florence and Modena (*Notes*, 1949 and 1950). Robert Stevenson, who was one of the first foreign musicologists to make a research tour of Spain after the war, brought back news of a previously unnoticed manuscript of more than eight hundred pages in the Medinacelli Library in Madrid containing all the Magnificats and all but two of the masses of Morales and a large quantity of works by other composers (*Notes,* 1952). In 1954 Luther Dittmer published his reconstruction of two rotulae in the Bodleian Library that help to illuminate a dark period in the history of polyphony in thirteenth century England (*Musica disciplina*). The repertory of Torino, Biblioteca Nazionale J. II. 9, a manuscript known for some time but only externally, was extensively discussed by Richard Hoppin in 1957 (*Musica disciplina*). Before he died, Bukofzer reviewed about three dozen manuscript sources found in recent years for the period between the twelfth and fifteenth centuries in an article, "Changing Aspects of Medieval and Renaissance Music," a precious legacy to the students of today. Quite a number of these sources he lifted out of obscurity and he succeeded in placing others in their proper historical contexts for the first time. In a brilliant report on the sumptuous, privately owned Medici Codex, Edward Lowinsky illuminated many aspects of the early sixteenth century Italian repertory contained in it (*Annales musicologiques* V, 1957).

Daniel Heartz has brought an acute critical sense and an impressive command of the history and geography of Parisian printing and musical life to bear on two newly available sources. One is a fragmentary copy of what is probably the first book of part-music printed by Pierre Attaingnant in the 1520's (AMS *Journal,* 1961). The other is a collection of guitar books, published in Paris between 1551 and 1553, the first devoted to that instrument (*MQ,* 1960). Together the two books nearly doubled the sixteenth century repertory of guitar music. The last of Heartz's finds, it must be added, was made possible by the files of the International Inventory of Musical Resources, coordinated by François Lesure at the Bibliothèque Nationale in Paris, which revealed the hiding places of these volumes, the Vadiana-Bibliothek, the town lending library of St. Gall, Switzerland.

Several others of the younger generation of Americans

have made significant discoveries through archival searches. Bain Murray has uncovered evidence in Modena of a visit by Obrecht to Italy in 1487 and further evidence that suggests he may have spent some of his youth there (*MQ*, 1957). Robert Stevenson has filled out the facts of the life of Cristobal de Morales through his gathering of documents in archives at Rome, Toledo, and Malaga (AMS *Journal*, 1953) and of many lesser known figures in his *Spanish Music in the Age of Columbus* (The Hague, 1960). Lewis H. Lockwood has thrown new light on the career of Vincenzo Ruffo, particularly with respect to his role in the Counterreformation (*MQ*, 1957). A thorough search in the archives of several Florentine churches by Frank A. D'Accone has disclosed a hitherto unsuspected flowering of polyphonic music around the Baptistry of San Giovanni and the Cathedral of Santa Maria del Fiore in the fifteenth century (AMS *Journal*, 1961).

Well-cultivated as they are, the Middle Ages and the Renaissance are likely to remain challenging fields to scholars for some time to come. The works of many composers, particularly French and Italian, have yet to be included in any series publication plans. Town and church archives in many European cities should be canvassed for names of musicians and composers, since biographical information is scanty on all but a few important figures. One of several problems whose solution partly hinges upon this kind of data is that of interrelationships between the musical cultures of various countries. The role of music in social life, theater, and church is imperfectly known, since musical sources, upon which the emphasis has been placed, disclose little about this. Contemporary attitudes toward music, and their relation to literary, philosophic, and scientific doctrines have only recently been subjected to special inquiries. Printed theoretical treatises whose titles and authors only are familiar are still in need of interpretation, particularly those in Latin. To this end there are several translations of theorists now in preparation. The *Journal of Music Theory* of the Yale School of Music has announced a series of them, but financial problems have so far delayed publication. The facsimile editions of printed treatises being published in Germany with the co-operation of the International Musicological Society are facilitating studies in this area. Finally, the greatest task of all —style criticism—has hardly begun.

The baroque period, in spite of the many challenging gaps revealed by Bukofzer's *Music in the Baroque Era*, has not been fairly represented in scholarly reviews. Individual discoveries in this period tend to have cumulative meaning rather than to emerge sensationally as missing links. When so much is unknown, a new fact or source is only a wild flower in a forsaken plot, no great ornament on an author's bonnet or in an editor's bouquet of titles. It is in such a situation that the publication of dissertations becomes necessary for the advancement of knowledge. More than one hundred doctoral dissertations have been completed on the baroque period. These light up such dark areas as the instrumental music of two composers noted for their operas, Leonardo Leo and Antonio Caldara; the music of Nicolas Bernier, Benedetto Marcello, Johann Ludwig Krebs, Johann Caspar Kerll, Giovanni Maria Bononcini, Johann Pezel, and Thomas Campion, to mention a few composers at random. Some of the theses written upon these subjects are voluminous typescripts, but few of them are so rich with new material that they could not be compressed into hundred-page monographs if the leisurely analyses and background-setting introductions were curtailed. Only when some of the information contained in these has been sifted and interpreted, can some syntheses be crystallized that may correct the many misconceptions rampant about this period and pave the way for further efforts. Two sectors particularly, seventeenth century opera and church music, remain today almost as little known as they were at the beginning of this century.

Few of our mature scholars have dedicated themselves to the baroque. David Boyden has reported on miscellaneous trouble-shooting tasks, like clearing up the meaning of the term *concerto* and explaining the tuning, tablature, and technique of certain string instruments. These have been off-shoots from his main task of writing a history of violin playing, and it is symptomatic that the stumbling blocks that begged most to be pushed aside were in the seventeenth and eighteenth century. Newman's large-scale plan for a history of the sonata became a wholesale investigation of the baroque sonata; this thick jungle had to be traversed in order to reach the relative clearing of the classic period. Henry Mishkin has focused some attention on the key Bologna school of instrumental music. Vincent Duckles and Carol MacClintock with their studies of early solo song in England and Italy helped to lift monody a little more out of the mist of legend into the plain day of facts. At least one creative personality in late seventeenth century church music has been placed into prominent relief, Marc-Antoine Charpentier, much neglected contemporary of Lully, by H. Wiley Hitchcock.

In the early eighteenth century, Donald Grout and Walter Rubsamen have contributed articles on Italian, French, and English comic opera, but both scholars have been too enticed by Renaissance music to continue piecing together uninterruptedly the fragmentary remains of early musical comedy. In the late baroque, studies of Bach and Handel have not been lacking, nor has their importance waned now that fresh definitive editions of the two composers' works are being prepared Yet Jacob Coopersmith's Harvard dissertation, a 4,114-page thematic index of the printed works of Handel, has remained in typescript since 1932. A valuable prelude to Arthur Mendel's present work on the New Bach

Edition was his earlier research on pitch and tuning in the period preceding and up to Bach's time. His articles on this work unraveled a complex knot that has impeded progress on several fronts in the study and proper performance of accompanied church music.

The early classic period—the half-century before Mozart and Haydn emerged to dominate European music—is beginning to be rescued from oblivion. It was neglected by the German scholars of the last generation partly because the host of Italians and Bohemians who populated this epoch wrote symphonies, concertos, and operas by the hundreds, few of them seemingly very profound Their works, moreover, were widely dispersed, and it was difficult to get a clear picture of their contributions. Now it is becoming evident that the origin of "Viennese" classicism must be sought in this multitude of nearly anonymous figures, among whom the truly creative personalities have still to be separated from the hacks. The wonderful world of the keyboard music of Domenico Scarlatti has been brilliantly revealed by Ralph Kirkpatrick's full-length study, yet this composer's operas and church music remain unknown. The stages leading to the ripe classical style of Johann Christian Bach's operas have been perceptively unfolded by Edward Downes in his giant two-volume Harvard dissertation (1958) In two studies Downes has published so far (AMS *Journal*, 1961; N.Y. Congress Report, 1961), he has shown how much the categories and terminology applied to eighteenth century opera need wholesale revision A parallel analysis of the genesis of the classical concerto and its forms by Edwin J. Simon (California, Berkeley, dissertation, 1954), also remains unfortunately mainly unpublished. It too upsets many conventional views. Reinhard Pauly similarly established links between the church music of the baroque and classic periods in his articles on Michael Haydn.

The disclosures concerning the theoretical background of the eighteenth century sonata by Leonard Ratner and William Newman have finally steered formal analysis of early classical music away from the "incipient sonata form" approach to one based on contemporary concepts and intentions. Jan LaRue's present work on the symphony promises to set accounts straight on the controversial background of Haydn's and Mozart's achievements. Meanwhile as by-products of this long-range project, he has contributed a number of very practical guides on research technique, particularly in the areas of thematic indexing, analytical symbols and graphs, and the identification of eighteenth century watermarks found on music papers (*Acta*, 1961). No account of American scholarship in this period should fail to pay tribute to the work of H. C. Robbins Landon, who at the age of thirty-six has earned a secure place among the outstanding researchers in musical classicism of past and present. His zeal in establishing authenticity and in ferretting out concealed copies has set a model for musicological detective work. While Paul H. Lang's book on classicism continues to be awaited, occasional glimpses into his workshop have been provided by his *Musical Quarterly* editorials and reviews of records and musical editions. He has particularly emphasized the need for studies of the contemporaries of Beethoven, composers who more than any others have suffered from almost total eclipse. In spite of recent gains, the classic period remains only spottily covered by critical research, and certain areas still languish in the shadow of the great figures of Gluck, Haydn, Mozart, and Beethoven.

It is generally recognized that the most neglected period of all is the nineteenth century. So great has been the distaste for romanticism during the last quarter-century that the period has been left mainly to a few devoted Wagnerites and romantic biographers. What is worse, this prejudice has been allowed to affect graduate teaching, so that the neglect tends to perpetuate itself. While it must be acknowledged that in the nineteenth century we are well supplied with printed editions, collections of letters, and testaments and confessions of all kinds, truly critical editions are scarce, and a large number of composers, from Hummel to Reger, are imperfectly known. The abundant links in this period between music and literature, philosophy, politics, and society in general afford excellent opportunities for original research. A revival of interest in the nineteenth century on the part of serious scholars, however, has been observable in the United States in the past decade. Some excellent contributions have come, for example, from Eric Werner, Mina Curtiss, Alexander Ringer, Donald Mintz, and Edward A. Lippman.

A similar neglect of twentieth century music by scholars has been less damaging. The vacuum has been partly filled by scholarly composers and musicians who would probably prefer not to be considered musicologists, though some of them have certainly earned the title. The excellent series of critical articles in the *Musical Quarterly*'s "Current Chronicle" by Richard Franko Goldman constitutes by itself a history of recent music. Some of the contributors to this department and to the portraits of contemporary composers that have appeared regularly in the *Quarterly* are scholars by profession: Everett B. Helm, Alexander Ringer, William Austin, George Perle, Robert Erich Wolf, and Irving Lowens. Others are articulate musicians and composers—Elliott Carter, George Rochberg and Milton Babbitt; another, Allen Forte, is a professional theorist. The fragments of a history of our times, although they are scattered, can best be found in these articles. Comparing them to present-day British criticism of contemporary music, one finds a more humanistic approach, less petty detail and technical jargon, and in comparison to the German and French literature, less faddism and partisanship. While these reviews show that musicological technique in the usual sense is not a prerequisite for significant work in contemporary criticism, greater participation by scholars would exert a healthy influence, for none are better equipped than they to relate the events of today to the traditions behind them. The early twentieth century is particularly open to scholarly investigation. George Perle's articles on Berg's operas and his penetrating book, *Serial Composition and Atonality* (1962), are exemplary of the fresh insights a scholarly approach to contemporary music can offer.

Thus far no American scholar has published a history of twentieth century music, although Austin has been at work on one. Joseph Machlis's recent *Introduction to Contemporary Music* (1961), though a textbook for undergraduate courses, is marked by thorough scholarship, musical perceptiveness, and an unusual flair for characterizing in a brief space the major contributions and styles of both Europeans and Americans. To the latter Machlis has accorded two hundred pages, a recognition as long due as it is unprecedented in a book of this kind.

Very few American musicologists can have an easy conscience about the subject of American music, for not many of them have even a passing acquaintance with the personalities and facts of our national musical history. This is a subject that has only a negligible role in graduate study and is treated as a serious research specialty by only a handful of American scholars, few of them in teaching positions.

If there is little justification for this neglect, there are some obvious causes. Many native American scholars, who would perhaps have been drawn to regional researches, were trained by Europeans The classic themes of European musicology, from organum to Beethoven's wills, dominated both their academic exercises and their subsequent independent efforts.

Moreover, the academic training as well as the daily occupations of the American musicologist are oriented toward European music, it is the subject of his teaching, and only by sidetracking his regular work can he turn his attention to American music. Even the problems of contemporary American music rarely involve the scholar in a consideration of our national past, since most of our composers share with scholars the same training, dominated by European music.

In academic circles, little recognition has been given in the past to scholars specializing in American music. Instead, the activity in this field has tended to be concentrated around several libraries The Library of Congress, with a collection of American material carefully gathered by Sonneck and expanded by his successors and through copyright deposits, has been a mecca for Americanists. On the staff of this library have been some of the most distinguished of them. Sonneck, Chase, Hill, Lowens, and Ellinwood. The New York Public Library, with its Americana collections, has also attracted champions of American music, such as Otto Kinkeldey, Carleton Sprague Smith, Hans David, John Tasker Howard, Philip Miller, and John Edmunds

A healthy trend has been observable recently toward closing the gap between American music studies and the academic world. A number of graduate departments have led the way by encouraging dissertation work in this field. Howard Hanson has been an enthusiastic supporter of American studies as director of the Eastman School of Music, where many dissertations in theory on little-known Americans of the past have been written. Several graduate departments have American specialists· Ralph Daniel at Indiana, Allen P. Britton at Michigan, Hans Nathan at Michigan State, and Charles Seeger at UCLA. Numerous theses in the field have been accepted at Catholic University, North Carolina, Harvard, New York University, Northwestern, Southern

California, Union Theological, Washington, and Pennsylvania.

The integration of American music studies with programs in American civilization and history offers an opportunity that has yet to be exploited sufficiently. Because American music has often been outside the stream of major musical developments overseas, part of the impulse for its study must come from the desire to know the total culture of our past American society. Besides such things as diplomatic relations, economic history, and Civil War battles, American historians should pay greater attention to cultural history, particularly that related to music.

Perhaps the most notable forward step that has been taken lately is the recognition of the fact that the study of American music demands a multilateral approach. The method has been amply described by Charles Seeger in numerous publications and demonstrated by Gilbert Chase in *America's Music from the Pilgrims to the Present* (1955). They have shown that the techniques of the musicologist and the ethnomusicologist must often converge upon a problem in this area before it can be satisfactorily solved. This is necessary because the musical past of this nation represents several strands that are only loosely woven together. There is the "colonial" thread: the music of the Puritan pilgrims, the Germans, Moravians, Dutch, French, and other national groups that settled here at different moments in history, bringing with them their old-world musical culture. Within each of these cultures there is a concert life, a music for worship, and popular music at various levels. The music of the Negro is another field, that of the American Indian yet another. Finally there is the music of the native composers, both serious and popular, and a further layer of anonymous popular and folk music with mainly oral traditions. While the specialist in Lutheran hymnody need not be an ethnomusicologist, and the student of Navaho music can get along without knowing New England psalmody, the well-qualified American specialist will need to be both. The welcome tendency toward including both traditional and ethnical musicological training in the graduate work of the American scholar, which is heralded in Mantle Hood's "Music, the Unknown," the following essay in this book, should not fail to stimulate a rebirth of American studies along truly comprehensive and scholarly lines.

MUSIC, THE UNKNOWN

୶ᠦᡫ

MANTLE HOOD

DIRECTOR, INSTITUTE OF
ETHNOMUSICOLOGY
UNIVERSITY OF CALIFORNIA
LOS ANGELES

He [Charles Russell Day] shows us the existence of a really intimate, expressive, melodic music, capable of the greatest refinement of treatment, and altogether outside the experience of the Western musician. What we learn from such inquiries is that the debated opinions of musical theorists, the cherished beliefs of those who devote themselves to the practice of the art, the deductions we evolve from historic studies—all have to be submitted to larger conceptions, based upon a recognition of humanity as evolved from the teachings of ethnology. We must forget what is merely European, national, or conventional, and submit the whole of the phenomena to a philosophical as well as a sympathetic consideration, such as, in this century, is conceded to language, but has not yet found its way to music.*

ALFRED JAMES HIPKINS

*From the introduction to Charles Russell Day's *The Music and Musical Instruments of Southern India and the Deccan* (New York Novello, Ewer, 1891).

1

MUSIC, THE UNKNOWN

In 1935, the internationally known biologist Alexis Carrel stated in the preface to *Man, the Unknown* (Harper) that specialists in the world of science would be disappointed in his book because it was not sufficiently technical and, further, that laymen would find it difficult because it was too technical. He defended his undertaking with the statement: "We must realize that an attempt, however awkward and though partly a failure, is better than no attempt at all." In the same spirit, I want to consider that part of the world of music that is appropriately the subject matter of a field known as ethnomusicology.

This branch of musicology—for many years referred to as *vergleichende Musikwissenschaft* or comparative musicology —has become increasingly broad during the eighty years of its development. The discipline is directed toward an understanding of music studied in terms of itself and also toward the comprehension of music within the context of its society. Ethnomusicology is concerned with the music of all non-European peoples—the civilized nations of the Orient as well as tribal societies—and includes within its purview the tribal, folk, and popular music of the Western world, as well as hybridizations of these forms. It frequently crosses into the field of European art music, although such material is only an indirect object of concern. In other words, ethnomusicology embraces all kinds of music not included by studies in historical musicology, i.e., the study of cultivated music in the western European tradition.

During the past few decades the range of subjects treated

by the historical musicologist has become progressively more restricted, so that we might say that the breadth of ethnomusicology has increased almost by default. At the twenty-fifth anniversary dinner of the American Musicological Society (Chicago, December 1959), the first president of the society, Otto Kinkeldey, mentioned early papers covering a wide variety of subjects—ranging from a consideration of musical logic (read by Charles Seeger) to a highly specialized topic such as the polyphony of two Japanese shakuhachi (read by Kinkeldey himself)—and he suggested that the broad interests that initially characterized the society had narrowed through the years. The next speaker, Oliver Strunk, then president of the society, said that in the preceding six months he had been asked the question "What is the future of musicology?" from three different sources. The first was connected with the twenty-fifth anniversary dinner, the second was a conference called by the American Council of Learned Societies, and the third was the Council of the Humanities at Princeton. Not wishing to rely only on his own opinion, he had written to colleagues in Europe and in America to get their views. He reported that all the musicologists, with one exception, had been in accord; the dissenter's point of view was that the fertile fields of the past would provide the fertile fields of the future. All of the others, according to Strunk, indicated that the promising future of musicological inquiry lay in what has been termed ethnomusicology. These opinions in no way minimized the continued importance of the study of Western art music, but rather pointed to the vast areas of unknown music that had yet to be explored.

The earliest notable example of attention to non-Western musics is the *Dictionaire de musique* (1768) of Jean-Jacques Rousseau, which contains the first serious notation of Oriental and folk melodies, giving transcriptions of "Air chinois,"

"Chanson des sauvages du Canada," "Danse canadienne," "Air suisse apellé le rans des vaches," and "Chanson persane." Neither Rousseau's interest, however, nor the perception shown by Hipkins' statement of 1891, quoted at the beginning of this essay, is typical of the attitude prevailing during the times in which each author wrote. In the late eighteenth and early nineteenth centuries, increased travel and contact with the non-Western world aroused a general curiosity that produced an assortment of quaint observations—as well as biased descriptions and evaluations—of unfamiliar musical cultures. It is not impossible that such early reports are still accountable for a certain prejudice among Western musicians and are therefore partially responsible for the continuing separation of the musicologies of the Western and non-Western world.

Commenting on this prejudice in *Ethnomusicology*, 3rd ed. (The Hague: Martinus Nijhoff, 1959), Jaap Kunst says: "There is among Westerners an inclination to regard all exotic music, even in its highest forms, as nothing more than either expressions of inferior, more primitive civilizations, or as a kind of musical perversion. . . . Neither is it generally understood that, as far as the higher musical forms of expression of the Asiatic civilized nations are concerned, their extremely refined specialization renders them difficult to grasp for us Westerners, who are equally specialized, but in another direction."

The difficulties of grasping the subtleties of Eastern musical cultures—elusive even in the twentieth century—proved insurmountable for most musicologists in earlier times. Their writings, which may accurately report some musical details, are nevertheless typically characterized by misunderstanding and misinterpretation.

From 1808 to 1810 a remarkable four-volume work by F. Baltazard Solvyns was published in Paris under the title

Les Hindôus. These four folios, richly illustrated with colored engravings, systematically describe—in both French and English—Hindu castes, customs, costumes, ceremonies, and musical instruments. Solvyns' work is practically unknown to Western musicologists, notwithstanding a review (actually a "discovery") by Jaap Kunst written for *Cultureel Indië* in 1945. Historically, *Les Hindôus* is especially valuable for the fine engravings it contains, showing in many instances the playing positions of a number of Indian instruments no longer in use today. Without this reference the actual method of playing many instruments would be largely speculative.

The judgments and criticisms of the text, however, are another matter. The following extracts, revealing the charming strangeness of the English text, show quite clearly Solvyns' complete lack of understanding of the music as well as of the character of the people.

> A great deal has been said upon the music of the Hindoos. The Transactions of the Society of Calcutta, among others, contain many treatises upon this subject, which is, notwithstanding, very imperfectly known in Europe, for this simple reason, that the instruments which they use have never been described with sufficient precision, which ought to have been the principal object, for they are much more remarkable than the music itself. Their instruments have been carried successively to a surprising degree of perfection; but those improvements have not reached their music, which still remains in its infancy. It is impossible not to make this remark in seeing a Hindoo play upon the Tamboora. In his hands is a magnificent instrument, covered with painting and gilding, ornamented to an excessive luxury, and we are naturally led to imagine that he is to draw from it the most enchanting sounds; but on the contrary he remains for hours together in the same attitude singing a monotonous air, and touching, from time to time, one of the four chords [strings] which compose this instrument. This is the only use he

makes of it, the only pleasure which he seeks from it. And for him even this is a great deal, seated on a carpet or piece of white cloth, he gives himself up to the pleasing sensations which the vibration of a single chord [string] produces, and probably he would give up even this enjoyment, if it required the smallest exertion. Everything about him must be proportioned to his natural taste for laziness and indolence.

. . .

The *Soorna* is our Hautboy; but the Hindoos play it so ill, that they can draw from it only shrill and disagreeable sounds, the European, the most accustomed to the stunning [*le tapage*] of Hindoo music, cannot stand a concert of several *Soornas* accompanied with some of their other noisy instruments. Every *Soorna* exerts his whole strength and entirely after his own fancy, without any respect to measure or harmony, at a distance one would imagine that it was the roaring of a number of wild beasts. The musician whom I have represented is before his house and not in a very easy attitude [See Plate 1.]

The *Soorna* players are men of bad morals, and pass the greater part of the day in the shops of the retailers of *toddy* and other spirits. There they recite at great length to those who will listen to them, the very shameful adventures of their lives, without omitting the most trifling circumstances of their gluttony and debauchery, with an exact account of all the feasts where they assisted, and the quantity of victuals and of betel which they received.

. . .

It is not necessary to remark that the music of the Khole is as monotonous as that of the other instruments I have been describing. But the Hindoos, on the contrary, find in it an extraordinary charm, and pretend that, accompanied by the voice, this instrument is capable of expressing all the emotions of the soul, from the most violent to the most tender

. . .

. . Still we cannot help being surprised that a people so evidently without the genius of music, should have been so anxious to multiply the means of this amusement, and have carried the number of their instruments much beyond what we have done in Europe

Solvyns' distaste for Indian music and his misunderstanding of an unfamiliar musical culture is obvious. The soorna, more properly termed sanai, or shanai, is an important instrument that at the time of Solvyns' book was a folk instrument traditionally played at weddings. Although in modern times it still has this important social function, it has become an instrument of art music in the hands of a virtuoso. The disparaging remarks about the player in the above quotation, representing an indiscriminate association of social and musical prejudices, reflect an attitude common to many early Western observers of Eastern musical cultures.

In the introduction to his book on *Chinese Music* (Special Series Number 6, Imperial Maritime Customs), published in London in 1884, J. A. Van Aalst notes the treatment of his subject by other writers: "Amongst the subjects which have been treated, with the least success by foreign writers, Chinese Music ranks prominently. If mentioned in their books at all, it is simply to remark that 'it is detestable, noisy, monotonous; that it hopelessly outrages our Western notions of music, etc.'" He dismisses such opinions summarily by saying that "I do not wish to create any discussions contradicting these and many other erroneous statements found in descriptions of Chinese music: it would take too long a time."

Having presented a fairly accurate descriptive account of Chinese musical instruments, providing us with some information that is still valuable today, Van Aalst reaches the following conclusion:

It is incontestable that Chinese music compares unfavorably with our European music. From our point of view it certainly appears monotonous, even noisy—disagreeable, if you please; but what matters this if the Chinese themselves are satisfied with it? And that they are satisfied, that they like it, that it is a necessity for them, is fully proved by the constant use of music in their ceremonies and festivities, by the numerous bands parading the streets and offering their services, by the strict attention with which they listen to their ballad singers—now exhibiting emotion at an affecting picture of suffering, now bursting into hearty laughter when the subject is of an amusing kind, and finally, by the large variety of instruments which, though often played without taste or feeling, are nevertheless remarkable for their beautiful simplicity of form, and their extreme cheapness. According to the Chinese themselves, music proceeds from the heart of man; it is the expression of the feelings of the heart.

Van Aalst's laissez-faire attitude was perhaps unusual, for low opinions of non-Western music were widespread. They were not, however, universal. Charles Russell Day, in *The Music and Musical Instruments of Southern India and the Deccan* (1891), expressed an unpopular viewpoint with great conviction and insight.

Almost every traveler in India comes away with the idea that the music of the country consists of mere noise and nasal drawling of the most repulsive kind, often accompanied by contortions and gestures of the most ludicrous description. Perhaps the traveler may have fancied that he has seen a nautch—he has possibly been asked to some such entertainment at the house of a wealthy native; or, more likely, he has possessed a treasure of a "boy" who has been able to make the necessary arrangements with the "nautchness" for a performance of a kind. [See Plate 2] But in certainly two-thirds of such cases the singing and dancing witnessed has been of the commonest, and the performers of the most abandoned and depraved of the city—and the traveler has therefore received a false impression, which may abide

through life, or impede the progress of a more correct appreciation of the real value of Indian music. But it is hardly fair
that an art so little really understood, even among the natives of India themselves, should be judged by such a criterion and then put aside as worthless because solitary individuals have been deceived by parties of outcast charletans
whose object is mere gain For that Indian music is an art,
and a very intricate and difficult one, can hardly be denied.
But to appreciate it one must first put away all thought of
European music, and then judge it by an Indian standard,
and impartially, upon its own merits—of the ingenuity of
the performer—the peculiar rhythm of the music—the extraordinary scales used—the recitatives—the amount of
imitation—the wonderful execution and memory of the performer—and his skill in employing small intervals as grace.

The illustration of the three Nautch dancers from *Les Hindôus* depicts the original beauty of the traditional dance and
provides historical interest because of the instruments and
setting; by contrast it also supports Day's comments about
travelers whose impressions were based on cheap and bad
performances. This, in my opinion, has been an important
factor in the faulty reporting of non-Western music and
dance practices to date. Too often, the German musicologist
of the late nineteenth and early twentieth centuries never
visited the field, basing his writings on the accounts of travelers, or sometimes anthropologists, who were not interested
in seeking out artistic performances representative of fine
quality.

In 1893 Richard Wallaschek put together what purported
to be a survey of the world of music under the title *Primitive
Music* (Longmans, Green), a potpourri of direct and indirect
quotations of most of the early studies of non-Western music
published up to that date. His subjects included Africa, Asia,
Oceania, the Americas, and the "Jews, Gypsies, and Hun-

garians of Europe." The following excerpts are representative of the tone of the work, and the inconsistency between the views expressed by Berlioz and by Lay introduces a fundamental problem peculiar to this field of study.

"Berlioz speaks in the following manner: 'The Chinese sing like dogs howling, like a cat screeching when it has swallowed a toad,' and their instruments are veritable instruments of torture." "The soft melodious tones of their music [the Siamese] offer a pleasing contrast to the monotonous noise of the Chinese, and hence, as Bowring declares, comes their preference for pleasure and polygamy." "The natives themselves [in Ceylon] are uncommonly fond of their music, and even prefer it to ours ['], which they say they do not understand." "Land quotes several [Javanese] orchestral compositions, but grants that it is impossible to reproduce all their *fioriture*. This seems to be the fate of all 'natural' music which happens to be reduced to writing in the modern notation; all the most important peculiarities are immediately lost. Mr. Lay experienced this when traveling in China, for he noticed that all original tunes lost a great deal of their beauty when played on the violin, and the same has been remarked by others."

In that same year, 1893, Francis Taylor Piggott published a different kind of work, *The Music and Musical Instruments of Japan* (London: B. T. Batsford), the first chapter of which discusses the basic problem of notation foreshadowed in the quotation from Wallaschek.

> If I say that Japanese music does not lack some reflex of the national grace, that it has some prettily quaint flashes of melody which strike the most inattentive listener at a tea-house festival, that it has some curious phrase-repetitions which seem to the attentive listener to indicate the possible existence of a science of construction, and that generally it is not altogether a concourse of weird sounds, it will appear

to many that I have not merely stated, but have overstated, the case in its favor.

. . .

Let us deal, then, with the music of this far-oriental people such as we find it I feel, however, both considerable difficulty and diffidence in laying the results of my investigations before my readers. An opinion, which I do in fact hold, that the case in favor of Japanese music may be put much higher than I have ventured to do in my first sentence, should, for full weight to be given to it, be supported by a far wider range of examples than it is possible to give at present. The only completeness at which it was possible to aim was in the investigation of the rudiments. To the many beauties, and to the great merits, of the structure which has been raised upon them, only my own ears can bear witness.

The difficulties which stand in the way of reducing the music into Western written forms are so great, that, unless Japanese musicians will come and play to us here in England, accurate knowledge of their art, due appreciation of their craft, can only come into being in the West very gradually. . . . We shall never hear it at its best until the deft fingers of the native musicians weave their spells for us. Much of the charm of the music, all its individuality, nearly, depend upon its graceful and delicate phrasing· and though I think that Western notation is capable of expressing these phrases to one who has already heard them, I feel a little uncertain whether their more complicated forms could be set down in it with sufficient accuracy to enable a stranger to interpret them satisfactorily.

These examples have been chosen from representative works devoted entirely or at least substantially to observations about music. The subjective prejudice apparent in all the writers except Day and Piggott is typical of the attitude encountered in travelogs and odysseys published in abundance during the nineteenth century. In spite of the lack of objectivity these excerpts support the two precepts mentioned earlier, namely, that non-Western music must be studied in terms of itself and within the context of its society.

The constant association of music with the ceremonies that accompany the crisis events of life, and the emotional and sometimes intellectual involvements of a given society with its music, suggests that ethnomusicology must rely on the collaborative efforts of the musicologist, the anthropologist, the ethnologist, the linguist, the psychologist, and the historian. And by the end of the nineteenth century it had become evident that sounds that did not fit the notation conceived and developed in the Western world represented a basic problem requiring the help of the physicist and the acoustician.

In 1884 the British mathematician and philologist Alexander John Ellis, whose primary interest was phonetics, presented a paper entitled "Tonometrical Observations on Some Existing Non-Harmonic Scales" (*Proceedings of the Royal Society*). This study and the enlarged revision published the following year, "On the Musical Scales of Various Nations," (*Journal of the Society of Arts*), earned for him the designation "Father of ethnomusicology." Ellis, who was tone-deaf, enlisted in his investigations the help of his contemporary, Alfred James Hipkins. In a summary of their findings Ellis states: "The final conclusion is that the Musical Scale is not one, not 'natural,' nor even founded necessarily on the laws of the constitution of musical sound so beautifully worked out by Helmholtz, but very diverse, very artificial, and very capricious."

His work demonstrated to the European musicologist that there exist tuning systems and scales that are built on entirely different principles from those employed in the West and that are accepted by accustomed ears as normal and logical. Ellis also developed a method for representing intervals between pitches in non-Western music, so that they could be readily compared to the familiar tempered tuning system of the West.

In 1890 the American archaeologist and ethnologist J. W. Fewkes made an important advance by using the recently developed phonograph to record the music of the Zuni Indians. He was assisted in the transcription and study of his recordings by Benjamin Ives Gilman, who in 1891 published an article on "Zuni Melodies" (*Journal of American Ethnology and Archaeology*), in which he confidently asserts that "a collection of phonographic cylinders like that obtained by Dr. Fewkes forms a permanent music museum of primitive music, of which the specimens are comparable, in fidelity of reproduction and for convenience of study, to casts or photographs of sculpture or painting."

Thus by the end of the nineteenth century two essential developments—the phonograph and a convenient method of tonometric comparison—gave promise that the study of non-Western music could proceed on an objective basis.

The oldest established phonogram archives began in the United States and collections now at the Library of Congress and numerous major universities throughout the country comprise, in Gilman's term, a gigantic "museum." An excellent collection of Canadian and Eskimo materials, assembled by the ethnomusicologist Marius Barbeau, is housed in the National Museum at Ottawa. The oldest European archive was established in Vienna around 1900 and somewhat later a rich archive was developed in Berlin. During World War II the valuable collection at Berlin was dispersed and at present less than one-fifth of the material has been recovered. The remainder is presumed to be in Russian hands. Within the last two decades other European and non-European countries, as well as Mexico and some of the countries of Latin America, have begun the establishment of significant archives.

An important center of study was developed in the last part of the nineteenth century by the German physiologist and psychologist Carl Stumpf. In 1902, in collaboration with Dr. Otto Abraham, Stumpf made the first German recordings of non-Western music—prompted by a visit to Berlin of the Siamese Court Orchestra. Through the dynamic energy of a pupil and younger friend, Eric M. von Hornbostel, the Berlin archives rapidly grew to the finest and best organized in all of Europe. Hornbostel was a psychologist who, often aided in his study by the physician Otto Abraham (who was particularly interested in the physiology of music), studied a wide range of musical styles from the non-Western world. The German school that formed itself around this brilliant leader concentrated its efforts on a study of tuning systems, scales, and instrumental measurements, and evolved a number of speculative theories on the possible origins of music. Most of the outstanding work accomplished by this group was based on museum studies of materials that had been deposited in the archive by anthropologists working in the field. Two of Hornbostel's outstanding students, Mieczyslaw Kolinski and George Herzog, later came to America, where Herzog was to have a profound influence on American scholars.

In contrast to the German concentration on the acoustics, psychology, and physiology of non-Western music comparative musicology in America was carried on primarily by anthropologists specializing in the culture of the American Indian. Between the German and American orientations, the two basic precepts of ethnomusicology were potentially represented: the German scholars were oriented toward a study of music in terms of itself, although they labored under the handicap of little contact with actual fieldwork; the American scholars, by virtue of their training, were interested in music within the context of its culture but de-emphasized purely musical considerations. Franz Boaz, a leading American anthropologist, recognized the importance of music as an invaluable aspect of cultural studies, and urged his pupils to record and transcribe melodies associated with rituals and ceremonies that they observed. One of these pupils was George Herzog, who published an article in 1928 ("The Yuman Musical Style," *Journal of American Folklore*) introducing Hornbostel's methods. His background, which includes training in linguistics and folklore, has made him one of the outstanding figures in ethnomusicology. Another whose reputation is well known as a collector and transcriber is Frances Densmore. Working primarily with the North American Indians, she collected and transcribed more than two thousand melodies, and her works, beginning as early as 1906 and continuing through 1957, form an important body of material. Helen Roberts, who published monographs and articles from 1918 through 1955, has made detailed musical studies of the Eskimos, Oceania, ancient Hawaii, the North American Indian, and the American Negro. These scholars, along with Fewkes, Gilman, and Metfessel (who will be discussed presently), represent most of the serious, early pioneers of ethnomusicology in America.

In 1936 Herzog made a survey of the work accomplished in America; this study was divided into two parts, "Primitive Music" (American Indian) and "Folk Music," and was published in the *Bulletin of the American Council of Learned Societies.* In his foreword he states: "The growing interest in primitive music and folk music all over the world indicates that the arts of the 'primitive' and the 'folk' have a heightened significance for our present-day culture." He suggests that this interest is stronger in the United States than elsewhere, but then continues with a rather discouraging summary:

Unfortunately, much remains to be desired from the efforts to guide and satisfy this interest. Lack of training, of proper technic, and of coordination has caused the waste of much energy in duplicating labor, while certain aspects of the study remain neglected. Much work is lavished on problems that might be better formulated or on material which is not beyond criticism. A good deal of work is so amateurish that the results are useless to the scientist, misleading for the public. Considering the amount of undirected effort and the lack of cooperation between the various interests involved—anthropological, historical, musical, etc.—it has seemed that a general survey of the field, such as is here attempted, might facilitate future efforts.

The next year, 1937, Herzog's "Musical Typology in Folk-song" (*Southern Folklore Quarterly*) sharply criticized both American and European publications of folk music in transcription:

> The nature of the drawback of formulistic representations becomes more apparent as one grows increasingly aware that most folk music material published in Western Europe and in the United States has in many respects become falsified while it is being heard, written down, and edited. We only begin to realize, through the help of objective phonograph records, that certain subtle elements in folk music, such as ornamentation, manner of singing, and so-called liberties of rhythm and intonation, are significant. Consequently, musical notation seems a very unsatisfactory means of recording and communicating a melody

A few publications appeared sporadically through the next decade or so, but as late as 1954 the American musicologist Manfred Bukofzer pointed out—in a communication addressed to the Cercle International d'Etudes Ethnomusicologiques, meeting in Belgium—that "only relatively few scholars have seen the need so far for entering the difficult

231

and seemingly remote field of anthropological musicology although the second World War and recent political events have suddenly brought into focus its immense practical importance." The communication from Bukofzer, who had been unable to attend the meeting, was later published as "Observations on the Study of Non-Western Music" in *Les Colloques de Wegimont* (Brussels: Elsevier, 1956). In this essay, Bukofzer underscored some of the problems suggested by Herzog almost twenty years earlier and, as the following paragraphs show, emphasized fundamental problems that still had not been solved.

Non-western music presents a great number of difficult problems differing radically from those normally encountered in musicology. The basic musical concepts in oriental music have almost nothing in common with those of the West and as a result Westerners cannot directly understand the music of the East and vice versa. The anthropological branch of musicology is attempting to collect the various musics of the world and derive from them new concepts for a proper evaluation. A comparison of the western and the non-western concepts will ultimately give musicology a truly world-wide perspective,—a perspective which is the goal of our study.

We are as yet very far from this ideal. The gathering of non-western music has only just begun and we have as yet but a sampling of the musics of the world They can be recorded properly only by means of phonograph, recording tape and sound film because they cannot be written down in our limited notation. The situation is aggravated by the paradoxical fact that phonograph and radio are destroying the native musical cultures at a pace more rapid than the same means can record them.

. . .

We still have to learn the important lesson that the nature of non-western music calls for specific research methods of its own. Due allowance must be made for the difference between western and non-western types of music. A thematic analysis appropriate for Beethoven quartets is not even valid for the music of Ockeghem, let alone for a comparative analysis of primitive melodies. It would be simple indeed to show that a Scottish folksong and a Chinese melody make use of the same scale, if not even the same melodic contour. But as we know, this would be an irrelevant observation based on our notation. The real difference can only be heard in actual performance. It is not the abstract scale that is essential in this case but the tone colour and style of performance,—precisely those features which resist notation.

It is one of the most urgent tasks of the study of non-western music to develop a method that permits clear reference to and comparison of the various forms of tone colour, attack, performance, and the like . . . So long as we lack the elementary tools we cannot hope to cope with the larger problems that a more profound study of non-western music is continually unfolding before us

To these warranted criticisms of a new and developing field of study I will add two basic observations: (1) a premature concern with the comparison of different musics has resulted in an accumulation of broad generalities and oversimplifications; (2) the underlying premise which supports all types of musical training in the European art tradition—namely, the actual performance of music by the student, no matter whether his ultimate goal be that of teacher, composer, performer, or scholar—has been too long ignored in the training of specialists in non-Western music

In connection with the first observation it seems a bit foolish in retrospection that the pioneers of our field became engrossed in the comparison of different musics before any real understanding of the musics being compared had been achieved. In connection with the second observation I refer to a statement made by one of the few ethnomusicologists

233

who acquired a performing knowledge of the music of his specialty. In 1934 Percival R. Kirby stated in the preface of his book on African music, *The Musical Instruments of the Native Races of South Africa* (2nd printing, Johannesburg, 1953): "On . . . expeditions I frequently lived in native kraals, and participated in the musical performances of the people, the only way, in my opinion, for a European observer to learn and understand the principles underlying native music."

All of these considerations force me to conclude that almost all of the so-called standard references in ethnomusicology, aside from some descriptive value, must be largely discounted in their analytical and comparative conclusions, based as they are on oversimplifications, generalities, compounded inaccuracies, and primitive methodology. Until the problems discussed in the following pages are taken seriously, Bukofzer's hope—that "a comparison of the western and non-western concepts will ultimately give musicology a truly world-wide perspective"—will not be realized.

Recently it has been suggested that the prefix *ethno-* is an unnecessary designation, and that any music is the rightful concern of musicology. Although this line of reasoning may eventually prevail—and although terminology in itself is relatively unimportant—the coexistence of two types of musicology demands some justification and explanation.

In his *Introduction to Musicology* (1941) Glen Haydon questions the aptness of the term *comparative musicology* and points out that the comparative method is one used in all branches of inquiry and that, conversely, the field of so-called comparative musicology must also depend on descriptive, analytical, experimental, speculative, and historical method to reach valid results. (Along the same line of reasoning one might question the appropriateness of the term *historical musicology*.) He says: "In fact, from a certain viewpoint, what we, as members of Western European culture, regard as the field of musicology, may be only one division of musicology conceived on a world-wide basis. Such a view is maintained by Charles Seeger."

Seeger's many publications, beginning in 1923 and continuing through the present, are concerned with the very bases of musical thought. As one of the founders of every international organization devoted to the subject of music, a charter member of the American Musicological Society, and the founder of the Music Division of the Pan American Union, Seeger has managed a more comprehensive view of the total requirements of the field of musicology than any other American scholar.

The need for a comprehensive, world-wide perspective, exemplified by Seeger, has received little recognition, even though, as Haydon points out, some early writers in the field of Western musicology did lay considerable stress on the importance of a discussion of extra-European and pre-Greek musical systems. Ambros (*Geschichte der Musik*, Breslau, 1862-82) devotes most of the first volume of his history of music to this subject, and Fétis (*L'Histoire générale de la musique* . . . , Paris, 1869-76) has almost three volumes devoted to similar subjects. Later, however, Hugo Riemann (*Handbuch der Musikgeschichte*, Leipzig, 1904-13) begins with the music of the Greeks, suggesting that other subjects should be the concern of comparative musicology. Nef (*An Outline of the History of Music*, New York, 1935) contents himself with a few pages given to the subject of origins and pre-Greek music, while Guido Adler (*Handbuch der Musikgeschichte*, Berlin, 1930) wisely asked Robert Lach, an excellent German comparative musicologist, to write his opening chapter. Finally, Hugo Leichtentritt (*Music, History, and Ideas*, Cambridge, 1947), although he believes that the history of music should actually begin with the music of the

Christian church in the later Middle Ages, does allow a chapter for the discussion of Greek music.

A notable crosscurrent to this accelerating notion of separating Western and non-Western fields of musical inquiry was provided by the work of Curt Sachs. This art historian and organologist collaborated with Hornbostel in devising a system of classification for musical instruments based on an earlier study by Mahillon. A recent article, "Primitive and Medieval Music" (*JAMS*, 1960), demonstrated that some of the living musical practices of the non-Western world afford considerable insight into the musical practices of our own Western past:

> Practically, we have no direct knowledge of secular music in the early Middle Ages before the advent of the *troubadours*. We studied later music preserved in an incomplete and doubtful notation and projected it backwards upon the earlier Middle Ages
>
> In this backward projection, in itself permissible, we overshot the mark; we took for granted that the early Middle Ages, being European, sounded like today's music, with the same singing technique, the same well-tempered intervals and the same habits of performance.
>
> When we finally realized that there is no proof and not even the slightest probability of similar voice placing, similar principles of performance, or similar intervals, except at best the three perfect consonances [in the present writer's experience with many types of Oriental music, even these are in doubt], then the gate is open for a re-evaluation This amounts to overcoming our prejudice and realizing that every facet in the oldest written music of secular Europe has its parallels in primitive music—melodic organization, structure, rhythm, polyphony Finally—and this is the most decisive fact—the two realms of music are non-literate. All history that relies on written sources alone is incomplete and of necessity misleading.

236

Still another important counteraction to the separation of West and non-West came in the form of a Report of the AMS Committee on Graduate Studies in musicology (1955). After eight years of deliberation this distinguished group of musicologists included non-Western music as part of their recommendations: "This period of graduate work . . . should include musical analysis, a thorough study of general music history, some acquaintance with musical cultures other than our own. . . ." This recommendation from such an important committee caught the major universities in the United States in an embarrassing position. Faculties already assembled were trained exclusively in the tradition of Western cultivated music. The only two institutions with programs of training in the study of non-Western music were the University of Indiana, where George Herzog had developed a program in the Department of Anthropology and Folklore, and the University of California, Los Angeles, where I had amplified existing courses initiated by Laurence Petran in the Department of Music.

The disposition of these two programs within the structure of a major university—one oriented toward anthropology and folklore, the other toward music—symbolizes a persistent problem in the assessment of a field like ethnomusicology. We might ask whether the student of ethnomusicology would be better equipped with primary training in anthropology (leading to musico-ethnology?) or in musicology. The *primary* field of training is not the important question, but rather the *final* training. The University of Indiana (George List in Music), UCLA (Mantle Hood, Boris Kremenliev in Music), Northwestern University (Alan Merriam in Anthropology), Wesleyan University in Connecticut (David McAllester in Anthropology and Robert Brown in Music), the University of Michigan (William P. Malm in Music), the University of Pennsylvania (Harold Powers in Music), and

237

the University of Illinois (Willem Adriaansz in Music) are training students whose undergraduate degrees may be in anthropology or music or, more often, a major-minor combination of the two.

To fulfill the obligations of his field, the ethnomusicologist must be prepared to undertake an unusually long and diversified training, including extended fieldwork. The necessity for such breadth of training in ethnomusicology seems to reinforce the viewpoint that the two types of musicology are perhaps wisely separate fields. There is, however, a discernible trend toward unity, indeed toward an even broader scope. During the recent Congress of the International Musicological Society in New York City (September 1961), the inclusion of a symposium on "Acculturation" and more especially one entitled "The Contributions of Ethnomusicology to Historical Musicology" was a significant indicator of possible future developments. In a number of publications, Charles Seeger has pointed out that many of the conditions that obtain in the proper study and approach to the music of the non-Western world apply with equal force to the study of Western music Sometimes he has spoken of the need for an "ethnomusicology of Western European art music." Such a phrase recalls the words of Kinkeldey, the forecast of Strunk, and the belief that the prefix *ethno-* may be in a state of dissolution.

Although in the course of the following sections of this essay, the reader may form his own conclusions, I might point out at this time that the music of our own past, prior to the development of the phonograph, can be studied only through the printed page or manuscript, which for correct interpretation ultimately depends on the oral tradition that supported it. Even that most familiar of all music, the music of the nineteenth century, is subject to the widest interpretation in performance. It is only fairly recently through the diligent efforts of musicologists that music of the eighteenth century may now begin to approximate the kind of performance it received during the time of Bach. It would not appear improbable that the dual responsibility of the ethnomusicologist —the study of music in terms of itself and within the context of its society—could be profitably applied to the study of any music.

2

IN TERMS OF ITSELF

In the mid-twentieth century the impact of technology and cataclysmic changes in political complexion are altering and sometimes destroying the musical cultures of many parts of the world. Therefore, it becomes an urgent responsibility on the part of the ethnomusicologist to define succinctly his problems in field and laboratory method before it is too late. He will need the help of his colleagues in the various sciences in modernizing methodology and developing scientific instrumentation worthy of an electronic age.

One of the basic precepts of ethnomusicology—*the study of music in terms of itself*—represents a challenge the very nature of which is insufficiently understood.

A few years ago the director of the Cairo Opera House told me that the opera season, opening appropriately with *Aida,* was usually sold out in advance. He said that audiences were made up of individuals who had received a European education. When I learned that the general public did not attend, I ventured the opinion that they stayed away because they did not like the European female singing voice. Genuinely surprised, he agreed that this was so and asked how I had come to know Egyptian taste.

Western audiences on first exposure to the various types of Oriental singing voice are inclined to say that the singing is thin, uneven in quality throughout its register, has no brilliance or carrying power, and may be summed up by the adjective *nasal.* The singing voice trained in the European tradition, on the other hand, is likely to offend the Eastern ear by (what seems to be) an extremely wide vibrato, an embarrassing dynamic range, and an exaggerated and unabashed opening of the mouth. From the Eastern point of view, the opera star in the European tradition wobbles about in an uncertain fashion (vibrato), absorbing in this wavy fluctuation of pitch the microtonal subtleties that in the Orient are synonymous with first-rate musicality. The control of a modest dynamic range as well as the practice sometimes encountered of averting the face while singing or shielding the mouth from view with a handkerchief may be further marks of refinement. Sometimes one hears all varieties of Oriental voices described as nasal, African voices as open or throaty, and the Spanish voice as hard. *Nasal, throaty,* and *hard* are not, of course, musical terms of reference, nor does any descriptive adjective allow for the great variety of voice qualities encountered in any one country or geographic area. The accustomed ear will readily distinguish the singing voice of Thailand from that of central Java, the traditional Japanese voice from that of the singer in India, the Persian vocalist from the Spanish singer of *cante jondo.* Gross similarities such as the usage of microtonal inflections and the reservation of vibrato for ornamental devices do not account for the many differences in voice quality and singing style that readily identify and characterize the individual tradition.

It was suggested at the close of Chapter 1 that even the study of European art music may proceed with certainty only if it is applied to that music with which we are intimately familiar, the music of which we are the carriers. The musical practices in Western tradition prior to the development of the phonograph exist today in the form of notes on a printed page or manuscript supported by the writings of theorists. These two sources, sometimes aided by a careful study of the musical instruments typical of a particular style period, provide the principal support for the musicologist who attempts to produce reliable modern editions. The extent

FIG. 5. Visiting Balinese musicians from Tabanan join UCLA students at the gamelan. Photograph by Mantle Hood.

to which a theorist has been objective in his writings, reflecting accurately the spirit of his times, may be difficult to determine. Since the musicologist is the inheritor of Western tradition, it is unlikely that he will be free from the prejudice of his heritage. In the study of non-Western music—as is evident in the excerpts from writers as early as Piggott and Day—objectivity is a *sine qua non* for the ethnomusicologist. If he is to communicate his findings, he must be first a thoroughly trained musician in the Western tradition. And it is a matter of record that the Western musician and even the Western layman (whose ears are inclined to be less prejudiced than those of the specialist) will, in spite of himself, "correct" unfamiliar intervals until they fit the nearest Western equivalent.

The solution to this problem of "objective hearing," as it has been worked out in the program of training at UCLA, rests on a simple premise—one which has long been applied to training musicians in the European tradition. In the education of a young Western musician—whether his ultimate objective be that of a performer, composer, theoretician, educator, or musicologist—his schooling begins with a course called Musicianship or Fundamentals of Music or Solfeggio, which includes sight singing, dictation, ear training, and performance. We have applied this principle in the training of an ethnomusicologist at UCLA, believing that a sufficient exposure to the live sounds of non-Western music and the challenge of producing the correct intonation or pitches with the voice or on stringed instruments or woodwinds will develop a musician with truly unprejudiced ears. Twelve different performing groups in non-Western music have included a complete Javanese gamelan (a total of forty-five instrumentalists and singers), a Balinese gamelan (thirty performers), a Balinese gendèr wajang quartet (in 1961 these three groups recorded two LP albums for Columbia Masterworks), a Japanese Gagaku ensemble (sixteen players), Japanese naga-uta (which accompanies the Kabuki drama), a Philippine kulintang, and groups of various size that perform the music of India, Iran, Thailand, China, and the folk music of Mexico and Greece. Altogether there are about one hundred students participating in these activities and of that number approximately half are general university students majoring in fields other than music; about half of the participating music majors are specializing in the field of ethnomusicology. Each performing group is under the direction of a skilled non-Western musician or American musician who has spent at least two years in practical training in the subject country. (See Fig. 5.)

The student participating in the program is encouraged to acquire a basic skill in each of the four large instrumental families—the chordophones (the string family), the idiophones (gongs, xylophones, and other types of percussive instruments), the aerophones (the wind family), and the membranophones (the drum family)—distributed among several different types of non-Western music. He is also expected to learn one or two vocal styles. This preparation, with his formal course work and seminars, enables him to go to the field to investigate an unknown music with highly discriminating ears, responsive hands, and a sincere respect and admiration for the finesse of a strange musical language. After spending two years in the field, advanced students return to participate in seminars with their instructors more on the level of colleagues than in a student-professor relationship.

The program is designed so that young non-Western musicians and American musicians may work together in an atmosphere of cultural exchange, each profiting from the experience and knowledge of the other. The past seven years have shown that persons involved in the program achieve a rare objectivity in their comprehension of the various musical cultures of the world and consequently are able to understand the unique value of their own musical heritage.

Recently, in a seminar of advanced students and instructors in the program, a curious question suggested itself· "What, precisely, is a musical language?" Many years ago linguists asked this fundamental question in relation to the spoken language and, although it has not been finally resolved to anyone's complete satisfaction, the constant search for an answer has nonetheless accelerated the development of precise descriptive and analytical methodology. May we speak of a family of musical languages, of brothers and half-brothers, of first cousins and distant cousins? Shall we find that there are root languages in music and dialects and chains of dialects? It is embarrassing to the whole field of musicol-

PLATE 1. An engraving from Solvyns' *Les Hindôus* (Paris, 1808-10) showing an Indian musician playing the soorna.

PLATE 2.
Another engraving from *Les Hindôus* showing a performance by Nautch dancers.

ogy, in my opinion, that these questions are only now being asked. But in defense of my colleagues in Western musicology, I might point out that there is an essential difference between a consideration of *music* in the Western tradition and a consideration of *musics* in their diverse Eastern traditions.

Through the early influence of the medieval church, art music has been reasonably unified in the countries of western Europe for many centuries. One readily distinguishes certain national characteristics and traits, but the great corpus of musical material in the western European tradition is characterized by a unity of expression lacking in the non-Western world. The same basic tuning systems, the same families of instruments aggregated in various ensembles, the interchange of poetic texts from one country to another, and the influence and counterinfluence of regional and national styles have produced, in the larger sense, a unified mode of musical expression in the Western tradition. In the music of the non-Western world and to some extent in the folk music of western Europe and the Americas, regional and even local differences exist in fundamental conception. As Glen Haydon has said, the tendency among historians of Western music to ignore non-Western and pre-Grecian and even Grecian musical cultures is evidence of the increasing narrowness of interest of the musicologist. As at one time in the field of linguistics all languages were evaluated in terms of Latin and Greek, so in the field of music the Western tongue, if the problem is considered at all, has been regarded as *the* language of music against which all others are logically evaluated. It is not too surprising, therefore, that my colleagues in Western musicology have not seriously asked "What is a musical language?"—much less the consequent question "How many musical languages are there in the world?"

245

In the fall of 1958, the International Music Council of UNESCO held a conference at the new UNESCO headquarters in Paris. Representatives of both Western and non-Western musical cultures participated. I had just returned from almost two years of study in Indonesia and was, therefore, particularly sensitive to the reaction of non-Western peoples to Western attitudes. It was disquieting to realize that among the Western musicologists participating, a good many were still in the Latin-and-Greek posture of the linguists before the linguistic revolution started by Bloomfield in 1926. The unconscious condescension that typified a number of papers read reached something of an apex in a proposal put forth that would, in effect, hand to the non-Western musicians an arbitrarily conceived tempered tuning system as a kind of lingua franca in which they could communicate with one another and perhaps eventually with the West. From the Eastern point of view, such a suggestion is as odious as a recommendation that the classics of Indian and Chinese literature, for example, be rewritten in Esperanto. In retrospect it seems strange that even at this conference no one asked the fundamental question, "What indeed is a musical language?"

With this question in mind I offered a special seminar during the spring semester of 1961 under the aegis of the Institute of Ethnomusicology at UCLA. This seminar, regularly given in the Department of Music under the title "Musical Instruments of the World," was reorganized to accommodate a greater scope. I was assisted by three other professors: Charles Seeger (Consultant in Musicology in the Institute of Ethnomusicology), William Bright (a linguist in the Department of Anthropology), and William Hutchinson (a member of the Music Department specializing in experiential psychology). Collectively, faculty and students represented extensive field experience in the musical cultures of Japan, the Philippines, Indonesia, Australia, Thailand, India, Iran, Turkey, Greece, and Mexico.

After a few weeks spent in reviewing the basic properties of the instrumental families distributed through the world, individual members of the seminar discussed the principal musical instruments of the culture in which they were specializing and illustrated their remarks by live demonstration and by tape recordings. Special emphasis was placed on the characteristic idiom of a given instrument in relation to the typical musical expression of the society. This *modus operandi* provided a focal point throughout the semester for a number of far larger questions. What are the essential features of a musical language? What fundamental and/or detailed attributes distinguish this musical language from another? To what extent is the quality of sound itself an identifying factor? Can we define and describe a musical language in terms of the relative balance or imbalance of the three basic elements of music: rhythm, melody, and harmony? Are we to account for the notable difference between the music of southern and northern Greece, for example, in terms of two dialects of the same language or half-brothers in the family of languages? What relationship is involved when we speak of the Turkish elements in Greek folk music? In what relationship does Persian music extend to the cultivated music of India? Sweeping from the western tip of Java to the eastern shores of Bali, are we confronted by a chain of dialects? How do these relate to the music of Thailand or the kulintang of the south Philippines?

It soon became apparent that there were questions to be asked that were even more fundamental. How critical are the refinements of tuning systems, and how does tuning system relate to scale? How are we to define mode on a world-wide basis? Can the concept of tonality and key be entertained if there is no clear tonic? What are the lines of distinction among melodic pattern, melody types and variants? What is the relationship between vocal and instrumental practice and how important does this become in the determination of a musical language? To what extent are rhythm, melody, and the quality of sound influenced by and perhaps even dependent on the spoken language?

Gradually it emerged that a sharp distinction had to be drawn between two orders of information necessary to these questions: (a) the pure physics of sound determined in the laboratory and (b) the conceptual or "musical" aspects of sound.

The tools of the ethnomusicologist used in the laboratory have lagged far behind the scientific instrumentation characteristic of an electronic age, although there are, of course, instruments that have been significantly useful. One such laboratory instrument essential to the study of tuning systems and scales is the Stroboconn, which in the measurement of pitch holds to an accuracy of 0.01 of a European semitone. A panoramic sonic analyzer is also valuable for studies of the quality of sound as it is represented on an oscilloscope and photographed by a polaroid camera. The most important instrument, the tape recorder, has been developed commercially to a high standard of performance; however, the particular demands of the fieldworker require the potentiality of multichannel recording on a relatively small and compact machine powered by an easily replenished battery supply. His particular requirements can be met only by very costly equipment especially designed and built to meet his individual needs. In anticipation of laboratory studies and analysis, the fieldworker recording the music of the African Bushmen for example, faces a different problem from the man who is interested in the large marimba bands of Mozambique.

The modification of existing scientific instrumentation has been successfully applied to the problems encountered

in notating and transcribing an important type of Balinese
music. In order to make an intensive study of the music literature of the gendèr wajang quartet, which in Bali accompanies the all-night shadow plays, it is necessary to notate the
entire repertory of at least three different quartets in south
Bali and three in north Bali. The gendèr has ten bronze slabs
that are resonated by bamboo tubes and that are struck with
two wooden beaters. The instrumental timbre of the four
instruments is the same, and the musical parts they play are
often of an interlocking or "shared" type of pattern. These
conditions make it impossible to transcribe the musical pieces
as recorded on tape. To transcribe all the parts in the standard
method of notation in the field would require many, many
months of concentrated work.

An operation or event recorder, a kind of graphic instrument sometimes seen at the edge of a busy street recording
the number of passing automobiles, was wired to operate
from batteries, so that contact between the copper foil wound
around the wooden beaters and the bronze keys closes a sole-
noid that actuates an inked pen on moving graph paper. This
simple adaptation makes possible the instantaneous notation
of the musical repertory as it is being played and yields a
transcription adequate for analysis.

One of the thorniest problems that persist in the field of
ethnomusicology is the search for an accurate and at the same
time practical type of notation in transcribing the music of
non-Western cultures. For many years in the field of dance,
"stick figures" representing the movements of the human
body and abstract footprints or a succession of X's or some
other symbolic representation were used as a kind of primitive notation of dance movement. Finally, a highly complex
set of symbols that could be combined to show precisely
every movement of the dancer—no matter how small the
details—was developed by Rudolf Laban. Labanotation and

some modifications of this system give the choreographer and the research scholar in comparative dance a notation far superior to any currently in usage in the field of music.

There are many forms of music notation in use throughout the world of musical cultures and, although they vary widely in their essential efficiency, it is not surprising to discover that each has been developed to accommodate the specific requirements of the culture by which it is used. Notation for the Chinese chin, for example, is based on the ideograms of the written language, and essential parts of different ideograms are combined into a form of tablature that reads vertically and from right to left. This notation achieves a surprising economy with one composite symbol describing the proper string, direction of stroke, and particular finger of the right hand; the correct point of stopping the string, the proper finger of the left hand; and sometimes ancillary techniques such as harmonics, or "left-hand plucking." (See Fig. 6.)

In central Java, although the musicians do not play from written music, they have developed a number of types of notation that preserve a record of the principal melodies played by the large gamelan orchestras. The most efficient type—known as "checkered script" or kraton (royal court) notation—appears to be one of the most efficient types of notation found in the world of music. Six or seven vertical lines represent the pitches of either of two different tuning systems. Horizontal lines crossing these vertical pitch lines represent basic pulsations of time, and every fourth one of these horizontal lines is made heavier so that it serves as a kind of fourth beat and barline simultaneously. Dots placed at intersections of the vertical and horizontal lines therefore indicate both pitch and, as one scans the vertical staff, time. Special symbols placed to the left of the vertical score indicate the structurally important occurrence of different gongs;

symbols shown to the right of the staff represent the basic drum patterns. Sometimes additional symbols are used and a few indications in the written language determine sections, number of repetitions, etc. (See Fig. 7.)

The music notation of non-Western melodies before the advent of the phonograph was not only handicapped by the prejudiced ears of the transcriber but also by the artificial conditions under which the performer had to work. Only through endless repetitions could the transcriber finally set down in Western notation an approximate record of the song. The intermittent stopping and starting on the part of the performer naturally interfered with the normal performance practice. Even though Fewkes, the pioneer in recording non-Western music, was working with primitive equipment, he had the foresight to record as many versions of songs as possible. Later, when these were transcribed by Gilman, a careful report of the margin of error in the equipment was given; but beyond these notes of mechanical deviation, no diacritical markings other than accents were added to the notation. In Germany both Hornbostel and Stumpf advocated the notation of only the important line of a melody in the belief that microtonal deviations in pitch and florid melodic embellishments would tend to obscure the principal flow of the tune. Even after the introduction of the phonograph, we find that a number of investigators paid little attention to the refinements and subtleties of the melody. George Herzog, on the other hand, stressed the importance of highly detailed notation, a form that perhaps reached its greatest realization in the transcriptions made by Béla Bartók.

Bearing in mind Wallaschek's concern that Chinese melodies played on the violin lose "a great deal of their beauty" or Piggott's concern that Japanese melodies could not be notated in sufficient detail to reflect their true character, we must return to the observation that any written notation in

高山

其一

其二

其三

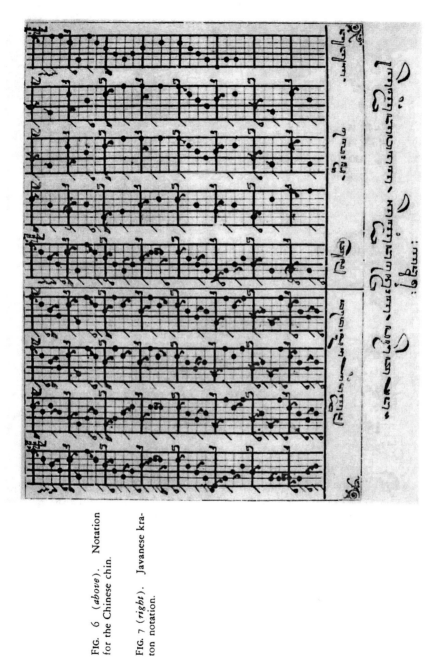

FIG. 6 (*above*). Notation for the Chinese chin.

FIG. 7 (*right*). Javanese kraton notation.

any musical culture is dependent for its accurate interpretation on the oral tradition that supports it. If the finesse of a musical language is accomplished through the details of its expression, these details must be noted accurately if the true character of the musical language is to be ascertained; detailed notation need not obscure the structural or important flow of the melody. These two extreme requirements of notation serve different purposes, depending on the users or readers for whom it is intended (see Chapter 4). Herzog and others introduced a number of diacritical additions to Western notation in order to achieve detailed accuracy. Unfortunately this requires the person reading such notation to forget the standard reference of the Western musical staff and the notes placed on it and to imagine the degree of deflection that the diacritical annotation represents.

In 1928 Milton Metfessel published *Phonophotography in Folk Music* (University of North Carolina), the first serious attempt to notate a given music (American Negro songs) strictly *in terms of itself*. The American psychologist Carl E. Seashore wrote a brief introductory summary of the scientific treatment of music in the Iowa laboratory for the psychology of music and speech. Early in his text Metfessel points out:

> This study describes music as it has never been described before. Many of the traditional terms of music have been scrapped, and new ones introduced. This is a serious disadvantage from the standpoint of the non-technical reader, but there has been no other way out. If there is a new concept, there must be a new name, and there have been many new concepts.

> · · ·

> Students of folk singing are quite frank in agreeing with Odum and Johnson [collections published by the University of North Carolina Press, 1925-26, and the Viking Press,

1925-26, respectively] that notating songs by ear is insufficient to indicate many allusive facts of folk music. Much of
the charm and distinctiveness of the singing Negroes lies in
queer pranks of their voices, but these twists and turns occur
too quickly. One seeking to analyze them or find out anything about them is only bewildered. As a consequence,
valuable detail and necessary accuracy have been lacking in
studies of folk music.

Metfessel demonstrates how a specially designed movie
camera can record a sound wave photograph that can subsequently be plotted and superimposed over a half-step musical
staff and finally summarized in a type of pattern notation.
In the course of his study he points out that the striking
difference in perception of musical sound by the human
ear varies according to conditioning.

> The same sound waves of Negro music affecting an Afri-
> can and a European musician create quite a different impres-
> sion. . . . In a subjective study of folk music there will
> never be a uniformity of description unless the musical talent
> and training of all students is the same. Only when musicians
> are confronted by an objective analysis of the sound waves
> in music will differences of opinion cease to exist as far as
> the factual problems are concerned. It is a disadvantage to
> be a trained, civilized musician in a solely subjective study of
> folk music.
>
> .   .   .
>
> Phonophotography, by laying the foundation for defini-
> tion of what a music is, by defining the terms used in music,
> by substituting objective experiments for opinions, and by
> the utilization of graphic and statistical methods, will assist
> in removing the uncertainties and prejudices that have per-
> vaded the study of folk music.

A few years later a different approach to graph notation
was undertaken by Charles Seeger. Beginning with his first

255

FIG. 8 (*above*). Charles Seeger operating the melograph.

FIG. 9 (*right*). Suenobi Togi, musician of the Imperial Household, Tokyo, demonstrating the Japanese hichiriki (oboe).

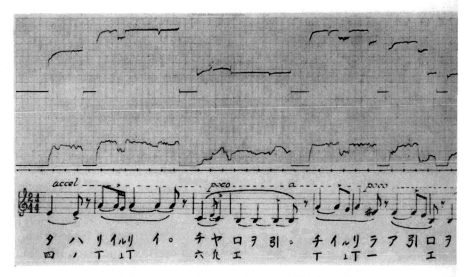

FIG. 10. A fragment of a part played on the Japanese hichiriki as automatically notated on the Seeger melograph. The upper half of the melogram shows the precise pitches and ornamental slides played, the lower half indicates the amplitude or loudness, and the evenly spaced markings at the bottom show one-second intervals at the rate of 10 mm. per second. The Western notation is a simplified transcription of the melogram. The lower line of Japanese characters represents fingering positions, and the upper line provides a syllabic key that modifies pitch, tone quality, and phrasing.

publication on this subject, "An Instantaneous Music Notator" (*Journal of the International Folk Music Council,* 1951), he has continued the development and refinement of a scientific instrument called the melograph. (See Figs. 8-10.) His method of graph notation seems to have several advantages over phonophotography: (1) the notation is instantaneous; (2) sensitivity to sound of the heated stylus recording on a special type of waxed graph paper can be controlled for as much or as little detail of the pitch line as desirable; (3) amplitude is reproduced by a separate stylus but on a graph moving in alignment with the pitch line; (4) a separate one-second time marker aids in the study of rhythm and tempo.

Currently preliminary engineering has been initiated that

promises an extremely important development of this machine. Continuous experimentation by Seeger and by myself over the past five years has demonstrated the great need for "seeing" in the graphic display of a melodic line the relative amplitudes of at least the first, second, and third partials that go to make up a sound. Thus far, a study of the partial structure of sound has been limited to isolated tones within a song. The melograph, which permits the continuous display of what the linguists refer to as "visible speech" (in this instance "visible sung-speech") as well as a graphic display of the total "partial structure" for purposes of spectrum analysis, will make it possible to determine to what extent, for example, the quality of sound itself is an important factor in a given musical language. Oriental cultures recognize many specific terms of reference for the qualities of musical sound. Laurence Picken, at a recent meeting of the International Folk Music Council (Quebec City, 1961), offered translations of an ancient Chinese musical dictionary that contained six terms for the sound of struck stone, six for jade, six for wood, etc.

In the speech laboratories the detailed analysis of sound has been termed *phonetics*. The objective in such methods disregards "meaning" in relation to the language. An interpretation of the data made available through phonetics and examined with reference to meaning in speech is termed *phonemics*. Both of these processes adjusted to the particular requirements of music would seem to be necessary to an objective study of non-Western music.

In "Language and Music," a paper read at the seventh conference of the Society for Ethnomusicology (Philadelphia, 1961), William Bright points to an important distinction to be made in comparing language and music:

> In seeking analogies between the content of music and that of language . . . it is necessary to distinguish two types of

content. The content of a sentence is in part derived from its associations outside of language—from the objects, actions, and relationships to which the sentence refers. But at the same time it also derives content from its linguistic structure—from the phonological and grammatical relationships between its parts, and between it and other sentences. The former type of content has been referred to as *exolinguistic,* and the latter as *endolinguistic.* In terms of this distinction, we may compare the content of music with the endolinguistic content of language. As Springer says, music "lacks 'dictionary' meaning" . . . ; a musical performance does not necessarily have any reference to specific non-musical phenomena. *Some* pieces of music within a given culture have, to be sure, extra-musical associations for the members of that culture; thus for us a military march may have content related to the emotion of patriotism But such content is not inherent in the nature of music, as exolinguistic content is inherent in the nature of language. In this respect music is especially similar to the language of poetry, which uses endolinguistic relationships of phonology (such as alliteration and rhyme) and of grammar (as in the Gongoristic style of Spanish verse) in a symbolic function, but without specific exolinguistic content. We may thus refer to the similar content structures found in music and in language with the term *endosemantic,* contrasting with the *exosemantic* structure which is an essential part of language but not of music. The existence of endosemantic structures in both systems suggests that both may yield to similar techniques of analysis— that basic units of one system may have analogues in the other system.

Techniques of analysis in the field of music are important to a consideration of musical style. And a proper understanding of stylistic analysis in the study of non-Western music is an interdependent consideration of music in society.

3

WITHIN THE CONTEXT

The flute of western New Guinea and the bull roarer used in initiation rites in the Congo are the exclusive property of men. The restriction is so severely enforced that if a woman catches sight of such an instrument accidentally she may be put to death. Among the Ila and Tonga tribes of East Africa certain songs are the personal property of either men or women. Each woman must have her repertory of impango songs, which she will sing at appropriate social gatherings in praise of her lover, her husband, or herself. Ziyabilo songs are composed, as one African writer has put it, "while men are still small boys." As he grows up, each boy will accumulate a modest repertory of these songs of manhood. At the time of death a mourning song known as a zitengulo is composed in honor of the deceased. The singer of the zitengulo, the wife or one of the relatives of the deceased, may show considerable emotion as she sings, but other relatives may not take the slightest notice of the song. This type of mourning song, functioning as a brief eulogy, is composed and sung only for such a specific occasion. (See further: A. M. Jones, *African Music in Northern Rhodesia and Some Other Places,* Rhodes-Livingstone Museum, 1949.)

A successful ethnomusicologist may have his primary training in either musicology or anthropology and, although he may strive to achieve a true balance by the end of his advanced training, one of the two disciplines usually receives more emphasis than the other. In a study of music within the context of its society, therefore, a characteristic attitude develops as a result of this emphasis.

The principal interest of the anthropologist is the behavior of man. Instrumental music, art objects, artifacts, song texts, folk tales, poetry, dance, and other manifestations of cultural expression are important to him not as objects or products of creativity but for what they symbolize in relationship to their users. Consequently, the role of music assumes significance for him as it is associated with the crisis events of life, with institutions and customs, with calendrical rites, and with other traditions of society. This social function of music is one of the essential considerations in comparative studies.

The principal interest of the musicologist, on the other hand, is likely to be centered on the music itself. He is concerned with the description and analysis of musical structures and instruments. Through synthesis he attempts to understand fundamental musical principles involved. In order to comprehend music in relation to its own society, he may study the choreography of the dance, the costumes, the paraphernalia, related ritualistic objects, song texts, poetry, chants, and other cultural expressions with which music is associated. In other words, he tends to be interested in the object itself rather than in what it symbolizes. This kind of study is essential to the comprehension of a specific musical practice. Comparative studies of different musical cultures must be based on knowledge of this type as well as knowledge of the social function of music.

If it is clear that both anthropological and musicological data are indispensable to the study of music, the unknown, and that the ethnomusicologist tends to emphasize one of these basic disciplines, what kind of inaccuracies are likely to result from such an emphasis? Giving primary attention to the social functions of music, the anthropologist may be content with an examination of only the most general musical features. It is likely that the extent of his musical training is too limited to support significant analytical studies. The musicologist may become so occupied with his concern for musical analysis and the reconstruction of musical theory that he pays too little attention to the function of music within its society.

Such overemphases produce two different orders of inaccuracy: analytical and comparative conclusions drawn by the anthropologist are likely to be musically inaccurate if they are based on the gross features of musical practice; purely musicological studies, through the omission of sociological data, may represent the machinations of the Western theorist's mind more than the living music used by a unique society.

Attempts at synthesis and comparative method prematurely applied have created a literature in the field of ethnomusicology that is couched in generalities and filled with compounded inaccuracies. The first significant attempt to present a theory of the world-wide distribution of musical instruments was Sachs's *Geist und Werden der Musikinstrumente* (Berlin, 1929). Although this work continues to have considerable value because it brings together in one publication a great diversity of material, its principal weakness is its organization into very large time periods (the smallest unit is a thousand years) and gross geographic areas. In a later study, *The History of Musical Instruments* (New York, 1940), Sachs modified his approach somewhat by further subdividing the geographic areas.

The anthropologist speaks of a *culture area,* a term used to designate a geographic area of greater or lesser extent whose inhabitants share a common cultural heritage. Such a people, for example, might know matrilineal descent, limited agriculture, rectangular houses made of bamboo, one primary literature and mythology and polytheistic religion. Dissatisfied with the breadth of the usual culture area, the ethnomusicologist Alan Merriam has applied a more refined grouping known to ethnologists as the *culture cluster*. The *cluster* is almost always smaller in size than the *area* and takes into account a *recognized* unity among the groups making up the cluster. In "The Concept of Culture Clusters Applied to the Belgian Congo" (*Southwestern Journal of Anthropology*, XV, 1959), Merriam points out:

> We are quite aware of the limitations of the culture area concept and regard it primarily as a taxonomic device; considered on this, descriptive, level the importance of a musical instrument is equal to that of a particular means of social organization. In describing a culture cluster, we attempt to give a brief sketch of the way of life of the people which considers all aspects of their behavior. The cluster concept, however, adds a dimension lacking in the area concept in that it *suggests* generic relationship on the basis of historic fact and in what we have called commonality. In a culture area, diffusion from one or more centers is assumed and can often be traced, but in a cluster, by definition we find not only diffusion but also the factor of commonality Thus, for example, the fact that the Mongo say they are all related and have myths and other means to "prove" it, makes them quite different from the Flathead and Sanpoil Indians who are grouped together in the same Plateau area of North America but who deny any relationship to each other. The cluster involves an acknowledged historic unity, while an area shows unity, but of a descriptive nature only.

The distribution of musical instruments, of specific types of singing voices, and of the most general stylistic features of music tends to correlate with anthropological data in establishing the broad features of a greater or lesser culture grouping. From a musicological point of view, however, the culture area itself or any one of its parts may tell us little or nothing; indeed, it may even lead to erroneous conclusions regarding the true musical practices of a specific tradition.

In examining some concrete illustrations of these problems, we should bear in mind *three interdependent considerations* that must guide the ethnomusicologist. The first two,
presented as a summary of the discussion thus far, are generally known and accepted; the third is unfamiliar to both the
anthropologist and the musicologist, but in my experience
it is vitally important.

1) The function of music as an aspect of the behavior of
man in his society.

2) Characteristic musical style identified in its own terms
and viewed in relation to its society.

3) The intrinsic value of individual pieces of music
viewed in relation to the world of music.

A person emphasizing anthropology might say that the
usefulness of these considerations in establishing reliable
culture groupings probably diminishes progressively from
the first mentioned to the third. The establishment of culture
groupings per se, however, is not the immediate concern
of the ethnomusicologist but rather of the anthropologist.
An evaluation of these three considerations will indicate
the need for caution in accepting fragmentary knowledge
of a music to reinforce an anthropological thesis and will
demonstrate the absolute necessity of the *interdependence*
of the three basic objectives.

The specific functions of music in a society, such as the
ritualistic usage of the flute by the Papuans of New Guinea
or the bull roarer by the Bapere of the Congo, are comparable
to such anthropological data as male-female lines of descent,
types of economy, architecture, bodies of literature and mythology and religion. Individual expressions of a society might
correspond in widely differing and separated cultures. The
flute and bull roarer, to continue the example, can be found
associated with ritual in many parts of the world and the flute
is regarded as a phallic symbol in many societies. It is true

that, as the number of cultural similarities between two neighboring tribes increases, the probability of a common origin increases. But in crosscultural studies such as those proposed by Jaap Kunst ("A Musicological Argument for Cultural Relationship Between Indonesia—Probably the Isle of Java—and Central Africa," *Proceedings of the Musical Association,* 1936; and *Cultural Relations Between the Balkans and Indonesia,* Amsterdam, Royal Tropical Institute, 1954) detailed information of a different type is needed. Even in the study of neighboring tribes particularities of musical style are necessary to posit a historical connection.

The examples of specific song types and their functions in the Ila and Tonga tribes afford more detailed information that would be valuable in a description of the culture cluster. Even this indicates only that the two tribes have personal property songs classified as male or female and a specific type of mourning song—representing again types of musical functions that are widespread. These facts, it is true, tell us something about the social behavior of the Ila and the Tonga; and if a neighboring tribe has the same three types of song functions we might postulate a cultural relationship on that basis. With only this evidence as a guide, however, we should be obliged to relate the Ila and the Tonga to societies on other continents as well.

Thus far the facts have told us nothing about the musical expression of these two tribes. In order to compare their song types with similar songs of a neighboring tribe we must include the second interdependent consideration: characteristic musical style identified in its own terms and viewed in relation to its own society. What are the types of information to be sought? For example, we learn that the text of the songs is in the Bantu language, a tone language with which the movement of the melodic line is closely correlated. It is also helpful to know that the mourning song is very brief and that both the words and the melody are made up by one of the principal mourners, who does not seek help from a "professional" composer. The composition of the female personal property song differs in that the words are supplied by the female who will own the song, although they may be modified by the professional composer who finds a suitable melody for them.

Although this type of information relates more specifically to purely musical considerations than do the details of social function, such facts must still be viewed as generalities of musical style. The musicologist studying the European art tradition is sometimes accused of ignoring the role of music in society in his intense preoccupation with musical analysis. Since both considerations are necessary, we should consider what the musicologist terms "stylistic analysis." The numerous techniques of musical analysis are often the subject of discussion, but no one as yet has offered a complete definition of *musical style*. When more of the fundamental questions posed in Chapter 2 of this essay have been answered, perhaps we shall come closer to a suitable definition. Meanwhile, we must be content with a consideration of the kinds of information about musical styles available through statistical and comparative methods and through a judicious use of critical methods.

In the field of non-Western musical studies probably more attention has been given to the determination of tuning systems and scales than to any other aspect of the musical culture. Although at first glance this order of information seems to afford highly specific details that can be interpreted as identifying characteristics, a number of factors suggest the need for caution in relying heavily on studies of this type.

A good many studies have been based on the measurement of musical instruments found in museums. The large family of idiophones—tuned instruments of the gong or xylophone type—are the most easily measured, since there is no appreciable skill involved as in sounding a flute, an oboe, a clarinet, tuned hand drums, or a bowed or plucked stringed instrument, all of which are likely to require a highly specialized technique. The large gamelan orchestras of Java and Bali are made up principally of the family of idiophones. Instruments of this type must be retuned fairly frequently during the first ten to thirty years after they are made, depending somewhat on the amount of usage, until, in the words of the Javanese, the bronze has finally settled. The metallurgist would say that the crystalline structure of the metal has stabilized. Even after this condition has been reached the entire gamelan is retuned periodically. Whether instruments of this type imported by a museum were in tune on arrival and the extent to which through years of storage the tuning has altered is extremely difficult to ascertain. An instrument like the Siamese ranad ek, a type of wooden xylophone, is finely tuned by applying a paste of beeswax, resin, and lead filings to the undersides of the wooden slabs. The erratic figures recorded by Carl Stumpf in his measurements of a ranad ek, reported in his "Tonsystem und Musik der Siamesen" (*Sammelbände für vergleichende Musikwissenschaft*, 1922), indicate that this critical tuning paste had fallen off some of the keys. Using a Stroboconn, I measured a similar instrument, which had been in storage for many years as part of the Eicheim collection at the Santa Barbara Art Museum. I found that the tuning of many keys seemed quite irrational; inspection of the underside of such keys showed that through the years the tuning paste had dropped off.

The measurement of musical instruments in the field is accomplished by means of a monochord. This device uses a single string that is tuned to a standard pitch, stretched over a logarithmic scale calibrated in cycles per second, and read by means of a movable bridge with an indicator. The limited range of the monochord often requires the investigator to match the sound of a plucked string in a central octave with that of struck bronze or wood or bamboo sounding several octaves lower or higher. The relative grossness of such measurements is further exaggerated by human elements such as physical fatigue, an insufficiently sensitive ear, and the tendency to "correct" if the pitch measured is in a different octave from that of the monochord.

How critical is the determination of pitch in ascertaining the structure of a tuning system? Characteristically, a good many non-Western musical cultures employ a variety of tuning systems, in which usually small differences are discernible from one area or region to another. If these differences are not too great, the investigator is likely to strike an average and thereby establish the tuning system of the culture under study. Recent laboratory research, however, indicates the probability that slight differences in tuning systems are much more critical than heretofore suspected and, further, that the accurate determination of the specific tuning system of one particular Javanese orchestra requires not just the measurement of one instrument with bronze slabs but rather precise measurements of every instrument in the ensemble.

(As a specialist in the musical cultures of Indonesia I beg the reader's indulgence for my frequent references to these cultures; the principles illustrated apply to many parts of the non-Western world.)

In the fall of 1958, UCLA acquired a very fine gamelan from central Java, the proper name of which is Kjai Mendung (Venerable Dark Cloud). The orchestra is about one hundred and twenty years old, and therefore through age and usage has long since acquired as much stability in pitch as can be expected. Shortly before it was shipped from Java to California, the orchestra was tuned by a skilled Javanese and on arrival all the instruments were promptly measured

268

with the Stroboconn. The actual tuning of all the instruments was then plotted on graph paper covering a range of over six octaves. The graph revealed that the tuning of the game- lan follows an open spiral, i.e., there were no perfect octaves (in which the higher of two tones should be precisely twice the number of cycles per second). It appeared further that two of the pitches within each octave seemed to move at a different rate of "spiral" from that of the other tones. Other multi-octave Javanese instruments not in Gamelan Kjai Mendung tend to corroborate this preliminary study.

A thorough investigation of the tuning systems of central Java will be possible only when an especially designed field model of the Stroboconn has been developed that will operate from batteries. Such an instrument would allow the quick and accurate measurement of a sufficient number of gamelan in the field to reach reliable conclusions. Even if our efforts and ultimate objectives were limited only to a study of the be- havior of man in his society, it is worth noting that a Java- nese musician playing in the gamelan of the princely resi- dence Dalem Ngabean in Djogjakarta will complain that the pitch djangga on the Solonese gamelan housed in the Pakualaman is too high. Behind this musical observation lie three centuries of rivalry between the two principal cultural centers of central Java.

The approximations of Oriental scales that can be accom- modated in Western notation are also of such a gross order that they tell us very little. An excellent illustration of this point and one reasonably accessible to the reader are two ex- amples of music included in Hornbostel's recordings, *Music of the Orient* (Decca). Among the excellent selections in this album is an example of Japanese ha-uta (the tradition of the short song) for which the program notes provide a brief description and an outline of the scale employed. Hornbostel calls our attention to the fact that this scale is identical in

its tonal material to the one shown in illustration of a Sundanese song from west Java. Stylistically the two selections
have little or nothing in common. If the precise pitches of
the scale material used had been expressed in a more accurate
form, the small but significant differences would have identified the individual character of each scale.

In the Western musical tradition there are several kinds
of minor modes: the natural minor, the harmonic minor,
the ascending and descending forms of the melodic minor,
and the so-called Hungarian minor. The numerical average
of these different tonal structures expressed in cycles per
second could hardly be referred to as *the* minor mode. Such
an average might suggest a minor (rather than a major)
character of mode, but it would not represent an existing
musical practice. By the same token, averages of non-Western
tuning systems and scales might, for example, suggest the
character of a seven-tone Javanese pélog tuning and at the
same time misrepresent the critical differences found among
a variety of Javanese pélog tunings in actual usage.

The most serious misapplication of such averages occurs
when they are used as bases for comparative studies of two
different musical cultures. If the basic tuning systems and
scales of each of the cultures under study have been rendered
in the form of gross averages, the margin of error has been
so compounded that any resulting similarity is likely to be
fortuitous rather than significant.

Another order of general musical information relates to
the predominant movement of the melodic line. The over-all
movement may assume a number of different patterns: the
melody may begin on a high pitch and slowly descend in a
diagonal sawtooth line or it may begin on a low pitch and
gradually rise to a high concluding tone; it may move in a
long graceful arch with the high point occuring somewhere
in the middle or this pattern may be inverted; it may undu-

late along a horizontal line; or it may have a compound shape of several of these patterns. Such information is of value in the study of a specific musical culture when one over-all melodic pattern tends to correlate with a specific song type. In a comparative study of different musical cultures, however, the value of melodic pattern is limited; its general nature demands considerable support from other modes of investigation.

Another type of information is concerned with a more specific description of melodic movement. The melody may move from pitch to pitch by single steps (conjunct movement) or by jumps of varying size (disjunct movement). A laborious count of conjunct and disjunct intervals will reveal either that one type predominates or that the movement is a fairly balanced mixture. An interval count will also yield the percentage of times each different size interval appears. Additional general statistics may be concerned with the number of times each pitch of the scale appears in the song, the number of times a tone is repeated successively, and the total rhythmic weight of the different pitches in the scale (important structural tones may be used in longer duration than less important ones). Attention may also be given to the use of stereotype melodic progressions as a function of mode.

This kind of information cannot contribute much to the determination of a musical style. Throughout the foregoing discussion—notwithstanding the fact that basic conceptions such as tuning and scale were involved—the critical need for highly detailed information was implied. Only through an intimate knowledge of the most detailed musical practices can we be sure of comprehending the larger framework of musical style.

For example, in Bali, Java, and Sunda (west Java), where the five-tone sléndro tuning system is used, each of the three cultures employs a distinct musical style that can be identified readily by the layman. In Sunda a complicated system of modes and submodes has developed with the addition of as many as twelve vocal tones within the five-tone system, thus producing seventeen different pitches in the concept of sléndro. In central Java, five vocal tones are added, giving a total of ten different pitches. In Bali the employment of sléndro is limited to a quartet of instruments that accompanies the all-night shadow plays; vocal music provided by the dalang (puppeteer), so far as is presently known, has not established a *system* of vocal tones.

The most complex form, found in Sunda, accomplishes subtleties of modulation and introduces mild dissonant clashes between vocal tone and "bronze tone" (fixed pitch) that might be completely missed if the investigator were content to record in his transcription only the five principal tones of sléndro. In central Java, where a large gamelan sléndro accompanies the all-night puppet play portraying the stories of the Hindu classic the *Mahabharata,* the employment of vocal tones and the occasional borrowing of pitches from the completely different seven-tone pélog tuning system follow aesthetic rules in relation to the emotions of the drama as well as musical rules connected with modal, rhythmic, and formal considerations. The use of vocal tones by the dalang in Bali is probably guided by a similar rationale, even though it has not led to the establishment of a known formal system.

These minute details of musical style might be dismissed as "nonessential" ornaments. *If they were, a study of the behavior of man in these societies would miss the important emotional reflex in his response to the centuries-old drama of morals, manners, and religion with which his mode of life has become inseparably identified.* In other words, it is a duty of the ethnomusicologist to advocate the study and comprehension of the most minute details of musical practice and to warn the anthropologist that a lack of interest in the object itself (the individual musical piece) may prevent an understanding of what the object symbolizes.

Thus we may state categorically that *a thorough stylistic analysis of music*—whether Western or non-Western—*must be founded on the most accurate and detailed information that the imagination of the investigator and the marvels of an electronic age can produce.*

Reference should be made to specific tuning systems and scales in actual usage, and the specific melodies realized on them made the object of a detailed stylistic analysis. In the study of purely vocal music, where no instrumental referent with fixed pitch is commonly used, a sufficiently large sampling will indicate whether "tuning system" and scale have stabilized in one or more forms. Phonetic transcriptions of the melograph type are necessary in order "to see" the more intricate kinds of ornaments and their relationship to structural tones. The recurrence and particular behavior of structural tones provide a key to modal concepts, such as cadential patterns occurring at the ends of phrases or sections, and establish the relative function of less important tones as they appear in passing or in the elaboration of melodic patterns. Substitute tones and stereotype patterns that effect modulations to related modes or auxiliary scales are subtle means of stylistic expression. The relationship of rhythmic pattern to melodic line and these in turn to text are important determinants of form and ultimately style.

Textual analysis should proceed with the help of a qualified linguist, so that the natural stress or accent of the words is thoroughly understood or, in the case of the tone language, so that the rising, falling, or level pitches are clearly indicated. The interplay between text and melody may achieve a rhythmic unity between the two or provide occasional cross rhythms, perhaps highlighting a particular meaning of the text or simply giving predominance momentarily to either text or melody. The especial importance of the tone language in relation to melodic pattern is a subject that demands far greater study than it has known to date. One period of Chinese music studied by John Hazedel Levis (*Foundations of Chinese Musical Art,* Peiping, 1936) indicates a very close correlation between language and melody; studies by the UCLA linguist William Bright of the Lushai tribe of India give little or, at best, residual evidence of such a relationship; George List at the University of Indiana has recently begun studies of the Thai language in relation to music. The close relationship between the Bantu tone language and melody was mentioned earlier. Among some of the Bantu tribes this has led to a curious type of humorous song in which the flow of the melodic line deliberately violates the natural rise or fall indicated by the pitch of the tone language.

Another important aspect of style is the influence and counterinfluence between instrumental and vocal music. Detailed comparison must be made not only of the melodic characteristics of each but also of the typical tone qualities. In Javanese and Sundanese musical cultures the finest quality of the male or female singing voice is that most closely matching the quality of sound produced on the two-string bowed lute known as the rebab. It is interesting to note that these two interpenetrated societies, sharing a common heritage, have developed different qualities of sound in the singing voice as well as distinct melodic styles. Suitable scientific instrumentation must be developed to allow thorough qualitative studies of "visible" or "sung" speech, as well as the characteristic timbre of the voice and instruments.

As the detailed practices that determine musical style become known and we acquire a true understanding of the fundamental musical concepts that shape a given musical expression, this precise knowledge affords a firm basis for

274

comparative studies. The music of central Java, again, will serve as an illustration. In spite of the prolonged and profound influence from the Hindu civilization, Javanese music until recently was thought to bear no practical resemblance to the music of India. After the details of Javenese modal practice became clearly understood, however, it was evident that the basic principles operative in the music of India and that of Java were very closely related. A thorough comparative study remains yet to be accomplished, but already there is sufficient evidence to warrant a positive working hypothesis.

Sometimes the quest of the more elusive aspects of musical style takes the investigator into the realm of the related arts. The dance drum of central Java (batangan or tjiblon), on first hearing, seems to produce an endless variety of subtle rhythmic patterns. Close study reveals that, in the very long spans of time between strokes on the large gong, short stereotype patterns are used intermittently and in varying order; these patterns carry the names of traditional dance movements. The rather long intervals between the stereotype patterns are filled up with what is termed "lagu," improvisations that ultimately form a kind of standard "drum vocabulary" for the individual player who originated them. Through the combination of stereotype and "standardized" improvisatory patterns, a good drummer will acquire a vocabulary that permits twenty to thirty minutes of drumming without repetition. It is little wonder that this long time span of constant rhythmic change strikes the listener as an endless variety of rhythmic invention. A knowledge of Javanese dance, in this instance, provides a key to understanding the rhythmic organization present in what at first appears to be endless, free improvisation. The word *lagu* promises to be of some value for comparative studies when we learn that the term is used in connection with the principal drum of southern India, the

275

mridangam, which in its shape bears a strong resemblance to the Javanese batangan.

The functional and contextual aspect of music is an interdependent consideration of stylistic analysis. Invaluable insights into musical style—whether in contemporary or historical perspective—may be gleaned from such related arts as the rituals of mythology and religion, poetry and prose, dance, puppetry, spoken and operatic theater, architecture, and even from such handicrafts as metalwork, weaving, and dyeing. Any one of these arts and crafts by action, word, imagery, movement, or conformation may provide a clue to some obscure musical practice that has previously escaped the attention of the investigator.

Architectural monuments and the findings of archaeologists may substantiate theories of stylistic change suggested by the living anachronisms often characteristic of non-Western musical cultures. The traditional Javanese house, for example, is divided into two main parts; the formal pendopo, the male part of the house, is a huge and elegant front pavilion open on three sides and providing on its fourth side access to the interior, the female part, of the house proper. This division not only is evidence of the ethnologically interesting mixture of male-female lines of descent but also suggests a corollary with two distinctive musical styles of earlier times. Formerly there were two types of Javanese gamelan—one of which used a loud style of playing to accompany outdoor functions while the other used a soft style of playing and was reserved for indoor functions. Since the sixteenth century, these two styles of ensemble have been combined into one large group housed in the male pendopo but led by the rebab, the principal instrument of the soft-sounding, or female, ensemble.

Literature, too, can provide many musical insights. In Java the seventeenth century epic poem the *Tjèntini,* the much older autochthonous Pandji cycle (about a culture hero who

276

numbered among his excellences and virtues outstanding ability as a gamelan player and gongsmith), the imported Hindu literature (the *Mahabharata* and the *Ramayana*), as well as lesser bodies of literature and mythology have proved to be rich sources. Investigators in this field, however, must take care to acquire a substantial knowledge of the appropriate languages, for the professional translator—not having a knowledge of musical practice—may not be able to select the particular shades of meaning that have musical significance.

Perhaps the very interrelatedness of the arts accounts for the difficulty in finding a pat definition of *musical style*. The challenge of thorough stylistic analysis can be met by the ethnomusicologist only if he is willing to augment his academic preparation and advanced training in the field with an acquisitive spirit for continued training in practical studies. In 1940, fourteen years before the first program of practical performance studies was made an essential part of training in ethnomusicology (UCLA, 1954), Charles Seeger made a prophetic remark in an article on "Music and Culture" (MTNA *Proc.*): "Perhaps I may suggest in passing that it would seem, in international music exchange, that actual performance of music of the other culture must carry far more weight than mere listening to it." This is not to suggest that the rigors of systematic method applied to stylistic analysis are to be equated with "mere listening," but rather to stress the importance of acquiring a reasonable competence in the performance of the particular music under study. My own experience and that of a number of advanced graduate students working in various parts of the world have convinced us that many of the accumulating errors in descriptive and stylistic studies in the field of ethnomusicology would have been avoided had the investigator learned such skills as how to manipulate a loose-haired bow in one hand and the slender neck of a two-stringed lute (which carries no finger board) in the other or had he slowly and painstakingly learned to execute the microtonal deviations characteristic of the style of the Japanese flute or trained his fingers to respond to the subtle requirements of hand drumming.

The social functions and style of a given music can be studied by historical, descriptive, analytical, and comparative methods, and, although somewhat furtively employed, critical method is also used in stylistic analysis. Every time the trained musicologist, utilizing the present inadequate methods of notation and transcription, finally "settles" for what he deems the most accurate representation of a highly ornamental passage or concludes that the peculiar melodic behavior and structural involvement of a given pitch justifies the term *tonic* or exercises choice as to phrase length, form, meter, and other niceties of style—he has rendered a kind of subjective judgment based on objective facts and referred to a wide and thorough knowledge of fundamental musical principles. The interpretation of facts, the interaction of subjective and objective methods, is the critical faculty in operation.

Objective scientific methods have been highly developed and the techniques of stylistic analysis, those employing objective methods, are frequent subjects of discussion. Critical methods, on the other hand, as though by tacit agreement, are not discussed and consequently remain relatively underdeveloped. Probably no adjective is so frightening to the research scholar in music as the word *subjective.* And he will be inclined to agree quickly that the examples given above of the exercise of critical judgment must be reinforced by a great variety of objective facts and tempered by pure and applied musical principles. Critical judgments can be made with even greater conviction, I must say again, when more of the questions posed in Chapter 2 have been answered. Meanwhile, on the assumption that every musicologist strives to be as "objective" in his subjectivity as possible, let us proceed to a discussion of the third interdependent consideration of the ethnomusicologist: the intrinsic value of individual pieces of music viewed in relation to the world of music.

It has been said recently that in the great metropolitan centers of the United States the music critic has all but disappeared, while the music reviewer—the reporter of programs, the man without an opinion of his own about performance or composition—seems to multiply, like the amoeba, by binary fission. Perhaps the quantity of diverse experiments in contemporary composition has snuffed out the flame of criticism. Perhaps the fragmentation of musical performance by the recording companies' "quantum" tape-splice theory has obviated criticism. A difficult contemporary composition rehearsed and recorded a few measures at a time with the best of numerous "takes" spliced together can hardly be considered "a performance." In the atmosphere of the concert hall further criticism of the nineteenth century repertory, by now, seems a bit pointless. One prefers not to believe that critics of today are less courageous than those of a few years ago.

Curt Sachs has stated: "Men of high civilization have become voracious hearers but do hardly listen. Using organized sound as a kind of opiate, we have forgotten to ask for sense and value in what we hear." (*The Wellsprings of Music,* ed. Jaap Kunst, The Hague, Martinus Nijhoff, 1961.) Modern Western man gives little attention to the increasing need for, much less to the development of, critical method in the field of music. This has not been true in other fields.

The cultural fabric of twentieth century Western man is shot through with countless threads of exotic color and texture. His architecture has been strongly influenced by that of Japan; the textile designs and patterns of his dress reflect the ancient traditions of many parts of the non-Western world; his intellect and to some degree his spirit have stretched out to meet the literature and philosophy of the East; his performing arts are fertile ground for the acculturative seeds of endless varieties of exotic dance and drama; his aesthetic sensitivity is receptive to the graphic and plastic arts of almost all societies on all continents; his food, his economy, his politics, his ever changing modes of government reflect the excellence of international commerce and communication systems. In such ways the critical faculties of Western man have been operative, have been selective.

A few years ago those same Papuans who use the flute in male initiation rites were extravagantly praised by the Western art world for their extraordinary abstract paintings on bark. The paintings were acclaimed for their fine sense of design, form, color, balance, points of tension, and other details of style familiar to the art critic. These extremely large paintings (there is an excellent collection at the Royal Tropical Institute in Amsterdam) were originally created as an expression of the native religion. Subsequently, European collectors visited New Guinea and persuaded the Papuans to create many more paintings, but these uninspired productions had little artistic value.

The cultural anthropologist might have said: "Here we have two types of paintings, one motivated by the mores of the tribe, the other by an outside commercial inducement. Their relative artistic worth substantiates the importance of the social function in the creative arts." It is probable that the cultural anthropologist, in this instance, had accepted the art critic's evaluation of their artistic worth rather than his own, for the European art critic, who may have been totally ignorant of the social patterns and motivations of the Papuans, without hesitation had proclaimed one type of painting masterful and the other contrived. In the *world of art,* which here is the concern rather than the authenticity of a Papuan tradition, the anthropologist would be presumptuous not to rely on the art critic.

Similar examples could be cited in relation to the sculpture of Bali or the carvings of Africa, where inferior objects are mass-produced to satisfy the ready tourist market and the inevitable import-export trade. These venal products of the art world serve to illustrate the fact that individual works of art have intrinsic value and may be viewed in relation to the world of art.

Modern practical editions of early Western music are reliable to the extent that the musicologist has been successful in his critical method. The same may be said about the study of all other types of music. We must exercise critical judgment not only in connection with the various levels of development in non-Western cultures but also in relation to the long-neglected expressions of our own contemporary times. Seeger points out that in order to comprehend music as a whole in the United States—including art, folk, popular, and jazz music as well as hybridizations—the various idioms must be known in themselves and in their cultural functions. It is necessary to know what kinds and sizes of groups accept, possess, or reject these idioms and with what intensity. He also admits that this is no easy task. "For any one of these idioms is in some ways like a language—one has to learn it in order to understand it and estimate its value—and sometimes even to discover it" ("Music and Culture"). The field of musicology has paid little or no attention to this problem, so that almost by default it has become the concern of ethnomusicology. Agreeing that *all* types of contemporary music in the United States deserve serious study while we can gather information and acquire knowledge about them that may be irrevocably lost tomorrow, let us consider the evaluation of individual pieces of music in the world of music.

I want to make it clear that my use of the phrase *world of music* does not refer to the winter concert season, its programs, managers, virtuosi, and composers, or to the "world of the aesthete" who swoons over the latest novelty, or to the solemn pronouncements of the quasi-critic (reviewer) who functions as part of the publicity racket. *World of music* refers to supranational, supra-ethnic musical value.

Art history and criticism are based on the assumption of a world of art. Music history and criticism have remained insular in their promulgation of Western theories and tradition. Any kind of insularity is hardly compatible with the demands of the last half of the twentieth century. A knowledgeable art critic may point to synoptic examples of Persian cloisonné, Chinese celadon, and Zuni pottery not with the purpose of *comparing* the relative worth of their different types of glazes but to explain the outstanding artistic achievements of each process within the world of art. In the same way he may discuss form, design, composition, color and even, what in this consideration becomes a secondary matter, the functional and utilitarian achievements represented by each object. It is the responsibility of the knowledgeable musicologist (N.B. the absence of a prefix) to acquire such a comprehensive knowledge in the world of music. I venture the opinion that potentially there are as many valid music terms as there are art terms to serve the needs of judicious critical method; the critical terminology of architecture, literature, philosophy, and other humanistic disciplines may be applicable as well. What evidence exists, however, to indicate that these cultural expressions are analogous to music when speaking of critical method?

If individual musical pieces have artistic value in their own right and may be viewed in relation to the world of music, why, one might ask, has the assumption of a world of music been so long in developing—if, indeed, it has developed at all? Why have the graphic and plastic arts, the philosophies and religions of the world, the literatures, the architectures, the foods, the costumes, and countless other arts from societies throughout the world—why have these been accepted in the West while the so-called universal language of music has not? For many years *universal language* has been applied to music by well-meaning writers, but the excerpts given from nineteenth century writers about non-Western music belie the phrase and, of course, *universal* in this sense refers only to the European art tradition. How, then, may we postulate a world of music?

Since 1955 I have been associated either directly or indirectly with a great variety of non-Western musical performances. It has been of great personal interest to note the reactions and remarks of lay audiences, a mixture of the academic community and the community-at-large. In much the same way that a layman might admire the depth of color and glaze in Chinese celadon, so he is fascinated with the brilliant contrasts of tempo and dynamics and the spectacular virtuosity required to produce the rapid melodic figurations of Balinese music. As he becomes more familiar with the refinements of celadon or of Balinese music, his pleasure in the aesthetic experience increases. I have watched performing groups in various kinds of Oriental music acquire an enthusiastic following in the community. Here laymen return to concert after concert, no longer attracted by the promise of novelty or an exotic first-exposure but by the artistic value of individual musical pieces from Bali, Java, Japan, India, Greece, Iran, and China. It is hardly necessary to point out that the audiences' pleasure in listening to these musical expressions is not dependent on a knowledge of anthropology or the technical workings of musical style. Some knowledge of these interdependent considerations, of course, increases appreciation; and individual members of the audiences, motivated only by their musical experience, have sought this type of information.

If we may take my experiences as evidence of a beginning development in the assumption of a world of music, the question remains, why has it been so long in realization? Although a complete answer to this must await the collaborative efforts of the "ethnopsychologist," the "ethnophysiologist," and other "ethnospecialists," we may venture some pertinent observations. Other cultural manifestations enjoying a fairly universal distribution are dependent on speech communication (the world of ideas) or on visual perception. From infancy, man is trained to express his thoughts and to understand those of others through verbal abstractions. From infancy his eye is trained in the realm of visual perception, so that design, color, form, inanimate and animate objects of all shapes and sizes are easily related to the symbols of abstract thought. Music is, in itself, a mode of communication, and we can speak of many different musical languages.

Imagine the reaction of a person hearing a foreign language for the first time: the only impression is one of strangeness and a sense of great frustration. A stream of undifferentiated sounds, a few of them perhaps vaguely familiar, offers no clues to separate words, phrases, or sentences—much less any indication of meaning. After increased exposure, the rhythm of the language and its inflections begin to convey a certain sense of structure; sentences, phrases, and finally words become apparent, although the elisions of normal speech remain unperceived. By studying, listening, and imitating sounds, the beginner learns a few phrases and brief sentences in the strange tongue, and his confidence grows until he is confronted by the challenge of communicating with native speakers of the language. Then he may find that his careful imitation of the strange sounds, with which he has come to associate a meaning, may evoke only a puzzled expression on the face of the native speaker, and he may realize that his ear has not been sufficiently sensitive to the refinements of sound on which communication depends. Repeated corrections by a native speaker, of course, will gradually introduce these subtleties until our beginner has "tuned his ear to the language" and is able to communicate and to understand—although an "accent" may persist for many years.

If it is difficult for the human ear to perceive the subtleties of sound in a foreign speech, is it not reasonable to expect the same order of difficulty in the perception of a foreign music? The first challenge in the assumption of a world of music is the need for sufficient exposure—strange sounds must become familiar, the stream of undifferentiated musical motion must be perceived as motives, phrases, musical sentences, and form. Until the Western ear has been exposed to the sounds of foreign musical languages, it has little opportunity to accept or reject that which in its strangeness may be perceived only dimly.

This line of reasoning seems to deny any notion of universality in music; yet if the word *universal* is considered within the assumption of a world of music, there is more to be said on this subject. By now it must be clear that the devotee of Italian opera may have no appreciation of Chinese opera. What, if any, are the universal attributes of music? Aside from minor exceptions, we may say that music throughout the world is directed toward the emotions, but we must turn to the psychologist to learn if there is any correlation between specific sounds, rhythms, tempos, melodic figurations, etc. and the particular emotions they evoke. Limited studies made up to this time indicate no universal correlations of this kind; even within our own society, an individual piece of music produces a different emotional response in different listeners. If, then, one piece of music does not produce a universal emotion in all listeners and if understanding one musical language does not necessarily involve understanding all others, why are Western and non-Western students of world music, as well as lay audiences, deeply moved by the beauty of such diverse pieces as "Koinju no Ha" in Japanese Gagaku and the *G Minor Symphony* by Mozart and "Rambu" played by a Javanese gamelan Sekati?

In "Universalism and Relativism in the Study of Ethnic Music" (*Ethnomusicology*, 1960), Leonard B. Meyer makes some remarks that are particularly germane at this point:

> Fifty years ago music was generally considered to be a universal language. Obvious differences between music of different cultures were explained away as being apparent rather than real. Beneath the profusion of seemingly disparate styles, it was argued, were fundamental absolute principles which governed the structure and development of all music everywhere [the Latin-and-Greek posture of old-fashioned linguistics] It was only necessary to discover these basic underlying laws. But when these laws were not discovered, this form of monism was largely discredited and went out of fashion.
>
> Then the warm winds of academic opinion began to blow in the opposite direction—towards an equally monistic relativism which sought to study each culture and each music "in its own terms" and which looked with suspicion upon any search for universal principles Although scholars of this persuasion gathered much valuable data, for various reasons—*perhaps above all precisely because it avoided cross-cultural questions such as those concerned with characteristics common to cultures unrelated ethnologically and geographically* [emphasis added]—relativism failed to produce fruitful hypotheses which might have led to new types of data and provided new insights into the nature of man, culture, and their interrelationships As a consequence, this form of monism has come to seem less and less satisfactory.
>
> There is, however, no transcendent logic compelling us to

choose between these antithetical positions Instead we can merely ask which features of music, if any, tend to be common to different cultures and which vary from culture to culture. The study and analysis of this material would presumably indicate which aspects of music are universal and which are culturally determined. Hypotheses might then be formulated to account for the findings, and, of course, to explain the exceptions.

Unfortunately the matter is not so simply solved. Appearances are often deceptive. For instance, two cultures may appear to employ the same scale structure, but this structure might be interpreted differently by the members of each culture Conversely, the music of two cultures may employ very different materials, but the underlying mechanism governing the organization of these materials might be the same for both. The possibility of such discrepancy calls attention to the importance of methodology and definition.

. . .

What we should ask about, when considering the problem of universals, is not whether the data itself is common to different cultures—any more than we decide whether there are scientific laws on the basis of particular physical events. What we should ask is whether, beneath the profusion of diverse and divergent particulars there are any universal principles functioning. Stated thus, it becomes apparent that the descriptive method is less than satisfactory for dealing with the problem of universalism vs relativism precisely because it ignores those psychological concepts which might provide common principles for interpreting and explaining the enormous variety of musical means found in different cultures.

Meyer calls attention to the difficulty of obtaining cross-cultural confirmation of common musical principles through the interrogation of native informants, and then continues:

. . . direct interrogation is not the only way to get evidence, nor the only way to discover what the norms and the permissible deviants of a style are and what rules and probabilities govern their use. Rather the ethnomusicologist, like the linguist, must learn to use the materials he wishes to study, he must learn to perform the music himself; for instance, by performing a group of carefully designed musical variants for an informant and asking questions such as: "is this a possible beginning phrase?" "which of these ways is better?" "can one do this?"—he can gradually discover the grammar and syntax of the style. Such a procedure supplemented by statistical, descriptive study of the repertory of the culture should provide a reasonably detailed and accurate account of the kinetic features of the style being studied. It would also enable cross-cultural investigation to be more rigorous, more precise, and more revealing.

From these remarks we must conclude that the rhetorical question referring to Gagaku, Mozart, and gamelan Sekati may take some long time to answer satisfactorily. In the quest that lies ahead, universalism and relativism, in the sense these terms have been applied by Meyer, are complementary necessities. Close observation of Western and non-Western students and many audiences, all of whom have been in contact with a number of different foreign musical languages, has convinced me and a good many others that the more familiar these different musical expressions become to the ear, the more readily they communicate; that persons of different ethnic backgrounds are able to perceive a given musical expression at different levels; that some kind of "musical meaning" seems not to depend on membership in the society carrying the tradition; and that the degrees and kind of "musical meaning" may be the same, may be similar, or may be different for members and nonmembers of that society.

Therefore, we may postulate a world of music with the tentative hypothesis: (1) that a given piece of music within a society may or may not have extramusical associations for members of the society, that it operates within a certain range of musical predictability within the tradition, and that it may produce varied emotional responses; (2) that the same piece will evoke different or no extramusical associations in nonmembers of the society, that perception by the nonmember will vary according to the length of exposure to the unfamiliar idiom, according to the natural limitations and capacities of the individual and the similarity or difference between his background and that of the ethnic group that carries the tradition; (3) that the potential of a universal aesthetic for this piece of music *exists,* independent of postulates 1 and 2, although an *explanation* of postulate 3 may ultimately derive from postulates 1 and 2.

I wish to state once more that the full responsibility of the ethnomusicologist must include three interdependent considerations: social function, musical style, and musical value. In these modern times, in our very modern Western society, the continued insularity of Western musicology is embarrassingly anachronistic.

4

OF SOCIETIES

In the latter half of the twentieth century it may well be that the very existence of man depends on the accuracy of his communications. Communication among peoples is a two-way street: speaking and listening, informing and being informed, constructively evaluating and welcoming constructive criticism. Communication is accurate to the extent that it is founded on a sure knowledge of the man with whom we would hold intercourse.

The significant trend in great universities of establishing integrated centers of study based on geographic areas and dedicated to the quest for comprehensive knowledge of whole societies offers the potential of accurate communication. Music and the related arts—which lie close to the heart of man as a fusion of mind, spirit, and emotion—are principal vehicles of cultural tradition and vividly reflect man's identity and aspirations. The diverse musical practices of the world are therefore invaluable in configuration studies.

Consequent to the ethnomusicologist's responsibility of developing and refining systematic and critical methods is the equally important responsibility of communicating his findings. In a field that is little known and even less understood, scholarly monographs and articles reach an important but extremely limited audience. Other levels of communication through which critically important cultural expressions of societies may be made known are too often disregarded by the ethnomusicologist.

The communication *of* music and the communication *about* music are two different kinds of communication. For many years Charles Seeger has been calling attention to this difference. In a recent article, "On the Moods of a Music Logic" (*JAMS*, 1960), he stated: "The musicological juncture, in which traditions of speech and music meet to form the sub-tradition of musicology, poses a unique philosophical situation—the report upon one technique of communication in terms of another. Music is reported upon by speech but speech is not reported upon by music. In this one-sided relationship, there is, thus, no direct check upon the former. Music can be studied as a datum in the physical universe by the extra- or non-musical sciences. But this yields the speech knowledge about music of the nonmusician and can serve but as a partial check upon the speech-report about the knowledge of music of the musician. This latter can, of course, be submitted to the consensus of musicians above mentioned ['known directly to producers and receivers of music . . . as a single, unified system of communication whose use they command at will']. But when musicians attempt to understand or deal with it, they have to use speech. And nearly unanimous as is the consensus of musicians in the making of music, as soon as they begin to talk about it, the consensus might as well not exist."

Many of the problems discussed in this essay exist because of this "unique philosophical situation." The "one-sided relationship" between two modes of communication not only imposes the need for a rigorous methodology on the musicologist but also demands consideration in the presentation of his findings. Again we may turn to Seeger for a concise statement of the problem: "Music must be viewed in three general classes of context, viz: (a) As a *concept* in the universe of discourse (i.e., of speech-communication); (b) as a *phenomenon* in the universe of nature; (c) as itself, a *communicatory medium* operating within . . . a universe of music-communication. . . ." ("Semantic, Logical and Political

Considerations Bearing Upon Research in Ethnomusicology," *Ethnomusicology,* 1961.) What the ethnomusicologist communicates *about* an unfamiliar music is of necessity only a supplement to the communication *of* that unfamiliar music itself. His responsibility in communications, therefore, includes using a wide variety of—or combinations of—different media at different levels.

The principal means of communicating music itself are live performances, motion pictures, television and radio broadcasts, and recordings. These are listed in a diminishing order of real or simulated "presence," a factor in communications that deserves special consideration. To what degree the success of communication is enhanced by a *visual* as well as an aural perception of musical performance has not, to my knowledge, received particular study. (It might possibly be that the current vogue of preference for stereophonic sound recordings is based partly on a transfer from one sense modality to another: instead of seeing two opposing sections of the orchestra on different parts of the concert stage, the listener hears the sounds from two different speakers. It is common knowledge that only a perfect balance of acoustics, speaker-placement, and room size can approximate the actual sounds heard in a concert hall.)

In the communication of unfamiliar music, live performance is certainly the most successful. As the famous Indian musician Ali Akbar Khan performs melodic and rhythmic subtleties on the sarod or Ravi Shankar on the sitar, the listener is better able to hear these nuances by visually associating them with the rapid movements of the performer's fingers. Or when the virtuoso par excellence Alla Rakha drums on the tabla and the bayam of north India, the movements of fingers, hands, arms, body, and head convey a composite visual impression of the masterful control that produces a rhythmic complex that, heard on the phonograph, would impress the uninitiated listener as being the collaborative efforts of several drummers.

Thirty or forty performers in the large orchestra of Bali, gamelan gong kebyar, comprise a flawless unit of rising and falling hammers on bronze keys, and the viewer-listener is able to see the relative activity of the various strata of melodic lines in operation. He will discern that two quartets of instruments are subdivided into four pairs of players sharing interlocking parts that require the flying hammers to behave like alternating pistons, with an occasional unison of movement to produce rhythmic cross-accents. He will see a slower and more important melodic line played by a larger pair of instruments. The hammers of another pair or quartet of instruments fall and rise at a still slower rate of speed in a fairly regular rhythm. And finally the deepest-toned melodic instruments, whose bronze keys are struck with large padded beaters, produce a slow and fairly regular melody that, because of the nature of the bronze slabs and bamboo resonators, has great sustaining power. His eye may follow the regular strokes on large and medium sized gongs as they subdivide the long melodic phrases. The interlocking rhythmic figures of two drummers can be seen as one rhythmic complex that guides the entire ensemble. The simultaneous or alternating tattoo of eight cylindrical hammers on a dozen bronze kettles becomes a visible metaphor as four players on the reyong perform the "flowers" in Balinese music or contribute harmonic-rhythmic shock waves to the total effect.

Although the most valid communication of Indian or Balinese music takes place in its native setting—where the rapport, reaction, and interaction between audiences and musicians are a considered part of the performance—concert performances of non-Western music in the United States can be further enhanced as a means of communication if the experienced ethnomusicologist adds a commentary to the visual-aural experience of the audience. The specialist should explain in layman's terms the musical meaning of the abstract sounds of unfamiliar music. Such an explanation should by no means take the form of a scholarly lecture, but it should by all means be delivered by a scholar; in the simplest possible terms it should illustrate by live demonstration the musical principles that guide a particular musical expression. If the melodic-modal potential of the India raga is explained and demonstrated, a performance by Ali Akbar Khan or Ravi Shankar becomes immediately more accessible to a Western audience. If the rhythmic implications of the Indian tabla are demonstrated and explained, a performance by Alla Rakha commands as much respect for the intellectual achievements of the artist as for his manual dexterity. If the Indian divisions of form into alapana, song, and swara are understood, they justify, on a conceptual level, the long time-span that sweeps from the tentative, free-rhythmic introduction to the final "competition" in improvisation among the participating players.

In addition to the virtuosity of native players, non-Western music finds expression in the live performances of two other important categories of musicians. One of these is exemplified by the groups of American students participating in the type of training program mentioned earlier. Ethnomusicologists responsible for such groups should permit public presentations, of course, only when a group has attained a standard of performance that represents both technical proficiency and artistic comprehension of the musical tradition. A few years ago it was a matter of conjecture whether American students were capable of reaching such a standard of performance; it has now been demonstrated that there was no need for doubt, but it is curious that the presence of Western-type symphony orchestras in the non-Western world was

294

not taken as an indication that musicality on the part of performers may be applied to any idiom of music.

"Professional" folk singers, singers of folk songs, and players of café music comprise a third category of musicians offering live performances of non-Western music. Sam Hinton, an American scholar-performer of folk songs, makes a sharp distinction between the folk singer—one who has "grown up" with a tradition—and the singer of folk songs— one who has learned the tradition. Either type in the mid-twentieth century may be heard in the cafés, on television, recordings, or radio. When his wares are disseminated by such a commercial outlet, the performer is considered a "professional." It is hardly necessary to point out that just as mass distribution does not guarantee artistic integrity, neither does it necessarily lead to artistic venality. Fifty or seventy-five years ago the true folk singer sang for his neighbors; today he may elect to sing for a microphone. The medieval bards and harpers of Ireland and Scotland, were they alive today, would most certainly seek out the local radio station rather than trudge from manor house to manor house. Hybridizations of folk music in popularized "folk style," it is true, are not accurate in the communication of a specific tradition; these hybrids in themselves, however, should be of more than passing interest to the musicologist lest his successors, fifty years from today, have to face the same historical vacuums that confront the contemporary musicologist.

After live musical communication the two most powerful media are television and motion pictures, the former through its almost house-to-house distribution in the United States, and to some extent in western Europe, and the latter through its distribution to all corners of the globe. Each has the same potential of presenting music and the related arts either as pure entertainment or as education or some combination of the two. With rare exception neither medium has begun to realize this potential—one that need not be considered financially unsound. Skillful camera work, editing, and direction, guided by the technical advice of a scholar-specialist, can produce accurate communication as well as the spectacle and colorful drama of good entertainment. In both of these media live performance can be simulated, even allowing the viewer-listener a closer inspection of the art form than he might otherwise be able to manage. Albeit "off-screen," commentary can be an integral part of the presentation.

Motion picture and television stories laid in foreign countries, of course, could offer a constant source of appropriate authentic music. It has been demonstrated time and again that the Western listener acquires a taste for his own early musical traditions—or the most contemporary experiments in music —only after repeated exposure. Authentic film scores of non-Western music, by the same token, could in time provide repeated exposures to the music of Africa, India, Thailand, Japan, etc. Expert guidance in the employment of the proper musical types, faithful to a given tradition and selected with discrimination to complement the requirements of dramatic action, can assure the production of filmed stories of high artistic achievement and accurate musical communication. Outstanding examples are the musical scores of the Indian motion picture trilogy *Pather Panchali, Aparijito,* and *The World of Apu.* Under the expert guidance of Ravi Shankar, these scores utilize both the folk and art music of India. American-made motion pictures having a foreign theme and setting complemented by an accurate musical score would not only contribute to international understanding through accurate communication, but would also invite an enthusiastic endorsement from the particular foreign culture that had been paid the compliment of respect for its musical practices. It is somewhat surprising that the motion picture industry itself, which includes in its resources a staff of expert researchers to provide authentic costume, settings, and historical facts, has so long ignored this important aspect of cultural tradition.

A few FM radio stations and some commercial recording companies offer the ethnomusicologist an opportunity, and thereby a responsibility, to present authentic material supplemented by brief commentaries or illustrated program notes. The current widespread interest in "folk" and "exotic" musical recordings has resulted in the mass merchandising of musical hybrids. Perhaps through the efforts of the recently formed American Folk Music Council this mushrooming interest can be guided into more accurate channels of musical communication.

Potentially all these media offer the accurate communication *of* music supplemented by commentary *about* music. Written communication, on the other hand, is entirely commentary; unable to be *of* music, it must be solely *about* music. As such, it has special problems of accuracy and special problems of media. The selection of the best avenues of communication for the written word is of particular concern to the ethnomusicologist.

Scholarly articles in the field of ethnomusicology are too often buried in a wide range of technical journals whose subject disciplines—anthropology, ethnology, linguistics, archaeology, physics, acoustics, folklore—do not necessarily suggest a musical interest. Worthwhile articles also occasionally appear in nonmusical encyclopedias, magazines, and newspapers. The extent of dispersion of scholarly articles sometimes entails considerable research merely to locate a study of possible interest. Fortunately there are several significant bibliographies that are indispensable to the specialist: e.g., "Bibliography of Asiatic Musics" by Richard A. Waterman and others (*Notes,* 1947-51); Jaap Kunst's *Ethno-*

musicology, 3rd ed. (Nijhoff, 1959); and Bruno Nettl's *Music in Primitive Culture* (Harvard, 1956).

Even with the aid of these the nonspecialist is justifiably discouraged by the difficulty of locating the heterogeneous array of publications pertaining to a specific musical culture. It is probable that for some time to come scholars in ethnomusicology will continue to rely on the good graces of technical journals in related disciplines, and that these organs, together with a few music journals interested in the publication of articles about non-Western music, will serve the needs of the specialist. The nonspecialist, however, even if he were to persist in the quest for widely scattered sources, would likely find the articles too technical and too restricted in scope. The scholarly monograph, although more readily available under its own title, also is proper fare only for the specialist.

During recent years, there has appeared a large number of books written by knowledgeable musicians about the music of the Western world and intended for an audience of laymen. These books are used by universities throughout the country as texts in classes in the appreciation of the various musical styles that are an important part of the cultural history of the West. Serious students of music criticize their musical content as being superficial; on the other hand, they may provide a comprehensive picture of music within its social context—a consideration too often neglected by specialized studies in music. The scholar in ethnomusicology has addressed the lay audience as a guide to the performance of non-Western music, as the writer of program notes accompanying authentic recordings, as a technical adviser on motion pictures (rarely), as the writer of encyclopedic articles —but seldom as the author of a popular book.

DeKruif's *Microbe Hunters,* Van Loon's *The Arts,* Hogben's *Mathematics for the Millions,* and Rachel Carson's *The Sea Around Us* are excellent examples of books describing fields of scientific inquiry for the layman. T. W. Ceram, in the foreword to *Gods, Graves, and Scholars* (Knopf, 1954), writes with admiration of Paul DeKruif, who "found that even the most highly involved scientific problems can be quite simply and understandably presented if their working out is described as a dramatic process." Citing the famous *Microbe Hunters* as an example of a genuinely exciting treatment of a highly specialized science, Ceram states that "since Paul DeKruif's pioneering efforts there is hardly a science that has not been skillfully popularized at least once."

The relatively large audience that this level of communication can reach justifies the inclusion of the "popularized book" among the responsibilities of the ethnomusicologist. Few have risen to the challenge. An American specialist in Balinese music, Colin McPhee, is a notable exception whose two books, *A House in Bali* and *A Club of Small Men* (John Day, 1946 and 1948, respectively), capture the spirit and significance of the related arts in Balinese society. These two publications have been very successful with lay audiences because at no time does the author's fund of scholarly knowledge obscure the reader's perception. A recent book of an entirely different order, but one that has the advantage of being a comprehensive survey written in reasonably accessible terms, is the book by William P. Malm, *Japanese Music* (Tuttle, 1959).

Unless the specialist is willing to face the challenge of this kind of book—replacing technical terms with nontechnical, viewing music and the related arts through the eyes of the layman but with the comprehension of the specialist, developing a style of writing that is worthy of the drama apparent in his subject—the innumerable popularized books that should be written in the field of non-Western music will go unwritten or will become the task of the dilettante.

Some years ago on board a ship bound for the Netherlands I asked a fellow Fulbright student what his field of special study was. "Cybernetics," he said. I confessed that although I knew the term I was not altogether clear on what, precisely, the field of cybernetics included. He proceeded over the next two hours to try to tell me. At the end of that time he said that perhaps after he had been studying a few more years he might be able to explain it more easily.

The ethnomusicologist who has written many scholarly articles and monographs on specific aspects of a non-Western musical culture, who has spent a good many years absorbing the wealth of ethnological materials that are inseparable from music viewed within the context of its society, who has ranged the field intensively and extensively until the very spirit of his subject pervades the most casual observation, who himself can play and sing the music and knows at firsthand the emotional and spiritual impact it makes on its society—this is the man who comprehends a complex subject within a complex society deeply enough to be able to communicate to a layman in simple, direct language a "popular" explanation. In this latter half of the twentieth century, when only accurate information can serve as the basis of effective communication, ethnomusicology may not be safely entrusted to the well-meaning dilettante, no matter how pure his intentions or how perceptive his powers of surface observation. The specialist must accept the obligation to produce popularized books as one of his many responsibilities.

Through the written word the specialist may reach still another kind of audience, one whose name should be printed in rubric among the ethnomusicologist's responsibilities. I am speaking of a very special audience, the particular people whose music is the object of study. I stated in the preface of my book *Patet in Javanese Music* (Groningen: J. B. Wolters, 1954):

The investigators of folk music and ethnomusicology represent a number of diversified attitudes, convictions and motivations. For this reason I want to say something about the intention of this study and the spirit with which it is offered. Although these remarks will be directed expressly to the Javanese niyaga, they may also be of interest to the general reader.

You, the Javanese niyaga and the peoples of Indonesia, are living in a time of great transition. Economic and political development is bringing you in contact with other countries. Standards of living will more and more be appraised in relation to the standards maintained by other peoples. It is a time of great learning, of increased education and the creation of a national language. For each of you it is a time of discovery—the discovery of individuality, of personal liberty and personal expression, of new ideas. In every way it is a time of great newness.

You are probably realizing that each new freedom brings with it a corresponding responsibility. I am thinking of a particular kind of responsibility. In the busy times of building a new nation you may not hesitate long in replacing the old with the new. That is understandable. But your music, your wajang, your literature and traditional forms of expression will never be replaced because they are part of you. They may change, just as you yourself will change, but that is only natural to a growing nation. I do not agree with some of my colleagues who think that changes in your music should not occur. We Westerners do not have the right nor are we able to "protect" your music, to try to preserve it unaltered. *You* are the ones who will take what suits you and reject what does not. The things in your own culture which continue to have meaning for you, you will retain, and the things which are no longer meaningful, you will no longer use. That is also understandable. But during the activities of your changing times some things may be lost which you will later want to recover. So you have a responsibility to your-

selves to preserve a *knowledge* of these things. A precedent
is already established Long ago the principal melodies of
the gendıng were written down in the kraton collections.
Even ıf some of them are not played for many years and fade
from the musician's memory, they wıll never be lost.

We Western musicians can learn much from you, the
Javanese nıyaga. We can learn something from your methods of musıcal training, from the rhythmıc structure of your
gendıng, from the function and preservatıon of a concept
like patet, from your voıce control (ıntonatıon) in singing,
from your gamelan conductor who ıs heard but not seen,
from your feelıng for playıng ın ensemble, from the ımper-
sonal qualıty of your compositıons

Part of my intentıon ın this study ıs to try to help the
Western musıcıan understand your music. If my conclusions
can also contrıbute somethıng to your knowledge of Javanese music theory, then the greater part of my ıntentıon wıll
be fulfilled.

Now, some years later, I must report that "the greater part
of my intentıon" was *not* fulfilled. Although my book did
ındeed succeed ın solvıng the rıddle of Javanese modal practıces, it was wrıtten for and directed to the Western-traıned
musıcologist. The very few Javanese musıcıans who could
read English with sufficıent fluency to negotiate a difficult
work did not, of course, have the years of technical training
in objective musical analysis required to understand my explanation.

Many of the musical cultures of the Orient have retained
their practices—encompassing change, acculturatıon, growth,
and development—through the powerful channels of oral
tradition. Even ın those cultures that have utılized some form
of written notation, oral methods have been the more important factor in ensuring contınuity. Through ımitation and
rote learning the most detailed and complicated musical
practıces have evolved with lıttle or no supporting "theory,"

written or oral. The practical musician in the Orient has at his command innumerable intricacies of a rich performance practice, but typically he is not able to communicate verbally the underlying principles that govern this practice. There are some exceptions. In India, for example, many publications written by Indian theorists have appeared, but even here the greater attention is given to details rather than to fundamental principles. So long as the delicate thread of oral tradition remains unbroken, methods of imitation and rote learning serve the heritage of master-disciple training.

> The success of an oral tradition is predicated on a lifetime of devotion by its practitioners. It has some merits over a written tradition in the development of tonal memory and quick aural perception. But the refinements of a highly developed art can be taught by this method only through months and years of painstaking imitation, until finally the student himself becomes the master; and having learned all that has preceded him—or at least all that his contemporary environment and society caused him to select—he in turn brings to his art an individual contribution that enriches the whole process. . . . In imitative methods of instruction a mistake made by the student is instantly corrected by the teacher, but on the basis of an almost intuitive knowledge. The mistake is likely to occur and reoccur in different contexts because the teacher himself is not able to explain *in principle* what is wrong. By this method after years of corrective imitation the student finally develops reliable "feelings" or intuition, but no conscious understanding. [Hood, "Changing Patterns in the Arts of Java," *Bulletin of the Institute of Traditional Cultures,* Madras, 1959.]

Today, however, the pressures of technology and political upheaval and the universal demands for formal education have snapped the thread of oral tradition. The imitative disciple seated at the feet of the master through years of daily devotion represents an anachronistic mode of learning in

an age founded on mechanization and its attendant requirements for general education.

To the ethnomusicologist, therefore, falls the responsibility
to communicate to those people whose music he has come to
understand the regulative principles underlying their tradition, for it is only in Western society that a long and conscientious effort has been made (with qualified success) to
establish objective methods for the study of music and
"speech" communication *about* music. To the extent that the
specialist fully comprehends his subject, he will be able to
explain it in indigenous terms—in written works substituting
figurative speech and perhaps even mythological reference
in place of heavily documented footnotes Textbooks should
include exemplary graded studies in composition and improvisation, as suggestions for a new mode of teaching compatible with the times, and should, of course, be written in or
translated into the appropriate language. (To my knowledge
only one serious attempt in this type of publication has been
made: in South Africa Hugh Tracy wrote a book called
Ngoma: An Introduction to Music for Southern Africans
[London: Longmans, Green, 1948].)

In the fall semester of 1961 at UCLA the composer Colin
McPhee offered a special seminar entitled "Compositional
Techniques in Balinese Music." Among American composers,
a few such as Henry Cowell, Lou Harrison, and Alan Hov-
haness have been attracted to the non-Western world as a
potential source of new ideas. McPhee's seminar is a beginning attempt to acquaint young composers and performers,
schooled in the Western tradition, with the compositional
practices of a specific non-Western musical culture. Unless
the American composer is willing to make a prolonged and
intensive study of a specific non-Western musical practice,
it is unlikely that he will be able to manage more than a
superficial acquaintance. The ethnomusicologist who has suf-

ficient acumen in the techniques of composition could therefore render a great service to the potential development of American music if he were to communicate to the American composer, in seminar or in publication, the musical principles of his specialty. This is not to suggest that the imitation of "exotic" sounds from the Orient or Africa is a worthy objective in the field of American composition, but rather that the African concept of rhythm and the Oriental development of melody are founded on principles still untried in the West.

In "The Viewpoint of Comparative Musicology" (MTNA *Proceedings,* 1936), Helen Roberts puts the matter this way·

> Like everything else in life, left to grow alone a musical art tends to become introverted, stagnant or set in special ways —ways so strangely limited among certain groups, despite the great possibilities for growth and development inherent in the musical material itself For new development there must seemingly be a fusion of different heritages. Musicians need to know with more complete understanding and sympathy, how alien musics are made, and to appreciate their beauties which to many, alas, are so obscure Only when some non-European forms are as clearly understood and as keenly enjoyed as our own will composers feel their way into new and greater music of the future, built up from their combined beauties.

The new and greater music of the future, dependent on international understanding of both Western and non-Western music, can be realized only through an accurate communication of music knowledge on an international level. The possibility of such communication is implicit in the words of Charles Seeger's essay "On the Moods of a Music Logic," which considers the extent of correspondence between music and language, between the communication *of* music and the communication *about* music, "between the original construction (of music-rationale) and the reconstruction of it (speech-rationale)." Seeger concludes that "between the communicable contents of the two arts and, hence, between the knowledge communicated by them and the rationale attributable to them there are points of identity (homology), of similarity (analogy), and difference (heterology)." This conclusion implies that there is a point in the process of comprehending music when speech fails, when only music itself may communicate.

It is necessary, therefore, in the world of music to place both Western and non-Western musicians in an international atmosphere and environment that allows the continuous interplay of music and speech. Participation in practical and theoretical studies by musicians of both the West and the non-Western world, including an involvement with both familiar and unfamiliar musical cultures, requires communication based on the interrelationship of the music-rationale and the speech-rationale. Such a program provides an international gathering of musicians with the most accurate and provocative mode of communication. It is encouraging that some of the major universities in the United States are taking positive steps to develop this *modus operandi.*

This person-to-person—or musician-to-musician—mode of international communication, having been demonstrated effective, should be accepted by governmental agencies and American foundations as evidence of the potential rapprochement possible in the field of humanistic studies.

A "Center for World Arts" should be founded to bring together resident scholars, composers, and artists from all parts of the world. Established by a university and perhaps endorsed by UNESCO this center might function like the Center for World Religions at Harvard or the Institute of Advanced Studies at Princeton or the one for Social Studies at Yale. Although more will be said presently about the particular importance of the arts in the non-Western world, the significance of a center devoted to the arts should be apparent.

The following vignette is offered as a rebuke to the unimaginative international training and assistance programs that do not take into account the humanities—the cultural achievements of man that lie close to his heart as a fusion of mind, spirit, and emotion.

After I had spent several months in central Java working with musicians I realized in great disappointment that my book explaining the intricate workings of patet (mode) was incomprehensible to the Javanese. The disappointment turned to alarm when I realized further that the tenuity of oral tradition had not successfully withstood the shock of World War II and the troubled years of revolution that followed. An awareness by the Indonesians of impending cultural loss, however, had resulted in the establishment of conservatories where Indonesian music, dance, theater, and literature are taught. But conservatory teachers told me that although a student might quickly memorize three different written parts (an innovation intended to supplant imitation and rote learning), he was unable to improvise a fourth one; and group improvisation is the very soul of Javanese music. It is a strange twist of fate that some of the American students studying Javanese music in California are quite capable of "improvising a fourth part."

An exceptionally talented young Javanese musician and dancer was my assistant. He was in his first year of study at the University of Gadjah Mada in Djogjakarta following a major in "Western Culture," since there was no major in music. It occurred to me that if this talented young man were trained in the objective methods of Western music, so that he could comprehend the need for analytical studies and understand and apply the principles that they reveal, he would be able to assist in establishing methods of teaching to fit the time-pressures of the twentieth century.

Inquiring about American undergraduate scholarships in the humanities, I found that none was available. The American Embassy, USIS, ICA, and several American foundations explained that undergraduate scholarships were out of the question—*especially* in the humanities. Sometimes this answer was defended on the grounds that the government of the country being assisted was not interested in such fields of endeavor (as though governmental interest were a measure of individual or social values!). I was quite distressed by my discovery, for I knew that a number of communist countries offer the foreign student three- and four-year undergraduate scholarships in the humanities, not to mention graduate fellowships. Finally, I was told by American colleagues working in Indonesia that if anyone might be interested in my proposal it would be the Humanities Division of the Rockefeller Foundation. Although they too felt that a three-year undergraduate scholarship was not possible, they suggested that they might make a grant available for the program in ethnomusicology at UCLA, and that I could bring the young man as my assistant.

Near the end of his second year of study at UCLA the young Javanese musician came to me and said that he was only then beginning to understand the importance of what I had been trying to do in Java, and that the formidable book, *Patet in Javanese Music*, was becoming *langkung mangertosaken* (more understandable).

In the summer of 1961 Hardja Susilo graduated with *Honors* in (Occidental) music, and in the fall semester began his first year of graduate study.

❧ 5 ❧

THROUGHOUT THE WORLD

In *Man, the Unknown,* Alexis Carrel points out that the field of medicine has proliferated into many highly specialized areas and that the rapid increase in knowledge and techniques has discouraged the young doctor from general practice and encouraged narrow specialization. He maintains that the specialist is incapable of viewing the *whole* man in his diagnosis, that because of his overspecialized training he misinterprets symptoms and prescribes badly. The greatest skill with forceps and scalpel or the most advanced marvels in medication can be misapplied without a comprehensive diagnosis. Carrel makes the (somewhat utopian) recommendation that a corps of superdiagnosticians be developed, composed of exceptionally gifted young men who would receive advanced training for a period of twenty-five years. This preparation would include not only a complete study of the physical man but also of psychology, psychiatry, metaphysics, and the spiritual man, as well as economics and sociology, becoming "the very science of the human being." The relatively small number of men who could survive this extensive and rigorous training would be ready to practice by the age of fifty.

The need for this supradiagnostic view of man-the-unknown might be compared to the urgent need for accurate configuration studies of societies throughout the world. Carrel rightly argues that the field of medicine must be concerned with the total man; so must configuration studies be concerned with the total society. If twenty-five years is necessary to the training of the superdiagnostician in the field of medicine, it is difficult to imagine the number of years required to train a corps of men in "suprasociology." In the 1930's Carrel put considerable emphasis on the importance of the mental and spiritual man in relation to his physical well-being; this emphasis has grown rapidly in the last three decades. In a consideration of configuration studies in the 1960's, it is interesting to note that the humanistic discipline—the studies of the cultural expressions that reflect man's identity and aspirations—are still weakly represented or conspicuously absent.

In the belief that the suprasociological view of societies can never be realized by a single corps of "diagnosticians" I maintain that *reliable configuration studies will be achieved only when the contributing specialists understand the absolute necessity of working in teams representing all the relevant disciplines.*

Too few individuals realize that the peculiar role of the arts in the United States (and to a lesser extent in Europe) may be significantly responsible for the lack of true communication between us and various foreign societies. The position in our society of music, dance, theater, painting, sculpture, and literature assumes a critical importance in international relations. I am not speaking of the banal products of our arts exported in the form of sexy motion pictures, which in a Muslim country, for example, create a false and odious stereotype of the average American. Nor am I referring to rock 'n' roll and similar forms of banality that have triggered riots in Indonesia, resulting in a governmental ban. There is no question that these forms of the arts, lifted out of the context of Americana, are inflicting irreparable damage to American prestige in a number of countries in the non-Western world. Under that often-abused term *free enterprise* or *freedom of press, communication, or speech* we irresponsibly condone this kind of indiscriminate distribution and disregard the need of compensating for it.

I am speaking of something far more insidious. Consider for a moment the relative importance of the arts in our society. In times marked by discussions of homemade bomb shelters and TV spot presentations showing the type of emergency rations to be kept at hand in the event of a nuclear holocaust, it is not unreasonable to ask "Where in a list of absolute essentials would we put music or dance or theater or literature or plastic art or graphic art?" Or would we put them on the list at all? If the question appears to be extreme, let me state that in some cultures of the Orient, the arts would be represented on such a list.

Apart from rhetorical questions of cataclysmic scope, we well may ask just how essential is music, for example, to our way of life in Western society. Some kind of music is performed in connection with weddings and funerals, and on the occasion of a happy birthday; it seems to be essential also in religious ritual. Beyond this, most of us purchase music for recreation in the form of LP records or concert tickets, or simply allow some disc jockey to free us from making a selection at all. I do not agree with European critics who say that the United States lacks culture, that it is a nation that buys art but does not foster it. The support and encouragement of the arts by American foundations and by universities and colleges give the lie to such pronouncements. The arts and practitioners of the arts are in abundance. I am merely pointing out that in our society we live by a scale of values that places the astronaut at one end and the poet at the other. Our major emphasis seems to be concentrated in outer space, on the guided missile and the missile-to-missile and the anti-missile-to-missile.

At least as critical as the successful launching of satellites is the need for *reliable* configuration studies, so that we may communicate with illiterate societies—men laboring in the rice fields of Asia or hunting or gathering food in the interior of Africa. And our failure or success in recognizing the *vital* role of music, dance, theater, painting, sculpture, and literature in non-Western societies bears a very direct relationship to the success of configuration studies.

Various modes of communication directed toward different kinds of audiences have been discussed earlier; the mention of an important audience—the nonmusician for whom this essay was prepared—has been reserved until now. A deep acquaintance with all the disciplines in the humanities is a desirable accomplishment for any humanistic scholar. The two companion essays in this volume offer the nonmusician in the academic community a thorough and critical appreciation of scholarship devoted to the musical traditions of his own European heritage. The relatively passive role of music and the related arts in our own contemporary society, however, should not lead us to underestimate the importance of the arts in other societies throughout the world.

An aura of belief that society is influenced by music has hung about the art of music from its earliest days. Philosophers, statesmen, and even generals have praised, often extravagantly, the importance of music in the affairs of men. Under authoritarian regimes, respect—even veneration—for music as a social force required no special apology. . . .

The converse belief, that music is influenced by society, is equally ancient. More credible than the first, perhaps, in the popular and learned mind of today, it has been given increased attention during the last fifty years or so. Music and society, we may agree, are both phenomena or functions of culture. So it is reasonable to assume that the various phenomena or functions of culture have definite relations, one to another and to the whole collection. Society being the most comprehensive concept, one might claim that music must be dependent upon it. Yet in spite of this reasonableness and its support by evidence of some of the larger events and processes of history, there seems to be very little tangible in it when we come down to details, even some rather large details. . . .

I must make clear that I am about equally impressed with these two beliefs. As I see them, ultimately (and that means basically) the two are complementary and interdependent. Concerning the first—that music influences society—the outstanding laboratory in operation at the present day is, of course, Soviet Russia. . . . Political control of music for social, including political, purposes is nothing new. It operated in ancient Greece and in 17th-century Massachusetts. It was highly successful in the Roman church (that is, in Western European society) up to about 1600 and in various sects of the Reformation. As for the second belief—that society influences music—the New World, it seems to me, has offered, and still offers, the outstanding laboratory. [Charles Seeger, *Music and Society: Some New World Evidence of Their Relationship,* Pan American Union, 1952.]

An awareness of the importance of these two "complementary and interdependent" beliefs seems not to have been within the purview of our recent international relations. The Music Division of the Pan American Union, it is true, has, within the limits of a restricted budget, taken into account the practical problem of using music in international relations. However, the misguided efforts of the American National Theater and Academy in various parts of the world may have achieved as much harm as good. An American symphony orchestra performing to half-empty houses in the Orient (because the price of admission was too high) reached, at best, some of the political elite. The performance of an operatic star in Jakarta before a Western-educated Indonesian audience made no contact with the ninety-three million people identified as the Republic of Indonesia. Some Americans have been puzzled why a Negro jazz musician was well received in the Near East but not in West Africa. One can only hope that the newly formed People-to-People program will follow the "two-way street" of accurate communications· listening first and then speaking, being informed and then informing, a process involving the *interchange,* not the imposition, of thoughts, opinions, and information.

External evidence of the importance of music and the related arts in other societies is reflected in the governmental support within countries whose economies hardly match our own. Frequent tours abroad by dancers, singers, and instrumentalists from such countries as Yugoslavia, the Philippines, Indonesia, India, Ceylon, Japan, and others (presented in variable degrees of commercial grooming) indicate a national pride in cultural identity. Fragmentary information from behind iron and bamboo curtains suggests that intensive and extensive research in the arts fostered by governmental support runs side by side with a recognition that "society is influenced by music" and conversely that "music is influenced by society."

Before seeking more evidence of the importance of the arts in other societies perhaps we should examine briefly the New World laboratory of which Seeger spoke. During four centuries of European colonization, beginning around 1500, three traditions were brought into contact in America: the indigenous Amerindian, the European, and the African. Each of these traditions had been subjected to a greater or lesser amount of acculturation. Seeger shows that in Colonial times the art, or learned, music tradition imported from Europe— a written tradition—had little or no place in the busy life of the frontiersman. The *oral* traditions, however, of European, African, and, to some extent, Amerindian music converged as the *principal* musical expression of the Americas. By the mid-twentieth century the products of this musical acculturation differ remarkably from North to South America as different aspects of the three traditions have been emphasized or suppressed according to regional social pressures and selectivity. Although in the last century the written tradition inherited from Europe has developed rapidly in the Americas, it should be noted that it is the oral tradition and hybridizations of the oral and written tradition that have the endorsement of an overwhelming majority of the populace.

The African elements of this acculturation have led to two interesting developments, one in North and one in South America.

Drawn into the neo-European tradition, rather than blanketed by it, as was the Amerindian, the African tradition also came into contact with a greater variety of European tradition than did the indigenous. The acculturation, I believe we will agree, is more spectacular and varied.

It is interesting to note that of the three main elements in African music—the instruments, the solo-choral song, and the dance—only the dance was retained by the neo-African tradition in both Latin- and Anglo-America. In the former it survived openly, in the latter, clandestinely, until the resulting acculturation blossomed in jazz

In the United States, the instruments were virtually banned. But choral song developed through what seems to be about fifty-fifty acculturation, a great new genre—the spiritual. In the Antilles, Brazil, parts of Venezuela, and Colombia, and some other areas, the instruments and solo song have lived, but choral song has not developed a product comparable to the spiritual.

Neo-African folk-music traditions have had little effect on the fine art of music in the United States, but has transformed the popular music. In Brazil and Cuba, however, neo-African traditions have permeated not only the popular, but the fine art of composition and maintains itself the while in exuberant varieties of form

315

If the preceding argument can hold, there should be nothing strange in these striking differences. Deriving logically from two distinct types of society bred respectively in the Protestant and Catholic faiths, they constitute most impressive evidence of the relationship I have been examining [music influenced by society]. [Seeger, *Music and Society.*]

In Western societies, and especially in the United States, music is divided into four genres: primitive, folk, popular, and art music. Although the term *primitive* is widely used, its connotation of "low musical value or worth" is entirely misleading. The more acceptable term *tribal music* suggests the important connection with magic or ritual or some other form of social function (music influenced by society). A suitable definition of folk music has been the concern of the International Folk Music Council for a number of years, and although complete agreement seems unlikely, certain factors are deemed essential· oral transmission, continuity through time (how long?), re-creation and refashioning by the community, and consequently the existence of a number of variants of a given text and/or melody. Popular music is described as a written tradition having a known authorship and being dependent on mass commercial distribution. When a "pop tune" becomes a "standard," by surviving the commercial process of saturation distribution, and exists in a number of oral variants, it might, theoretically, with sufficient continuity (how long?) link the past with the present and become a folk tune. Popular music of sixteenth and seventeenth century England seems to have undergone this kind of transformation. Art music is a written tradition (although it, too, is dependent on an oral tradition for correct interpretation), cultivated by learned musicians who are schooled in the consensus of practice and theory that surrounds it. There are also hybridizations of these various musical genres.

We need not have at hand specific percentages to realize

316

that the vast majority of our society most readily appreciates popular music or some form of hybridization. The recent surge of interest in folk music—by individuals who are learning the tradition, rather than by those who have grown up with the tradition—probably qualifies this particular audience as next in a quantitative ranking. A relatively small percentage of our society is interested in art music, and the fraction of a per cent involved with tribal music (not collectors but rather "users") can practically be ignored. Of these four types, it is significant that art music—a written tradition whose total audience and performers represent a very small percentage of our society—has developed as part of its tradition an attitude among its adherents of "musical superiority." The intellectual and pseudo-intellectual devotees of art music have convinced themselves and to some extent individuals outside their coterie of this superiority.

Here we may summarize the complex of factors that prevents us from realizing the significance of music and the related arts in other societies. Since we are predominantly listeners rather than performers, collectors rather than creators—whether we are speaking of popular music, folk music, art music, or hybridizations—we seem to be incapable of realizing that in other societies active participation is the rule, passivity the exception. The few who claim a superiority for art music (the written tradition) assign a "low value" to the taste of the many who prefer popular, folk, and hybrid musical expressions (a mixture of oral and written traditions)—thereby suggesting a false double standard of musical values: one for written traditions and one for oral traditions; or still worse, a single standard with written traditions standing at the apex. The latter is, of course, nonsense; much of the music of the Orient has attained a high level of cultivation largely or wholly through the oral tradition.

The problem is further compounded by the fact that the

317

four terms used to describe the music of our society—*tribal,
folk, popular,* and *art music*—are not clearly distinguishable
even in their application to our own culture and, when applied
to other societies, often become altogether obscure. The
highly cultivated music of the gamelan orchestra in central
Java may be performed in the palace of the Sultan of Djogjakarta by an orchestra of about forty instrumentalists, a male
chorus of fifteen, and three female soloists. The performance
may include a large company of dancers trained in the classical tradition of the royal court. This same music and dance
—an oral tradition—may be performed in one of the nearby
villages on a gamelan much smaller in size whose instrumental keys are made of iron rather than the costly bronze of
the royal court and whose dancers are clad in costumes that
only simulate the richness of the court dress. These same
songs, praised by the literary scholars of Europe for the high
quality of their poetry, will be sung by the laborer in the rice
fields. Perhaps, if his work is suddenly interrupted by a tropical rainstorm, he will huddle inside his kowangan, a large
hood made of dried palm leaves, which protects him from
the rain. Inside some kowangan, attached to the supporting
framework, will be six or seven palm fibers tuned to the
pitches of the five-tone sléndro tuning system or the seven-
tone pélog system; two additional fibers will be tuned to the
deep- and high-pitched heads of the drum. Sometimes three
kowangan are put together as a common shelter, and the
three men will sit back-to-back, huddled inside, plucking out
the principal melody of an orchestral piece on their fiber
"keys" and singing the classical songs of central Java until the
rain stops.

If the term *popular* has any meaning applied to music,
the great body of Javanese musical literature can be said to be
truly "popular." Many of the pieces in the repertory are also
associated with various types of ritual and by our earlier defi-

nition would therefore be termed *tribal.* Javanese music also
fits the definition of *folk music* in that it is dependent on an
oral tradition, has great continuity linking the past with the
present and is re-created and refashioned by the society, producing many variants. It is, of course, in the first place, an
art music by virtue of its conscious cultivation by professional
instrumentalists and singers as well as practitioners at the
amateur level.

There are, it is true, other genres of music in Java, but
since the predominant musical expression is so difficult to
classify in our terminology it is perhaps better not to attempt
a discussion of such hybrids as krontjong—a type of song
based on the folk songs of Portuguese sailors who came to
Indonesia in the sixteenth century—or certain ritualistic
residues persisting in the villages since the days of animism,
or a type of Arabic song "sung in the Javanese manner" under
the name of santiswaran.

In Java and more especially in Bali countless gamelan
clubs, dance clubs, various forms of dance theater, puppet
theater, bodies of solo songs, and types of opera involve a
vast majority of the people, probably to the extent that popular, folk, and hybrid idioms in our own society involve us
—with the important difference that theirs is an active, participating involvement and ours is a passive, "spectator" involvement.

"The Music of Africa" by Alan Merriam, which appears
in *Africa and the United States, Images and Realities* (Background Book, 8th National Conference, U. S. National Commission for UNESCO, 1961), presents one view of the
importance of music in African societies in terms of three
levels of functionality.

The first involves music as an everyday and all-pervading
aspect of life, a feature which is shared by all the arts in
Africa. The distinctions between "the artist" and his "audi-

319

ence," which are so sharply drawn in our society, do not seem to be of particular importance in Africa. Almost everyone sings, hand-claps, and participates in group performance, and it is generally assumed that almost all individuals are equally potentially "musical" or are at least of a higher level of musical competence than is usually attributed to the non-musicians in our own culture. Music in Africa, then, finds a higher degree of integration into everyday life and a high proportion of participation by the people.

Music in Africa is functional in another sense: its use in almost all aspects of life. Music may be organized for formal or ceremonial occasions such as festivals or occasions of worship, or for informal occasions such as recreation, or to accompany some forms of manual labor Sex or age differences may be a basis for musical organization, and thus there are specific musical forms and performances for men and women, children and adults. Kinship may form the basis for musical performance, and many kinds of music reflect associational groupings. There are strong connections between music and political, social, and economic behavior, to say nothing of the obvious relationships to religion, dance, drama, and folklore. In a more specialized sense music is used as a historic device, as a means of educating children, and as a form of social protest both within a culture and in reference to Europeans or others outside it.

Finally there is evidence to indicate that music—in some African cultures at least—is functional in the sense that it is not abstracted from its cultural context. Thus among the Basongye in the Congo, the total body of music is a known rather than an unknown (as it is in our own culture) and, further, individual songs are recognized instantly in terms of their function. . . .

· · ·

Our knowledge of African music is fragmentary at best. . . . At a time when the Africans themselves are laying even greater stress upon the humanities as vital and basic parts of their cultures, we should devote more concentrated attention to these aspects of African music. For they can lead us to a clearer understanding of the basic values and sanctions in African life.

In spite of the fast encroachment of Western technology, or perhaps because of it, many societies throughout the world are awakening to the importance of their own cultural identity. Sometimes this intensification of interest and pride in cultural identity has occurred after the pressures of rapid "modernization" have already destroyed some of the vital root stock of the culture. Reconstruction in such instances may be extremely difficult, if not impossible. In the most recent times, however, the young nations (made up of very old societies) seem to realize, as they achieve the status of independence and self-determination, that their artistic expressions, integral to their society, represent that fusion of mind, spirit, and emotion that is their unique identity and that shapes their aspirations.

It is understandable that the men responsible for our international relations are unaware of the critical importance of humanistic studies. The statesman, the politician, the economist, the space scientist, the military man of necessity may have had little opportunity to discover that any one of these humanistic expressions, as Seeger put it, "is in some ways like a language—one has to learn it in order to understand it and estimate its value—and sometimes even to discover it." We need only glance at the frustrations of the past decade or so to realize that too little has been learned, too many values have been underestimated, and too much has been left undiscovered.

It is not easy to know and understand the values and sanctions of societies that differ widely from our own. And yet, if we are to establish reliable communications we must know and understand. The ethnomusicologist who has discovered, understood, and evaluated the cultural expressions of a society can make a unique contribution toward the solution of these problems. Even during the course of his study true communication will begin.

My own experience in Indonesia is typical of the attitude encountered by the ethnomusicologist in the field. Early in my stay in Java I was puzzled that my activities, in fact, my every move, seemed to be common knowledge. The most casual acquaintance or even a person to whom I had just been introduced would comment with assurance on my whereabouts of the past few weeks. I began to be faintly alarmed when such comments referred to events that were still in the planning stage. The mystery was cleared up, however, when I was informed that one of Java's most popular radio commentators and the editor of the leading Javanese language newspaper between them kept the public informed about this American professor who had succeeded in communicating with the Javanese people through his involvement with their music, dance, theater, language, and other aspects of their culture.

It might be argued that as the new small nations of the world achieve modernization and develop sound economies, taking their place in the chain of international commerce that girdles the globe, the "anachronisms" of ancient traditions will be relinquished. It might be reasoned further that these "shackles" of tradition, unless discarded, will prevent progress —a half truth quickly embraced by human beings facing for the first time the challenge of Western technology and economic pressure. It is this kind of Western-oriented, superficial analysis that has led us down a one-way street of communication speaking, but not listening, informing, but not being informed. Let us be immediately aware *that modification of traditions, but not destruction of traditions, will occur through modernization, that the old societies making up new nations shall decide what of their traditional identity is to be retained, changed, or relinquished.* We need look no further than to the fate of the American Indian to find the dear price paid for loss of cultural identity—and we should bear in mind that, unlike the American Indians, blanketed by a foreign culture, the new nations have the opportunity of self-determination.

The reader may point out that the young people from Asia and Africa studying on American campuses have little knowledge of or concern for the traditions of their own societies. I readily agree that a good many foreign students give such an impression, but the impression may not be entirely accurate.

During the past few years, I have come to know a number of highly educated Javanese who hold responsible positions in their own national government. A typical example is a man who has served as Indonesian ambassador to several foreign countries, a man fluent in half a dozen European languages and several Oriental languages, who is conversant with English, French, German, Dutch, and American literature, as well as the principal bodies of literature in Indonesia and other parts of the Orient. Having spent three-quarters of the last twenty years living outside Indonesia, he knows the manners and niceties of European societies, and he knows these aspects of his own culture and those of other Oriental cultures. He believes that it is as important for him to know the *Iliad* and the *Odyssey* as it is for the Westerner to know the *Mahabharata* and the *Ramayana*—how many of us share this belief in practice? During the course of many long evenings, this man, and many others not so internationally schooled, explained to me in detail the importance of the literature of wajang purwa. These "old stories" from the *Mahabharata* and the *Ramayana* have persisted for a thousand years as a rich treasury mirroring the manners and mores, the sanctions and beliefs of the Javanese people, who regard the gods and heroes of these Hindu religious cycles as their own ancestors. Presented as puppet plays or dance dramas or a kind of opera or related in the form of solo songs, they serve as an educative medium for all ages. For children they teach etiquette and the requirements of fine breeding and manners, for young adults they portray the ideals and virtues of Javanese society, for those who have achieved a maturity in wisdom they hold an inexhaustible wealth of philosophical concepts. For individuals of any age, any rank or station, any degree of social attainment—the stories of wajang purwa are brought to life through the long night perfectly integrated with the classical music of the large gamelan orchestra, a deftly woven fabric including the finest poetic imagery, classical songs, subtle and ribald humor, ancient formalities and topical witicisms, political commentary and satire.

The ambassador told me that his teenage children, who had spent most of their lives outside Indonesia, were woefully ignorant of this literature and that having returned to Java they must now begin to appreciate and understand this cultural heritage. "Because," he said, "to understand our wajang is to understand our people."

Some of the young Javanese students now studying on American campuses, grown to young adulthood through the hectic period of the revolutionary years, have spent their youth in troubled times that twisted and confused their standard of values. The older generation seems to have become aware of this loss and it is significant that in the public schools of Indonesia, the Indonesian language, regional language (e.g., Javanese, Sundanese, Balinese), regional music, dance, and other aspects of the cultural heritage are included. The English language, political science, economics, the pure sciences, and other studies needed in the modern world are also important components of the curriculum. I might add that a good many of the young adults who have gone abroad from Indonesia to spend several years working or studying among foreign societies have expressed regret that they were not better versed in their own cultural heritage.

In the September 1961 issue of *Jakarta Dispatches,* published by the Indonesian Embassy in Washington, D. C., the following announcement appeared:

Indonesia Sets Up Cultural Centers Abroad

The Indonesian Government is planning to establish a number of cultural centers abroad, including one in London, Paris, Washington and Cairo, according to Secretary General Supardo of the Indonesian Department of Education and Culture.

Mr. Supardo said the decision had been reached after a recent conference in Prague of Indonesian cultural attachés in Europe. The aim of the cultural centers will be to promote cultural exchanges with foreign countries and to "improve the mental development of Indonesian students abroad."

Both his department and the Indonesian Foreign Affairs Department, he said, concurred in the decision, regarding it as an effort to make Indonesian culture popular abroad and to help Indonesians abroad retain their national identity.

Alexis Carrel's concern with the total man lies close to the thesis of this essay with its concern for the total society. His insistence that the study of the *inner* man has been neglected is analogous to our present concern with the neglect of music and the related arts.

The historian, the archaeologist, the ethnologist, the psychologist, the linguist, the political scientist, the geographer, the anthropologist, the economist, and specialists from other disciplines are each contributing to configuration studies. It is necessary that the vital role of the interrelated arts in non-Western societies become a part of the comprehensive

325

objective. These cultural expressions, representing the heart and soul of a people, can serve as a kind of camera obscura, reducing the vast and complex panorama of their multifarious activities to a sharp image in miniature. Through language and literature, through music, dance, and theater, through the graphic and plastic arts can be revealed in natural color and living images all of those essential attributes making up the very identity of a people. The passive nature, the recreational role of the arts in our own society must not be allowed to dull our comprehension when the Javanese says: "To understand our wajang is to understand our people."

In this essay no attempt has been made to refer to all the important contributors to the field of ethnomusicology. Specific references to names and works have been made only as convenient illustrations of specific points. There appears to be no practical way in which to acknowledge the many individuals who through conversation and reflection have contributed immeasurably to the ideas expressed here. I am particularly indebted to the small but increasing number of scholars represented by the ethnomusicologist who has written many scholarly articles and monographs, who has spent a good many years absorbing the wealth of ethnological materials that are inseparable from music viewed within the context of its society, who has ranged the field intensively and extensively until the very spirit of his subject pervades the most casual observation, who himself can play and sing the music and who knows at firsthand the emotional and spiritual impact it makes on its society. This is the man who has begun to know the *inner* man of the total society.

INDEX

329